L VE
BEYOND BELIEF

For my teachers: John B. Cobb Jr., Jane Dempsey Douglass, Amos Funkenstein, and Jack C. Verheyden. Their commitment to truth made my spirit soar.

In loving memory of Kenneth M. Morrison and Jaak Panksepp. Our conversations buoyed my soul.

And with prayerful praise and gratitude to Desmond Tutu, the Archbishop Emeritus of Cape Town. The name Thandeka, which he gave me in 1984, reminds me daily to love beyond belief.

L♥VE
BEYOND BELIEF

Finding the Access Point
to Spiritual Awareness

Thandeka

POLEBRIDGE PRESS
Salem, Oregon

Polebridge Press is the publishing arm of the Westar Institute, a non-profit, public-benefit research and educational organization. To learn more, visit westarinstitute.org.

Cover and interior design by Robaire Ream
Cover image by D'mitri Sobol

Library of Congress Cataloging-in-Publication Data
Names: Thandeka, 1946- author.
Title: Love beyond belief : finding the access point to spiritual awareness / Thandeka.
Description: Salem, OR : Polebridge Press, 2018.
Identifiers: LCCN 2018029149 | ISBN 9781598152012 (alk. paper)
Subjects: LCSH: Psychology, Religious. | Love--Religious aspects. | Emotions. | Spiritual life.
Classification: LCC BL53 .T45 2018 | DDC 204--dc23 LC record available at https://lccn.loc.gov/2018029149
10   9   8   7   6   5   4   3   2   1

Table of Contents

Foreword

Thandeka has written a book of rigorous scholarship, brilliant original insight, and great practical importance. Few will agree with every detail. I do not. But having read it, I will never be able to think of my theological heritage in the same way again.

We theologians have always known that in our theological heritage there are ugly elements. Augustine called for burning synagogues. Luther called for slaughtering rebellious peasants. But I, along with others, have passed over these horrors to get to the "truly theological" part of their work. Thandeka shows that these teachings are integrally connected to their whole theologies.

I, along with many others, have identified the villain in Christian history as the legalism that repeatedly recurs in the church despite its teaching of grace. I have often commented that Christian legalism is worse than Jewish legalism. Thandeka shows that this is far too abstract an analysis. She explains how and why it is worse.

Thandeka identifies the villain as the "Gentile conscience." This was introduced into theology by Paul as functioning for Gentiles as the Mosaic law functioned for Jews. For him, Christ frees us from both. But Thandeka shows that the theological tradition has been far from liberated from the Gentile conscience. This is associated with a dualism from which Jewish legalism is largely free. As a result, this conscience has drastically distorted Paul's gospel. In the United States it has overwhelmed the gospel, and the consequences for the spirituality, which is her primary concern, have been horrendous.

Thandeka's deep commitment is to the experience of "love beyond belief." The theologians most respected by Protestants have incorporated teachings that work against this experience. The

Enlightenment reinstated the Gentile conscience, now thought of as the Protestant conscience. This has not been an improvement.

Thandeka has devoted her life to the study of research on affects, namely, "ancient brain processes for encoding value" (Panksepp and Biven, Archeology of the Mind, 31). The theologian she has found most promising is Friedrich Schleiermacher. Her chapter on his theology is magisterial and important for all of us. Schleiermacher shows how we can liberate authentic spiritual experience from any specific religious interpretation, while at the same time showing us Christians how we can interpret it in our way. Nevertheless, Thandeka also shows how dominant the Protestant Enlightenment conscience has been in the United States. This has turned the churches in this country away from any spiritual experience and into support for American exceptionalism and imperialism.

Thandeka sees in the emergence of the "spiritual but not religious" community a great potential for her goal of "love beyond belief." She has demonstrated in practice how, by paying close attention to the affects, dying established churches can come alive. She hopes that those who are alienated from these churches, often for excellent reasons, can develop community activities that will lead them to experience love beyond belief. With her leadership and the support of progressive churches, perhaps this project will succeed.

—John B. Cobb, Jr.

Acknowledgments

I could not have completed this twenty-year book project without the support of an extraordinary community of family, friends, teachers, and colleagues.

I thank President Martin B. Copenhaver and Vice President of Academic Affairs Sarah B. Drummond of Andover Newton Theological School (ANTS) for the opportunity to teach various parts of this book in courses on ethics and ministry to an amazing array of ANTS seminarians. I also thank Sarah for awarding me the position of Affect Theologian in Residence to complete the work on this book. Special thanks to the students in my classes at ANTS for insights I gained as they courageously undertook the task of rereading Western Christian theological history and emerging from the journey transformed. The generosity of time, attention, and care that Nancy Lois, ANTS's librarian, gave to me in helping identify and locate articles, essays, and books for my project was a godsend.

Many thanks to Sarah Lammert, Co-Director of Ministries and Faith Development at the Unitarian Universalist Association. Without the generous financial support of the UUA I would not have been able to complete this book project.

I offer deepest appreciation to Circulation Supervisor Laura Whitney and Access Services and Resource Sharing Coordinator Michelle Gauthier at Andover-Harvard Divinity School Theological Library. I could not have conducted the years of intense and extended research required for this book project without their gracious, extensive, and unstinting support and care.

Special thanks to Lawrence Alexander, former publisher at Polebridge Press, for not only accepting my book for publication, but also for reading each of the chapters of my book as I developed them. Larry offered incisive critiques and advice for the project as it unfolded. After retiring, Larry continued work with me until the first major draft of the entire project was completed. He has my heartfelt gratitude and is now a cherished friend.

Special thanks also to Polebridge Press staff. Editor Cassandra Farrin's editorial work on my book tightened arguments and made the narrative line more evident. Copy editor Barbara Hampson is a master reader and critic who identified and called for revisions that advanced the clarity of this book project. Executive Director David Galston's attention to this book project as well as his work with me as a Westar Fellow have given me a new community of colleagues.

Edite Kroll, my literary agent for more than two decades, never gave up hope or support for me as we worked to move this book to production. She is a dear friend whose support and encouragement, critical eye, and ongoing *joie de vivre* make it possible for me to let hope spring eternal even when it's hard to find.

Two friends and colleagues spent innumerable hours reading, critiquing, and editing various drafts of the chapters of this book. One was Kenneth M. Morrison, who was professor of religious studies at Arizona State University and a dear friend for thirty-three years. And the Rev. Constance L. Grant, a Unitarian Universalist minister and a wonderful friend, confidante, travel companion, spent countless hours reading every draft I sent to her with a spirit of goodwill. Her steadfast presence anchored me. From beginning to end, Constance's removal of excess words was a wonder to behold!

The ongoing support for and belief in my work by my brother, Merrel D. Booker, Jr., helped me reached the end of a dark tunnel to find the light of a new day. He is a wonderful reminder of what it means to have the gift of family in my life: love beyond belief.

I met Jaak Panksepp in 2006 in Evanston, Illinois, before he delivered a public lecture. I had read his book, *Affective Neuroscience: The Foundations of Human and Animal Emotions*, and assigned it to my students at Meadville Lombard Theological School in Chicago. I had been in search of a way to advance and expand upon the neuro-conceptual analysis of affect, namely, the immediate experience of one's own emotions such as rage, anger, lust, fear, and care, *before* one thinks about what was just internally felt. Friedrich Schleiermacher, the nineteenth-century father of liberal theology, defined *Affekt* [affect] as the product of stimulated "nerves or whatever else is the first ground and seat of motions in the human body."[1] Jaak Panksepp, who is the father of the contemporary brain science of emotions, defined affect as the way we experience specific states of our own nervous system.[2] Could I use insights from Jaak's work to understand, correct, and expand Schleiermacher's affect theology, namely, his analysis of how human affections become religious feelings?

I asked Jaak if he would be a consultant as I analyzed Schleiermacher's affect theology using insights from Jaak's affective neuroscientific research. He agreed and thus began an eleven-year conversation. He sent me numerous articles of his that had not yet been published. He carefully read many of my essays in which I used insights from his work and he added nuance to my claims. So, too, did he write commentaries that I added to the first chapter of this book.

Myra and Darwin Smith played a critical role as dear friends. Their folk art festivals as well as their support of theatre and public art projects created opportunities for me to dive into the creative wellsprings of life. Special thanks to them also for grants from their donor-advised fund at The Dallas Foundation to congregations to beta test the Love Beyond Belief™ initiative linked to my book project. These onsite consultation experiences gave me the practical insights needed to keep my academic research project linked to the heart of my mission: strengthening religious and secular congregations in order to build a national network of Love Beyond Belief™ communities working together for the greater good.

Abby Raeder and Robert Sarly walked with me through the last decade of the work on my book project, providing weekend Vermont getaways in their wonderful country homes, with music, art, dialogue groups, movies and feasts. I found laughter there with these two dear friends as we walked through the woods and journeyed anew into a life filled with hope.

My sister-in-law Rickie Booker also walked with me through the last year of this book project, providing laughter and support when my spirit sagged. She remained steadfastly present awaiting breakthrough moments as bright as the noonday sun.

Heartfelt praise and gratitude to D'mitri Sobol, Senior Business Analyst at ValorBiz Professional Services, who is spearheading a social media campaign for my Love Beyond Belief™ initiative and creating ever-new ways to link it through social media to my book. I am deeply grateful for his enormous generosity of time and creative energy to help make the Love Beyond Belief™ initiative a beacon of hope in hard times. He is a master craftsman who transforms dreams into realities. The Rev. Randy Lewis, a community minister, introduced me to D'mitri. Both Randy and D'mitri have been steadfast and visionary in their support of my work.

Special thanks to my colleague and friend James M. Brandt, Professor of Historical Theology and Director of Contextual Education at Saint Paul School of Theology. His fine critiques of my chapters on Schleiermacher were enormously helpful and our conversations have been open-minded, open-hearted, productive, and celebratory.

Many thanks to Kathleen E. Corley, Oshkosh Northwestern Distinguished Professor University of Wisconsin-Oshkosh, for critical suggestions and advice on my chapters on Paul. Kathleen and I have been friends since graduate school. I count this renowned New Testament scholar as a hallowed grace note in my life.

I offer enormous thanks to a reader of my chapters on Paul who strongly urged me to read Daniel Boyarin's *Border Lines*. I had already used other books by Boyarin in my work but *Border Lines* was on my bookshelf, unread. I spent a week combing through Boyarin's arguments, utterly fascinated and finally convinced by his critiques of the received histories of Christianity and Judaic traditions.

The primary argument and line of reasoning framing my analysis of Paul began when Bernadette J. Brooten, who is the

Kraft-Hiatt Professor of Christian Studies; of Women's, Gender, and Sexuality Studies; of Classical Studies; and Chair of Religious Studies at Brandeis University, invited me to teach her Introduction to Christianity course when she went on sabbatical. In preparation to teach the course, I began to research the question: What do the origins of Christianity look like from various Jewish and Judaic perspectives? A new narrative about Paul began to develop in my mind. To test my theory, I asked Bernadette to listen to my theory and then tear it to shreds. Only when she agreed to do so, saying "better me than someone else," did I tell her my theory. In response, Bernadette set up a meeting for me with Krister Stendahl (1921-2008), a former dean of Harvard Divinity School and a Church of Sweden Bishop of Stockholm, whose book *Paul Among Jews and Gentiles, and Other Essays* opened a new era of interpretation in Pauline Scholarship. We met for tea and Bernadette said, "Tell Krister your theory." He listened intently, was silent for a short while, and then gently smiled and said, "This could be right." He agreed to be a reader for my chapters on Paul as I developed the narrative, but, unfortunately, he died a few months later.

Special thanks also to Bronson Brown-de Vost, a former graduate student at Brandeis, who worked on the translation of Hebrew texts.

This book is dedicated to my beloved teachers John B. Cobb Jr., Jane Dempsey Douglass, Amos Funkenstein, and Jack C. Verheyden because their extraordinary scholarship, their rigorous insistence on close textual readings of primary texts, and their love of and commitment to truth, turned me into an impassioned defender and also a severe critic of Western theological traditions. Jane Douglass read my chapter on Luther and offered invaluable suggestions including the recommendation of more texts to fill out my argument. John Cobb read the last chapter of this book and added critical insights about the history of Methodism as part of the American story I unfold there.

My teachers inspired me. And it is my good fortune to count all of them as friends. I still mourn the loss of Amos, who died in 1995. I spent countless hours playing chess with him, going to dinner with him and his kids, and arguing—always arguing with grand humor—as we interpreted texts and explored the secrets embedded within the words.

I would like to thank my former partner Naomi King. We walked down so many roads together as I endeavored to gather together arguments and insights into a coherent narrative. Her astutely critical eye strengthened the work in this book in countless ways. I also thank her extended family for their loving support.

A network of dear friends and associates infuse my daily life with extraordinary care: Peggy Alexander, Arnold "Brad" Bradburd, Kate Braestrup, Sheila Briggs, Philip Clayton, Phyllis Cutler, Jerry Dancis, Dolores Maniscalco-D'Alfonso, Noreen Dean Dresser, Susan Gottlieb, David Keyes, Lydia Kleiner, Michael Lerner, Rebecca Maida, Bobbi Murray, Hnia Sophia Nediri, Michael Robinson, Mikel E. Satcher, Yvette and James Shepard, Julie Steinbach, Don Streets, Richard Sweeney, Jesús Salvador Treviño, and The Square Radishes Lori Granger and Iris Sachs. Their belief in me and my work has been magical, helping me to transform loss into gain and fatigue into the laughter of precious moments packed full of deeply familiar faces.

Finally, I thank Nobel Peace Prize Laureate Desmond Tutu, the Archbishop Emeritus of Cape Town (1986-1996), who in 1984 gave me my Xhosa name Thandeka, which means "lovable" and "beloved." I made Thandeka my one and only legal name in 1985, but it has taken me decades to know the meaning of this name as a lived experience in my life.

All these people have help me with the work to complete this book. Any errors in the scholarship found in this book are mine.

Abbreviations

1,2 Chr	1,2 Chronicles
1,2 Cor	1,2 Corinthians
Dan	Daniel
Eccl	Ecclesiastes
Ezek	Ezekiel
Exod	Exodus
Gal	Galatians
Gen	Genesis
Isa	Isaiah
KGA	*Christian Faith, Der christliche Glaube nach den Grundsätzen der evangelischen Kirche im Zusammenhang dargestellt*
Lev	Leviticus
LW	Luther, *Lectures on Galatians*
Phil	Philippians
Rom	Romans
1,2 Thess	1,2 Thessalonians

Introduction

We are on our way to spiritual awareness. Let's walk with John Cage as he enters a small, six-walled, echoless chamber constructed with special soundproofing materials to eliminate all external sound. He expects to experience absolute silence. Instead he hears two sounds: one is the high-pitched tinsel sound of his nervous system in operation; the other is a lower sound made as his blood courses through his veins.

Think about what Cage heard. He heard the universe—not figuratively, but literally—strumming his nervous system and drumming the life pulse of his blood. This experience of his own nervous system, namely, the experience of his own "intrinsically biological"[1] feelings—his affective states of consciousness—happened fifty years ago to the experimental composer and musician. But something also just happened to us. We followed Cage into the place between thoughts where he and the universe met.

This meeting place is found in the luminous darkness of feelings enveloped by infinite life.

Cage felt the floor and his shoes and the skin on his feet as they met and altered the pattern of his nervous system. He saw light patterns sparkle the walls in the room, which altered his retinas and thus colored his nervous system. He felt the air in the room enter his lungs. The quality and temperature of the air affected his breathing and thus the flow of his blood.

His turn inward led him into the very heart of cosmic interior life. Here's how he described the interior journey:

> The turning is psychological and seems at first a giving up
> of everything that belongs to humanity.... This psychological turning leads to the world of nature, where gradually or

suddenly, one sees that humanity and nature, not separate, are in this world together; that nothing was lost when everything was given away. In fact, everything is gained.[2]

Cage experienced what the Harvard psychologist William James calls cosmic consciousness in his classic book *The Varieties of Religious Experience*, published in 1902. James cites in his book the major characteristics of cosmic consciousness delineated by the psychiatrist Richard Maurice Bucke:

- a consciousness of the life and order of the universe
- an intellectual enlightenment that places a person on a new plane of existence as if a member of a new species
- a state of moral exaltation
- an indescribable feeling of elevation, elation, and joyousness greater than the enhanced intellectual power
- a sense of immortality
- a consciousness of ethical life, and
- not a conviction that one shall have all of this, but a conviction that one has it already[3]

Love Beyond Belief is a roadmap to cosmic consciousness. My book uses insights from affective neuroscience (the brain science of emotions) and related fields. I investigate and reaffirm a type of human consciousness core to mystical experience, in which a person feels connected to all of life at once, and experiences awe, wonder, and an intoxicating love of life itself. The access point to this cosmic state of consciousness, I will argue, isn't thinking; it's feeling. It's a strictly interior domain of human experience in which one feels quickened, enlivened, compassion, ultimate care, love beyond belief, and thus is resonant with all of life. Accounts of this inner life of the self *per se*[4] become stories about affections, shifts in feelings, namely, triggered affect that raises feelings to their highest and noblest state.

The narrative in this book makes five basic points about affect as the access point to cosmic consciousness.

First, Christian faith has two emotional foundations: cosmic consciousness and the Christian conscience.

Second, cosmic consciousness, namely the exalted experience of love beyond belief, was lost when *ideas* about the Christian conscience replaced *affective experiences* of infinite life.

Third, the story of the Christian conscience as a *replacement* for cosmic consciousness begins with a linguistic accident made by Paul, the first-century Apostle to the Gentiles, who urged his followers to love others beyond the reach of their former beliefs. He called this new kind of selfless love the "law of Christ" (Gal 6:2) and the "law of Spirit" (Rom 8:2). This law has also been called the "law of love"[5] because it required from Gentiles unfailing compassion for others and prompted acts of lovingkindness (1 Cor 13:1–10). But a term used by Paul kept his followers from understanding this law of love for Gentiles as their nonreligious state of cosmic consciousness he tried to affirm.

Fourth, the loss of access by Gentiles to the state of cosmic consciousness was especially evident at three points in the history of Christian thought: (1) the autobiographical *Confessions* of the fifth-century Catholic Church Father Augustine; (2) the two kingdoms theory and the "religion of conscience" created by Martin Luther, a sixteenth-century father of the Protestant Reformation; and (3) the "moral sense" affirmed by liberal and traditional Christians two centuries ago during the American Enlightenment.

Fifth, Friedrich Schleiermacher, the nineteenth-century father of liberal Christian theology, separated the history of the Christian conscience from experiences of cosmic consciousness in order to retrieve the lost access point to God-consciousness. Master theologians Reinhold Niebuhr and John Cobb, Jr. also set aside the received theological tradition of conscience as the affective foundation of Christian faith.

This five-point schematic is a lost-and-found story about the access point to cosmic consciousness in the Christian West, namely, resonant, uplifting feelings of infinite life. The narrative line helps explain drug-free personal experiences of bliss that the poet Rilke called "cosmic space."[6] Etty Hillesum, killed in Auschwitz, described her own experience of this exalted affective state in her letters and journal entries as "heaven [which] is inside one, like Rilke's 'cosmic interior.'"[7]

I write this book because I discovered, quite by accident, this cosmic interior in myself.

I was a lonely, despondent college kid filled with emotions I didn't think I was supposed to have. To end the internal war against my feelings, I swallowed forty sleeping pills, went to bed in my dorm room, and waited for the disturbing feeling of my own life to die. But much to my surprise, when the moment of death finally arrived and I could no longer breathe, I bolted out of bed gasping for breath, demanding to live. I struggled until finally I cleared my lungs of the vomit I had aspirated.

As I inhaled, I felt life without end, joy without remorse, and an unbounded love that resounded in me like the heartbeat of God. This momentary experience was too vast and fleeting for religious belief, too unfamiliar for sensate knowledge, too remote for emotional feelings, and so intimate that the distance between my inner and outer worlds collapsed. I felt at home in my life, at one with the universe, and free.

A tidal wave of feeling enveloped every aspect of my life as a surge of energy, a rush of impulses rhythmically moved as the ebb and flow of the universe renewed and transformed my life. This stream of life felt infinite as a mother's first embrace of her child. The embrace was as wide as the stars, the galaxies, the firmament pirouetting together.

My cosmic state of consciousness made me feel loved beyond belief—not by some higher being or deity or other object of human thought—but by life itself. I fell in love with my life, the life of others, life on earth, the All of life.

And I refused to reduce this feeling of infinite hallowed life to religious notions and doctrinal beliefs. The feeling was too big for thought. My access point to the feeling was not reason or sensation, but emotion, shaped, informed, and infused with infinite life.

I now wanted guidelines, maps, and instructions: a beginner's handbook. There must be a way to find this place of unfathomable beauty and infinite depth again.

My search for maps and instructions began with writings of people who had turned inward and felt an infinite expanse within themselves.

William James entered this state of consciousness when he took nitrous oxide to experience firsthand something akin to the mystical experiences he studied. According to James, he saw opposites meet and watched the contradictions and conflicts, which make human life so difficult, reconcile and meld into a unity.[8]

Thomas Merton explored this cosmic state as a twentieth-century Catholic monk and mystic who called this kind of cosmic inner experience "full spiritual reality." The search for one's true identity, Merton said, is to be sought not in separation from all that is, "but in oneness ('convergence'?) with all that is."[9] In short, in the cosmic interior.

John Cage drew on Buddhist teachings to make sense of this cosmic state: "Without my engagement with Zen (attendance at lectures by Alan Watt and D. T. Suzuki, reading of literature) I doubt whether I would have done what I have done."[10]

I wanted to understand this experience in Western Christian terms. The search led me to Friedrich Schleiermacher because his description of a "mysterious moment" of sense perception when objects flowed into one another and became one, before returning back to their original position,[11] had a strikingly similar pattern to Cage's cosmic experience and to the drug-induced experience of William James. Schleiermacher called his experience the "natal hour of everything living in religion."[12]

This experience, Schleiermacher insisted, wasn't about religions, which are cultural creations, social artifacts, and human constructions of rituals, beliefs and practices. Religion, according to Schleiermacher, "never appears in a pure sense," but rather "clings to" the extraneous parts created by cultural biases and vested interests. Schleiermacher strove to get rid of the excess so that the "essence of religion," namely, its "pure form"—a personal intuition, an "immediate perception" of the universe—is experienced.[13] He claimed to have experienced religion in its "pure state,"[14] which he called the "interhuman dimension of our experience,"[15] the "inner side of human nature and the world,"[16] the inner experience of the "mysterious moment" in which consciousness "hovers" between the universe and the self.[17] According to Schleiermacher, the experience is

The first mysterious moment that occurs in every sensory perception… where sense and its objects have, as it were, flowed
into one another and become one, before both turn back to
their original position.… It is as fleeting and transparent as
the first scent with which the dew gently caresses the waking
flowers, as modest and delicate as a maiden's kiss, as holy and
fruitful as a nuptial embrace; indeed, not *like* this, but it *is itself*
all of these. A manifestation, an event develops quickly and
magically into an image of the universe.… I lie on the bosom
of the infinite world.[18]

This cosmic experience, for Schleiermacher, is an innate spiritual capacity of human nature.[19]

What have we missed because this access point was lost? And
what can we gain if we find it again?

Part One

Affect Neuro-Theory and Theology

Chapter One

The Loss

Several years ago, a Catholic priest I knew did famine relief work in an Ethiopian village. The villagers, as they awaited the next shipment of food, moved rhythmically in a circle to the beat of a single drum. They danced this way for hours.

The priest joined the circle dance, which seemed by his account, to consist of a "one, two, three, jump" sequence. But he never managed to jump at the right time. He jumped too soon or too late, or sometimes he simply forgot to jump at all.

His missteps gave the villagers countless hours of laughter. The children frequently fell out of the circle and onto the ground in fits of giggling delight. The laughter was neither intended nor received as ridicule. Instead, the priest said, it felt like the bemused jesting that goes on in a community when someone marches to the beat of a different drummer.

Hour after hour the priest labored to learn to count and then jump in just the right way. How many times did he move into and then out of step with the group's rhythm? Too many to count, he confessed. But as time wore on he felt something that surprised him.

Tears now welled in his eyes and he was silent for a long moment. And then he whispered to me, saying, "You know, until that experience I thought I had known God all of my life. But only as I danced with the members of the village did I actually *feel* God's presence in my life."

The priest had danced his way into cosmic consciousness.

He set aside all mental distractions and focused steady attention on the internal alignment of the movements of his body with the external, rhythmic movements of the world.

Thanks to this cosmic interior experience, the priest entered the difference—the space *between* his lifelong beliefs in and thoughts about God—and became one with the cosmic *feeling* of eternal, abounding life. This difference between what he thought and what he felt, however, disappeared when the priest called his cosmic experience an encounter with God.

This book analyzes the difference between cosmic consciousness and the religious concept "God" used by the priest to encode, order, and explain his awareness of the felt experience. The story of the dancing priest is thus an easy way to introduce the subtle distinction and its subsequent loss highlighted in this book.

The work of Friedrich Schleiermacher, the nineteenth-century father of liberal theology, is the first systematic way this book investigates the distinction between cosmic consciousness and what is then said about the experience in culturally-defined, religious terms. This initial focus on Schleiermacher's work is merited because he made cosmic consciousness the experiential foundation of liberal theology. But something went terribly wrong.

Schleiermacher did not explain the difference between religious thoughts and the cosmic feeling in terms his readers could understand. Part of the difficulty was not his fault: as this chapter will demonstrate, his inchoate neuro-conceptual analysis of affect, which is a triggering impulse that activates feeling, as the experiential foundation of and access point to cosmic consciousness was two hundred years ahead of his time.[1] But he also mistakenly assumed, as he confessed in a letter to his friend Dr. Friedrich Lücke, that the personal study by readers of their own shifting feelings and triggered emotions would make self-evident his claims about the foundational function of affect in the creation of pious feelings and religious ideas.[2] His pathbreaking analysis of affect as an access point to cosmic consciousness was thus lost.

The consequence of this loss was disastrous: liberal theology appeared foundation-less from its inception.[3] Liberal theology, after all, is more than an Enlightenment narrative created by Schleiermacher that critiques and replaces outmoded church doctrine and reaffirms human nature as grace-filled rather than fallen. But upon what basis are these core values of liberal theology and faith made? Schleiermacher did not provide an adequate answer to this question. Rather, he gave liberal theology and liberal faith a foundation no one could understand, explain, or find: affect-triggered, cosmic interior feelings. His affect theology, which tracks the way emotions become religious feelings, was not understood.

A few examples of the resulting confusion—and its legacy—illustrate the point: the affective foundation of Schleiermacher's work could not be discerned and affect as the access point to cosmic consciousness was lost.

Schleiermacher's work was therefore called self-contradictory, a reintroduction of paganism, a system perfectly compatible with the papal system of the Roman church, and a venture that made faith in God inconsistent with Schleiermacher's own position.[4] Moreover, Schleiermacher, himself, was called a Gnostic, an Alexandrian, a proponent of monastic morality, a Cyrenian, someone influenced by Schelling, or by Jacobi.[5]

Two centuries later, the barrage of conflicting claims about Schleiermacher's theological project continues.[6] Modern and contemporary scholars, as Ulrich Barth's survey reveals, believe Schleiermacher's explanation of the foundation of his theological claims and their reference to Christian doctrine is satisfactory (Friedrich Wilhelm Gess); psychological (Christoph von Sigwart); pantheistic (Wilhelm Bender); ontological (Martin E. Miller); a specific mode of time-consciousness (Hans-Richard Reuter); the basis for interpreting religion as mystical, anti-moral and anti-intellectual (Emil Brunner); the basis for a system of aesthetics as the process of an ethical activity (Rudolf Odebrecht); inadequate as the basis for a philosophic doctrine of art (Edmund Husserl); platonic (Bernard Tidt); Kantian (Wilhelm Dilthey); Fichtean (Immanuel Hermann Fichte); Spinozistic and Schellingian (Christoph von Sigwart); or Jacobian (Eilert Herms).[7]

Liberal theology in America became prodigious in its creation of offspring of this convoluted legacy: postliberal and postcolonial theologies, gender, racial, and ethnically defined identity-based theologies, and more.[8] The main achievement of American liberal theology toward the end of the twentieth century, Gary Dorrien observes, was diversity. And as American liberal theology became progressively "more liberationist, feminist, environmentalist, multiculturalist, and postmodernist," Dorrien concludes, the contested pronouncements of these diverse theologies, devoid of a unifying essence, revealed the present impossibility of American liberal theology claiming for itself an uncontested foundation of and for liberal Christian theological studies as a secular, academic field of inquiry.[9]

The requirements for academic membership in these respective theological guilds also created a gap, as Carter Heyward, professor emerita at Episcopal Divinity School observed, between the theological studies of students in the progressive seminaries spawned by liberal theology's heirs and the ability of these students upon graduation to communicate with the congregations they were hired to serve. As Heyward pointedly notes, the students "spoke of transgressing religious and cultural boundaries while American politics and religion moved to the right."[10]

Seminaries, theology schools, and religious studies programs became progressive collections of interest groups without a shared foundational ground,[11] namely, the study of cosmic consciousness as the shared affective spiritual ground of religious experience. The lack of attention to human affections closed off the access point to cosmic consciousness and created, as Ralph Waldo Emerson noted two centuries ago, "corpse cold" liberal churches.

A personal example illustrates this last point.

Several years ago I attended the Sunday worship service of an evangelical mission church in a blighted, inner-city community in Roxbury, Massachusetts. I had gone to Boston earlier in the week to attend a national meeting of liberal clergy. While there, another minister and I decided to attend the Sunday service led by a newly credentialed minister who wanted to combine her liberal, social justice work with traditional, Christian mission work.

The small sanctuary was packed to overflowing with the truly dispossessed and downtrodden in this drug-ridden, desperately poor, black and brown Roxbury community. But the evangelical spirit of the minister's traditional black Protestant background was present in full force. Toward the middle of the service, there was an altar call.

The congregants lined up, music played, and everyone sang. Each person in line had a chance to whisper something into the minister's ear. Each person then received a personal blessing and now, aglow, rejoined the larger congregation.

As my friend and I left the church after the two-hour service, we talked about the altar call we had just witnessed.

"What do you think would happen if we initiated such a ritual in our mainline congregations?" I asked my friend. He replied, "Here's what would happen in my congregation. Everyone would line up. Each person would whisper into my ear: 'After the service, I want to talk with you about your sermon.'" We didn't laugh.

The joke wasn't funny because it exposed a primal flaw in Schleiermacher's liberal theological legacy: enlightened ideas are hawked while triggered feelings are shortchanged.

Today mainline Protestant churches like the Methodists, United Church of Christ, and the American Baptist still have the most church buildings. But they have the fewest people in them: about seventy-five on a typical Sunday. And less than 2 percent of these adults are twenty-five or younger. There are, of course, countless reasons for this decline.[12]

The work in this book, beginning with Schleiermacher, highlights a major overlooked factor in the self-decimation of liberal theology: affect as the access point to cosmic consciousness, which is the spiritual, nonreligious, foundation of liberal faith.

Eight steps take us into the heart of Schleiermacher's affective work and prepare us to move beyond his compromised legacy.

The first step is the easiest one because it's about an experience most of us have felt: loss. The steps become progressively more difficult as we explore the core of Schleiermacher's analysis and we must call upon insights from contemporary affect theology to help us out.

First Step

Schleiermacher's Story of Loss

On October 9, 1805, Schleiermacher received a letter from Eleanore Grunow, the unhappily married woman with whom he had been in an unconsummated love affair for seven years. He expected to marry her as soon as her divorce, already underway, was final. In her letter, she announced her decision to return to her husband and she renounced any further contact with Schleiermacher.

Devastated by the sudden and unexpected loss of his "soul mate," he fell into a depression, which he described in a letter written nine days later. The sorrow was "crushing" and the unity of his life was sundered. He wondered if the pain would ever leave him. He cut short his letter saying, "writing is like death to me; I cannot continue."[13] By December 2, his grief had deepened, stifling every creative activity of his life except for his lectures and preaching. In a letter to another friend, he called the depth of his grief unutterable. Writing was irksome, he said. He felt relief when in the classroom and behind the pulpit. His life in service to others freed him from "the sorrow that touches the individual alone." His refuge was the public and assurances from friends. Alone, his life was unbearable.[14]

On this same day, the grief-stricken Schleiermacher cancelled a class to attend a solo performance by the preeminent flautist of Europe, Friedrich Ludwig Dülon (1769–1826). Schleiermacher went to the concert knowing what to expect from a Dülon concert: a change of heart.[15] He wanted an emotional uplift—and he got it.

The review of the concert in *Berlinischen musikalischen zeitung* (*The Berlin Musical Newspaper*) leaves little doubt that Dülon was in improvisational high form during the concert Schleiermacher attended. His great and small concert and solo performances were deeply appreciated, the reviewer noted. But special praise, the reviewer continued, was reserved for Dülon's anticipated soul-filled free fantasies, which delighted and moved his audience the most.[16]

Second Step
Schleiermacher's Emotional Regeneration

After the December 2, 1805 concert, Schleiermacher stood by his stove trying to make sense of what had just happened to him. He felt an explosion of creative energy and an astonishing thought came to mind: Music isn't enough! Music and religious ideas and feelings must be in harmony. In his own words: "every fine feeling comes completely to the fore only when we have found the right musical expression for it." And, "it is precisely to religious feeling that music is most closely related.... What the word has declared, the tones of music must make alive, in harmony, conveying it to the whole inner being of its hearers and holding it fast there."[17]

Three weeks later he had written and sent off to his publisher the most artistically creative work of his career as theologian and preacher: *Christmas Eve,* a dialogue framed by music, filled with effusive feelings and an array of theological reflections.[18]

The dinner party guests in his mini-drama took turns describing what Christmas meant to them. Each speaker in Schleiermacher's mini-drama thus sustained or amplified the affections in Schleiermacher regenerated by Dülon's concert religiously. The final speaker is Josef. Christmas, he confesses, creates within him a "speechless joy, and [he] cannot but laugh and exult like a child." All human beings are children on this day, "and all the dearer on that account." The pain from Schleiermacher's own broken relationship with Eleanore Grunow is expressed in Josef's confession that even his Christmas joy does not cancel his pain.

Josef's Christmas Eve confession of speechless joy in the midst of a non-cancelable pain is in keeping with Schleiermacher's statement to his friend Georg Reimer on December 21, four days before he completed his manuscript: "What I must give up, as Eleanore must, is marriage, the forming of a wholly undivided life.... Thus I cannot but keep on saying that I shudder at my life as before an open wound that cannot be healed, but peace dwells within my heart, dear friend, whole and unalloyed—a peace which, wherever it comes, is by its very nature eternal and cannot wither away."[19]

Schleiermacher had parlayed his emotions regenerated by Dülon's music into exalted religious feelings. His own experiences illustrated and exemplified the foundation for the liberal theology he would later formulate and write. His devastated emotions had been gathered together and ultimately cared for and he felt the natal hour of everything living in religion.

He now set out to explain what he felt using music not as metaphor, but rather as the language of his affective science—his *Affekt Theologie*, namely, his neuro-conceptual analysis of consciousness as an access point to cosmic consciousness.

Third Step
Music and Schleiermacher's
Affekt Theologie: the Cultural Context

In Schleiermacher's era, the expectation that music would trigger affect that would regenerate the listener's sentiments, moods, feelings, and dispositions was pervasive. It even had a name, "the doctrine of human affections" (*Affektenlehre*), which referred to the art and science of the use of music to stir up human affections. The term *Affektenlehre* was coined by the German composer Johann Mattheson (1681–1764), who believed that different major and minor scales evoked different affective states within the listener.[20] The basic claim of this doctrine was that music was resonant and thus stirred and altered dispositions. Music, so it was believed, moved emotions.

Dülon is a case in point. He took it as a given that music moved human affections. Thus, when he described his own experience of listening to C. P. E. Bach perform an original composition, Dülon could use the language of human affections not as metaphor or analogy, but as a scientific description of the effect of the musical event on the listener:

> His tones were words, his performance spirit and life, his expression enchantment; each human passion [*jede menschliche Gemüths-Bewegung*] was subservient to his playing and before the power of his exalted genius, as Schubert said, must the listener shudder in bliss.[21]

For Dülon, musical improvisation and "fantasy" were a major musical means to this affective end. C. P. E. Bach, after all, as Dülon's teacher for a short time, frequently reminded his young pupil that improvisation is foundational for composition. Knowledge of harmony and some of the rules of construction were not enough. As Bach noted in his *Essay on the True Method of Playing the Clavier* (*Versuch über die wahre Art das Clavier zu spielen*), free fantasy, unmeasured and modulated, define the master composer.[22] In keeping with the era, Bach first assessed Dülon's worthiness as a potential pupil by asking him to improvise. Invention, inspiration, and innovation took precedence over theory and rules.[23]

Schleiermacher's own life is a playbook that tracks this era. While he was a theology professor at the University of Halle (1804–06), he spent Thursday and Friday evenings talking about, listening to, and learning more about music theory and performance in musical salons at the homes of friends. The home of the Thursday evening salons was called the "Lodging of the Romantics" (*Herberge der Romantik*), because so many of the leading Romantic artists spent time there. These gatherings, as Gunter Scholtz notes in his groundbreaking book *Schleiermacher's Music-Philosophy*, functioned as the heart and soul of the network of Romantic interests in musical expression. Here, discussions of music and religion blended together with musical performances.[24] Schleiermacher's vocabulary for music came of age in these settings.[25]

Music, to use Schleiermacher's term, consists of "moments of affection" (*Affektionsmomente*).[26] These moments are the result of the actual impress of sensations upon the ear and thus within the self. The internal result of the impress of sensations is an affect, a moment of sensible self-consciousness felt. Music, according to Schleiermacher, is thus quite literally, affect attunement (*Stimmung*). This transformation of physical impulses (sound) into rhythmic feeling (music) is a nonconceptual activity of human consciousness. It is an act of understanding by the human spirit (*Geist*) explained from the standpoint of that which it orders: human affect (*Affekt*).

Schleiermacher analyzed music to track the physical movements of human emotions. For him, as Gunter Scholtz rightly notes in his book *Ethics and Hermeneutics*, the beginning point of human experience "is the anthropological fact that the agitated/excited feeling, the affect, will express itself directly in a somatic reaction, in sounds, gestures, and actions."[27] In other words, the human body is anatomically designed so that strong surges of affect produce external somatic expressions.

To this end, Schleiermacher redefined the term *Affekt* to make the link between emotional and physical behavior evident. According to Schleiermacher, the human body is constructed in such a way that strong surges of affect must be expressed through bodily movement and gesture.[28] Music, he argued, can trigger these affective surges and the accompanying physical behavioral displays.

His innovative use of the term *Affekt* is best understood when placed in its immediate, etymological context. This historical context, as Karl Bernecker notes in his book, *A Critical Outline of the History of the Concept of Affect: From Descartes to the Present,* was created in the seventeenth century when Germans began to use this Latin-based term (*affectus*).[29] As Bernecker notes, the terms "affect" (*Affekt*) and the "movement of the disposition" (*Gemütsbewegung*) of a person very quickly became equivalent terms. The German term *Affekt* was used to describe the spiritual condition (*vestige*) of a person. This term, however, was almost never used to describe the physical condition of a person (*körperliche Befinden*). Schleiermacher broke this rule.

Schleiermacher now used the term "affect" and its related terms "being affected," "affection," a "moment of affection," and "affected" (*Affiziertsein, Affektion, Affektionsmoment, afficirt*) to identify the organic "material" (i.e., affect) the human spirit/mind (*Geist*) mentally organizes through acts of making sense of (*Besinnung*) one's own stirred up and agitated affections. This sense-making activity of the human mind together with the affective "senses," Schleiermacher concluded, is a moment of human consciousness as a created and creative moment of reason and feelings.

This new definition of "affect" is found in Schleiermacher's work on aesthetics. Aesthetics, for Schleiermacher, is the study of how the physical movement of human feeling becomes art. And art, according to Schleiermacher, is the creative external expression of an internal state of affective consciousness.

Schleiermacher made affect the bedrock reference for his new theological system even though he did not make affective studies part of this new academic field.[30] Thanks to Schleiermacher, affect rather than God, the Holy Spirit, Christ, the Bible, church tradition or doctrine, was now liberal theology's first and primary reference point for assessing the adequacy of religious claims.[31] And affective consciousness—the immediate feeling or experience of being moved by and embedded in the creative pulse of eternal life—was its touchstone.

Affect, for Schleiermacher, is thus foundational to the creation of religious community. Pious communities, he argued, are created by the reproduction of affective states "by means of facial expression, gesture, tone of voice, and indirectly by means of the spoken word."[32] This reproduction of similar emotional states of consciousness in persons is the *contagion*[33] that transmits and marks the collective affective displays as the temperamental signature of a specific religious community and church tradition. These affective displays create and maintain pious communities through this shared emotional state of a "consciousness of kind."[34]

Schleiermacher, in the Introduction to his major theological work (*Christian Faith*), called the primary affective state of consciousness for theological reflection the feeling of absolute dependence.[35] The term "God," Schleiermacher argued, refers to that which is felt reflexively *in* this human feeling as a co-determinant "push back" movement within this human state.[36] (The dancing priest, for example, thought about what he felt and called the feeling the presence of God. The priest was a missionary because he wanted to teach the Ethiopians to think about what they felt as the presence of the Catholic's God.) Schleiermacher wanted to spotlight the movement within us without reducing it to or confusing it with religious beliefs.

This movement within us is not our consciousness of God's internal nature, Schleiermacher argues, but rather refers to our human state of "God-consciousness" aligned with our feeling of absolute dependence. Accordingly, the immediate reference for the notion "God" is that which is co-posited in the *human* feeling of absolute dependence as a determination of the self from beyond itself.[37] This means that Schleiermacher's delineation of "God-consciousness" is not a doctrine of God *per se*, but rather a doctrine of God-consciousness in human experience.

For Schleiermacher, the notion of "God" is (1) *a result of* the personal, immediate, human feeling of absolute dependence. The term "God" is thus the first *idea* that comes to mind to explain a source co-posited with and also in the human feeling. Schleiermacher also explained the notion "God" as (2) *simultaneous with* the feeling.[38] But to claim that something is simultaneous with the feeling and also a direct reflection of the feeling is confusing.

Fourth Step
The Design Problems in
Schleiermacher's Affect Theology

Schleiermacher's theology, so it seems, was rife with conflicting claims, "concealments and ambiguities," according to Karl Barth. Barth, who was one of Schleiermacher's most influential twentieth-century critics, concluded that the basic source of these logical problems was Schleiermacher's attempt to put human emotions where the Holy Spirit belongs. By so doing, Barth argued, Schleiermacher compromised "a proper theology of the Holy Spirit [by offering up a] theology of [human self-] awareness."[39]

According to Barth, Schleiermacher stripped theology of its "third" element, the Holy Spirit, which is theology's principle of mediation, namely, the way everything that needs to be said, considered, or believed about God the Father and God the Son is shown and illuminated through God the Holy Spirit.[40] As a consequence, the distinction between man and God was lost. Schleiermacher, Barth concluded, had put culture—the acculturation and socialization process of human emotions—where it did not belong: in the "innermost sanctuary [of] his theology."

Thus Karl Barth's core complaint against Schleiermacher is that he had created a theological system that explained all Christian doctrines, practices, beliefs, and precepts as a study of the different ways in which human feelings are modified by the beliefs and practices of a particular religious community. Human experience rather than the Holy Spirit was now the foundation, namely, the place where pious feelings began.

Barth's critique was half right. Schleiermacher had indeed made the first reference for theological reflection triggered human emotions and their affective expressions, rather than the Holy Spirit. But Schleiermacher placed the study of triggered human emotions—and how they show up affectively—outside the academic field of theology. So Schleiermacher, contra Barth's claim, did not make the actual study of human emotions an immediate theological topic and concern. Instead, he relegated the actual study of the affective foundation of his theological scheme to ethics, philosophy, aesthetics, and other academic fields and disciplines.[41]

By consigning the study of the affective states of consciousness—the experiential foundation of this theological system—to other fields, Schleiermacher kept human feelings out of the realm of his theology. And by so doing, he created a theological system without a delineated exploration of how human emotions function in religious experience and shape doctrinal beliefs. Schleiermacher expected his readers to put in what was missing by drawing on their own personal experiences.

Schleiermacher concluded, through his own personal experiences, that the primal affective states (e.g., seeking, rage, fear, lust, care, panic, and play) are not relative but innate. He also thought that the ways these states are determined and expressed are not innate but relative to the cultural and social environment in which they are acculturated. Accordingly, Schleiermacher turned the primal affective states into the non-relative foundation of liberal theology. And he made the way these neurological states of

consciousness are determined as "pious," the empirical, cultur-
ally-linked relative foundation studied by Christian theology.

His liberal theology is thus a cultural theology, but the emotional foundation upon which it rests is not cultural: it's triggered
affect. Everyone, Schleiermacher insisted, can feel this innate capacity, namely, this neural movement within themselves. This
movement, when discerned with steadfast attention, sweeps one
into a state of cosmic consciousness.

The only thing required to enter this state is a critical ability for
self-understanding that differentiates and separates pious feelings
from their primal affective ground. Remember, Schleiermacher in
this work is not focusing on the particularity of Christianity, but
rather on the universal human experience of cosmic consciousness. And for Schleiermacher, this state is not a universal religion
because all religions are cultural creations and thus always refer
to particular faith traditions. Rather, Schleiermacher refers to that
which is found between thoughts, which can be called spiritual
experiences or cosmic consciousness or the feeling of love beyond
belief.

The assumptions that (1) religion is a man-made creation and
his belief that (2) theology's positive claims always entail a cultural bias created the following four structural design problems
for the readers of his theological system.

The dependency problem. Christian theology, set up by
Schleiermacher as a newly defined independent academic field
within a university, seemed dependent upon philosophy, ethics,
aesthetics, and psychology (i.e., the study of the psyche/soul) for
knowledge of its own foundation.[42] Schleiermacher thus seemed
to confound his own claim that liberal theology was a distinct academic field of inquiry.[43]

The obscurity problem. Schleiermacher's foundation for liberal
theology was obscure to the readers of his *Christian Faith.* So his
references to the non-rational, affective state of self-consciousness
foundational to his theological system were not self-evident to his
readers.

The problem of self-contradiction. The complex structure of independence and dependence coupled with the obscurity of its

foundational affective reference in human consciousness set off self-contradictory perceptions of Schleiermacher's liberal theology in its readers' minds.

The measurement problem. The measuring rod used by many of liberal theology's nineteenth-century Protestant evaluators judged Schleiermacher's system by the standard from which he had intentionally discharged it of duties: the doctrines of human nature formulated by Martin Luther or John Calvin. Both of these Reformers included their doctrine of human nature *within* their theological systems. Their use of conscience was the lynchpin here.[44] In contrast, Schleiermacher established liberal theology's foundation (i.e., its doctrine of human nature) *outside* his theological system. His *Affekt Theologie* explained this foundation in spiritual but not religious terms.

Schleiermacher expected his readers to understand what he was doing by looking beyond his theology and into themselves. But their vision did not extend that far, nor did the science of his era. Two centuries had to elapse before Schleiermacher's neuro-conceptual analysis of the affective foundation of his theological system could be reaffirmed in affective neuroscientific terms.

Fifth Step

Schleiermacher's Brain Science—A Translation Project

Schleiermacher invented the modern brain science of theology. More precisely, he invented affect theology, a theology of emotions designed to explain emotional development in religious terms and settings. He did so by creating academic theology as a secular university field of inquiry that studies how church communities create and sustain pious emotions in their members. The recitation of claims by Christian Church Fathers or references to the Bible or personal confessions of faith would no longer serve as the proof texts for the adequacy of religious claims and church doctrine.[45] Rather, the cogency of religious ideas was now linked to the way they explained, illustrated, created, and maintained pious affections in a given church community.

Pious feelings were now defined, in part, as a product of neurological processes. How do these affective neurological processes become the pious feelings that (1) bind individuals together and (2) create a religious community with its own set of traditions, beliefs, rituals and doctrines?

To answer this twofold question, Schleiermacher analyzed three domains of human consciousness: (1) affect, that is, a triggering impulse that activates feeling, (2) sensations/appearances, and (3) our unitive experience of personal coherence as the link between our internal affective states and our sensate states triggered by the external—in neuro-conceptual terms. So, too, the relationship between feeling (*Gefühl*) and affect (*Affekt*) uses these same terms.

This analysis, first presented in the 1799 publication of his book, *On Religion: Speeches for its Cultured Despisers*,[46] can be translated into contemporary neuroscientific terms. His neuro-conceptual analysis of human consciousness is, in effect, aligned with scientific advances of the past forty years. Thanks to the brain science of emotions (affective neuroscience) summarized in 1998 by Jaak Panksepp[47] and thanks to the "new ontology ... in modern experimental neuroscience" co-authored by Jaak Panksepp and Georg Northoff eleven years later,[48] the neuroscientific tools are now at hand to translate Schleiermacher's analysis of human emotions into what it actually was: the beginning stages of a mind-brain science that can illuminate religious emotions.[49]

A translation project of Schleiermacher's analysis into twenty-first-century neuroscientific terms "corrects" the two mistaken assumptions that framed this theological work. He had underestimated the extent of his own pioneering insights about the human brain and how it works. And he had underestimated his readers' ability to grasp what he had felt and what they could similarly feel: primal emotions uplifted into exalted pious experiences.

Two brief examples illustrate what his analysis affirms when translated into contemporary neuroscientific terms.

The first example. Consider Schleiermacher's twofold invitation to the readers of his 1799 *Speeches* (1) to observe the ways in which their own nervous systems are altered by the impress of external objects upon their sense organs, *and then* (2) to observe how these neural movements, prompted by exterior events, become linked to a completely different, internally generated, spontaneous movement of their emotions that alters their state of mind.[50] This twofold invitation to his readers, translated here into contemporary brain science terms, becomes Schleiermacher's call to focus attention on "actual brain processes as opposed to a conceptual entity."[51]

The second example. When Schleiermacher invites the readers of his *Speeches* to let their attention go back and forth between their sensations and emotions in order to see how these two areas of the mind oscillate together as one living moment of immediate self-consciousness,[52] he is actually calling for the reconceptualization of the core of the self in "new neuro-materialistic and neuro-dynamic ways."[53]

As Schleiermacher pointed out in his explanations of and commentaries on his *Speeches*, no one can command someone to have a particular feeling. So Kantian moral imperatives cannot function as the foundation of religion for two basic reasons. First, religion, according to Schleiermacher, originally is "feeling stirred in the highest direction,"[54] and "all higher feelings belong to religion."[55] Second, religion thus cannot be constructed by moral imperatives because religion pertains to the realm of human emotions and no one can command another person to feel.[56]

Schleiermacher focused attention on *how* individuals and communities learn to feel as a religious experience. Their affective values, Schleiermacher argued, are coded by the nervous system and exalted into culturally-determined pious feelings and dispositions. This affective coding process, Schleiermacher concluded, is the foundational reference for his liberal theological system. And he experienced this foundation as the heart-felt emotional integrity of his own religious life.

Sixth Step
Schleiermacher's Three Domains of Consciousness

Schleiermacher laid out his analysis of human consciousness in his *Speeches* and in the Introduction to his 1830/31 second edition of *Christian Faith*.[57] These two works, as Schleiermacher noted in his commentaries on his *Speeches*, have "many points of contact."[58] In neuro-conceptual terms, we first draw on these "points of contact" to highlight basic claims Schleiermacher makes in his *Speeches* about the structure of human consciousness. This translation project then goes on to explain Schleiermacher's most basic claims in contemporary neuroscientific terms.

Three of Schleiermacher's propositions in his *Speeches* set the stage for the present translation project:

- Our mind is the real world of religion.[59]
- Talk about religious emotions is thus talk about states of mind.[60]
- The religious content of our mind is discerned not through contemplation of the external world, but rather through self-contemplation, that is, through immediate self-consciousness or the soul's immediate awareness of itself.[61]

Schleiermacher, in effect, has just told his readers where they must look if they want to talk about religion and make sense of its claims: the human mind.

Commentary on these three propositions is found in the Introduction to his *Christian Faith*. In this text, Schleiermacher places feeling (*Gefühl*) and self-consciousness (*Selbstbewußtsein*) side-by-side as equivalent terms. Both terms, as he notes, refer to a nonreflective objectless state of the self, rather than to objective self-knowledge about a particular experience.[62] As such, the term *Gefühl* (feeling) refers to an emotion such as joy or sorrow or any other genuine state of feeling.[63]

In his Introduction, Schleiermacher also identifies the triggering impulse that activates feeling: *Affekt*.[64] He thus makes a fundamental distinction in his analysis of human consciousness between feeling and affect.

A simple example illustrates Schleiermacher's critically important distinction between feeling and affect. Imagine two persons who have just experienced the same shocking event and as a result anger is triggered within them. Both persons display the same initial spontaneous movements: their jaw muscles tighten; their eyes bulge; and their lips turn downward. But there the similarities end because of the ways the two persons immediately handle their triggered anger. One person has an emotionally volatile personality and begins to rant and rave, flailing his arms, shouting, and punching at the air. The other person tends toward emotional quiescence so the anger does not peak with a bang but ends with a whimper, a sigh of sadness, and a tear.

This example spotlights the difference between (1) the triggered anger with its spontaneous somatic displays (the facial expressions, etc.) by the two persons, and (2) the way the anger is then handled by their respective dominant and pervasive emotional dispositions.[65]

Schleiermacher noted the difference. And he used two different German terms to track this difference: *Affekt* and *Gefühl*. Moreover, he designed his new theological system to take note of *how* one particular kind of feeling—pious feeling (*Frömmigkeit*)—is created as a management regime for triggered emotions.

The term *Gefühl* (feeling), for Schleiermacher, refers to a religious disposition. It is, as such, an emotion that has been moved in a particular way. In short, piously.

The function of religious and spiritual communities, from this perspective, is to establish the dominant affective temperament—the ethos—that mediates all emotional states. This emotional framework is the felt value-structuring affective principle of the community that transforms the raw emotions of the congregants into uplifting feelings of awe, gratitude, joy, and so much more. Schleiermacher called this experiential ethos of a congregation Gefühl, namely the uplifting spiritual feeling created within the self by the community. This dominant affective state determines how triggered emotions are handled "piously." A religious community, from this perspective, can thus teach its members, affectively, how to hate beyond belief or how to love beyond belief as their dominant "pious" state of consciousness.

According to Schleiermacher, the original task of religion is to stir up emotions in the highest direction. In short, to exalt them. Religion, says Schleiermacher, originally is "feeling stirred in the highest direction."[66] Moreover, "all higher feelings belong to religion," says Schleiermacher.[67] Religion thus functions for

Schleiermacher as the affective trigger for inspiring/inspirational emotional states of the mind.

Religion, from this perspective, pertains to the *way* in which emotional states are determined affectively as pious states of mind.[68] This is why religion, according to Schleiermacher, should be the mind's overarching emotional disposition: religion functions as the way in which triggered emotions are handled piously by the mind. All healthy sentiments, according to Schleiermacher, are or should be pious in order to avoid emotional dis-ease,[69] namely, toxic emotional relations to self, others, and the wider world.[70]

Schleiermacher, in his *Speeches*, thus identifies three domains of consciousness, giving *Affekt* its own domain in human consciousness in the following way.[71]

The First Domain: Affect. Schleiermacher refers to *Affekt* as the "mover" of emotions, "the stimulus of single feelings."[72] He calls the area of the mind where this shift in feeling takes place a domain of consciousness pertaining to what is strictly interior to the mind. It is here, says Schleiermacher, that we become aware of a domain of our consciousness that pertains to the inner life of our self *per se*.[73]

To help his readers find and understand this domain, Schleiermacher directed them not only to turn their attention inward to their own consciousness, but also to descend into the "inmost sanctuary of life" found therein.[74] This inmost sanctuary, according to Schleiermacher, pertains to human feelings generated within the self rather than to human sensations that are prompted by events exterior to the mind.

The Second Domain: Sensations. Schleiermacher, in his *Speeches*, now identifies a second domain of human consciousness. This area of the mind pertains to our awareness of sensate appearances (call it mass, material, or element or whatever you wish, Schleiermacher says). In short, sensate appearances. Perceptions. According to Schleiermacher, this domain of consciousness pertains to that which occurs exterior to the mind. Here one discovers how the exterior world is first expressed in consciousness as sense data. A person finds, in short, appearances.[75] This domain thus refers to perception, that is, to that which can be intuited and perceived,[76] rather than to that which is immediately *experienced*: feeling.

The Third Domain: The In-between. Schleiermacher's third domain of human consciousness pertains to that which is between the interior and exterior domains. This domain might seem fanciful to many of us, so I begin with an example of it and then, using the example, explain what is entailed in this domain.

The example is a story about Margaret, a research assistant who worked with me several years ago.[77] She is a master horse rider and gymnast. During a horse show jumping competition, Margaret's horse stopped unexpectedly at one of the hurdles, thus throwing Margaret over it. In midair, she realized that she was tumbling almost in a somersault fashion. She gained control of the tumble, thus turning it into a gymnastic somersault and landed on her feet with both hands raised above her head as if she were in a gymnastic competition. The judges and audience applauded. She bowed.

Margaret's transformation of the uncontrolled tumble into a controlled somersault is what Schleiermacher means by his definition of artistic activity as the act of expanding the interval between initial agitation into an ordered, artistic movement and expression.

This kind of shift from agitation to ordered movement—illustrated by Margaret's story—is Schleiermacher's most basic reference for artistic activity. Art is the act of changing agitated activity into ordered movement. The agitation originally awakened a capacity of the human being to express this activity externally. The external expression appears (e.g., Margaret's somersault) as an ordered movement and, as such, it is an artistic expression internally modeled by *Geist* (the mind).

Geist and *Affekt* are thus the limits between which human consciousness is calibrated as a determinate moment of consciousness.

The narrative about my research assistant can now be used to help clarify what Schleiermacher means by the third domain of human consciousness.

In midair, as Margaret tumbled, she realized that she could shift the way in which she expressed the sudden jolt to herself caused by her horse's unexpected halt. At the moment of realization, she created a space between the way she was falling and the way she could tumble.

This space between the two is the dawning moment of a new conception. It is also the open and opened capacity of her body to respond to physical movement in a variety of skillful ways. In other words, the unity of her awareness of the difference between agitation and expression gave her the space she needed for a creative act. The wider the space we create for improvisational skills, the more masterful our artistry.

Both her body and her mind negotiated this terrain together. Her theories about the way gymnastics works informed the way she moved her body, which then informed her theories through praxis. Margaret thus ended her tumble as an artistic activity, a moment of sustained creativity, a duration of creation, a moment of lived experience perfected through the co-determinate coordination of theory and practice. In short, praxis. Her performance was an artistic activity.

Every human being engages in artistic activity, Schleiermacher argues, because human affections (and sensate experiences) are always astir—our nervous systems are always being triggered—and some of these shifts can be comprehended by and as a spiritual (mental) act. The difference in artists pertains to degree and depends upon interest, talent, and personal character. Because such acts of coordination are a birthright, Schleiermacher believed that all of us can achieve some form of creativity.

Our bodies and our minds negotiate this terrain together. Through this back-and-forth negotiation between our bodies and our minds, says Schleiermacher, we become aware of a binding of the other two areas (affect and sensation) together achieved through a going back and forth, an inward and outward awareness or mental state that by this very movement unites both domains together. Peace of mind is achieved, Schleiermacher tells us, only with the acceptance of this unconditional, intimate (*innigsten*) union of the inner and outer domains.

This domain between the other two domains is the realm of the individual, Schleiermacher concludes, because it is the domain of the consummate, the accomplished, the perfected (*des in sich Vollendeten*); the place where everything that is art in nature and in the works of humans is found.[78] It's the place that lets us land on our feet as the co-determinate coordination of theory and practice we have achieved.

In this place, Schleiermacher tells us, we experience our original unity, which I call cosmic consciousness. Here we experience "the original relation of feeling and intuition from which alone their unity (*ihr Einsein*) and their separation (*ihre Trennung*) is to be understood."[79]

Schleiermacher, in effect, linked the human act of understanding to physical and sensate activity—and to insensate *Affekt*. *Affekt* is thus included as part of every human experience in Schleiermacher's scheme of things. And the co-determination of the self between its whirl of the emotional and the sensate domains is the space where the unitive experience of the self, namely, cosmic consciousness, is found. Schleiermacher's third domain of consciousness is located where this "co-occurrence"—this convergent unity between emotions and sensations—takes place. This unity is felt in the space between thoughts as the sweep of cosmic consciousness astir with life itself.

Another way to think about this unity is to visualize the transition point between the integers minus one and plus one: zero. Zero is not the meeting point of these two whole numbers. Rather it's the transition point of their incommensurable differences. It's the domain in which one number comes to an end and the other number begins. This space of transition between them is akin to the place where human consciousness shifts from emotions to sensations, thoughts to feelings, and ideas to affections. There is nothing in this domain except the movement of life itself, the oscillation of consciousness that affectively resonates as an actual occasion—and actual movement—of life.

The next step in this translation project can now be taken: Schleiermacher's three domains of human consciousness will be translated into twenty-first-century, affective neuroscientific terms.

Seventh Step
The Translation of Schleiermacher's Three Domains of
Consciousness into Contemporary Neuroscientific Terms

The translation of the three domains of consciousness delineated by Schleiermacher into contemporary neuroscientific terms focuses attention on the neural operations of the brain. This neurological perspective on human consciousness takes into account a paradigm shift begun more than three decades ago. The shift, as neurobiologist Allan N. Schore notes in his book *Affect Regulation and the Origin of the Self: The Neurobiology of Emotional Development,* has moved psychology away from the narrow constraints of a strict behaviorism: multidisciplinary studies of cognitive and affective processes are now investigated as proximal internal causes of overt behavior.[80]

This present translation project is also framed by three basic affective neuroscientific guidelines summarized as follows.

First, we *experience* feelings. We feel them as internal affective states. These primary felt states (such as rage, fear, grief/panic, and play) are generated by the emotional operating systems of our brain.[81] We feel (experience) specific states of our own nervous system.[82] When we are enraged, for example, we feel rage. We are feeling in that moment an actual occasion of our life: rage. We are in this affective state of consciousness as a living moment of personal experience.

Panksepp found three basic types of affect: (1) homeostatic (i.e., internal bodily needs and processes) affects: affect that make us feel/experience shifts in the internal state of our body (e.g., hunger or fatigue) as internal organic value judgments that become the noncognitive motive for action to ensure survival and flourishing; (2) emotional affects: affect that makes us psychologically feel/experience the type of emotional system that has been triggered and thus aroused (e.g., the feeling of being enraged, afraid, cared for) as internal organic values judgments that prompt behavior to ensure survival and flourishing; (3) sensate affects: affect that makes us feel/experience the intensity of bodily sensations (e.g., tactile and visual stimulation from sources exterior to the body) as internal organic value judgments that prompt behavior to ensure survival and flourishing.[83]

These affective commentaries on changes to various homeostatic bodily process, changes to our sensations, and changes to our emotions, Panksepp concluded, are the way we initially, consciously but non-conceptually, feel/experience what has just happened to our body. This felt state is indeed a state of consciousness, defined here functionally as the "bare awareness of 'something.'"[84]

Referring to affects as "pre-propositional feelings," Panksepp found that they alert us, not through ideas, but through a felt sense of life—called affective consciousness—about how we are faring in the world, within ourselves, and with others at the somatic level of our lives.[85] To be sure, Panksepp argues, these affective triggerings can be mediated by rational consideration as well as through dream work on alternative ways of responding behaviorally to the triggered feelings.[86] Nevertheless, they are a way in which the brain neurologically assesses and thus values the surrounding environment in order to make affective judgments (linked to motor movements) that dictate approach or retreat. Affects, in sum, are physical neurological value judgments of internal shifts within the body that prompt actions by the organism to ensure its survival and thriving in its exterior environment, its world. They measure shifts within us and value them to alert us subjectively/neurologically to what has just happened to us.

Second, we can also *become aware of* what we felt (e.g. rage) by turning the felt experience into a cognitive object of inquiry. When, for example, we think about how enraged we are, we conceptually cognize the experience and reflect upon it. This act of reflection is a mental act of awareness different from the personal experience of rage itself. This state of awareness is thus not rage experienced but rather raged parsed.

Third, affects are value-coded. More precisely, the intensity of the experience is measured, registered, and felt as, for example, pleasant or unpleasant, too intense or not intense enough. These values are "intrinsically biological," as Jaak Panksepp and Georg Northoff demonstrate in their groundbreaking 2009 essay, "The trans-species core SELF."[87] The values are "indexed" affectively "by positive and negative affects."[88] These valuations alert us to the "relevance" of an experience. Will it enhance or harm our life?[89] Approach or retreat is based on these felt and thus experienced affective emotional value codes.

Accordingly, we filter external stimuli affectively. Sensations get shifted and coded.[90] Our brain screens what is felt before our mind knows it. Neuroanatomist Jill Bolte Taylor states all of this quite succinctly when noting, "Although many of us think of ourselves as *thinking creatures that feel*, biologically we are *feeling creatures that think*."[91]

From this contemporary neuroscientific perspective, there are two systems of self-knowledge: (1) an explicitly conscious, cognitive, self-reflective, evidence-based self-knowledge processing that can be termed "awareness" and (2) a non-cognitive, conscious, automatic, and implicit affective valuation process communicated "non-verbally [and] independently of any linguistic abilities," which is pure "experience."[92]

The non-verbal communication system, as Panksepp and Northoff note, enables us to feel an emotional state as a self-relational process and also to relate emotionally to others. These two neuroscientists thus characterize this self-relating processing as "affective felt but automatic [insensate rather than] self-conscious awareness that is cognitive and explicit."[93]

In Panksepp and Northoff's terms, Schleiermacher attempts to show how "one experiences one's self, one's body and one's environment singly and in relations to others."[94] The entire progression entails a process by means of which the self not only relates to itself but also creates the experience it feels.

In sum, we do not first reflect upon what is happening to our brains and bodies; we simply feel it. What we then become aware of is more—or less—than the feeling itself. Our conditioning and thoughts, our affective history, learning and memory value code what we felt. The original experience is now a socially-constructed, affect-encoded awareness of what the experience cognitively means to us.

Thus the result is "what becomes represented in our perceptions are not just [externally produced] environmental objects and stimuli, but neurobiological-environmental relationships and social interactions that are mediated affectively."[95] We have become socially-constructed selves with socially-constructed others in an embedded wider social world.

From this perspective, Schleiermacher's three domains of consciousness pertain to how external and internal stimuli get linked together *within* an organism and valued.[96] The two neuroscientists call this internal linking process "co-occurrence."

Schleiermacher's first two domains of consciousness, in these contemporary neuroscientific terms, refer respectively to what Panksepp and Northoff identify as internal states (affects) and external stimuli (sensations).[97] The third domain refers to how these two domains "co-occur."

Schleiermacher's first domain of consciousness, from this contemporary neuroscientific perspective, can now be affirmed. The content of this first domain is explained by Panksepp as the link between what goes on within the brain and how it shows up in the body and the mind.[98] Affects, as such, are bodily and brain state experiences. They "are all within-brain barometers that signal survival utility."[99] Schleiermacher's claims and those of Panksepp and Northoff about the "within" or entirely internal content of this domain are thus aligned. The content of this domain is affect.

Affects, in contemporary affective neuroscientific terms, are primary processes, namely, spontaneous ways we make organic value judgments about how our bodies are faring in the world. The emotional, behavioral movements of our bodies and the simultaneous generation of corresponding psychological states of experience are called "dual-aspect monism" because the brain creates both at the same time.[100] More precisely, the same circuits that were triggered in our brain and prompt physical movements of our bodies and our facial expressions also prompt psychological experiences (i.e., affects) of these changes happening within our brains and bodies at the same time.[101]

This contemporary affective neuroscientific perspective coheres with Schleiermacher's claim that the human body is constructed in such a way that strong surges of affect must be expressed through bodily movement and gesture.[102] Music, to reiterate, can trigger these affective surges and accompanying physical displays and behavior.

Schleiermacher's second domain, from the present neuroscientific perspective, is also affirmed here through the discussion of the co-occurrence of external and internal stimuli.

For Schleiermacher, the third domain is the link between affect and sensate awareness. This is an interfacing domain. It's the Margaret moment. Our act of creativity. It's where self-coherence as one organism with multiple events is orchestrated. These disparate events now cohere as a unitive moment of experience called "mine." This symphony orchestrates our soul and attunes us. Our "lowest integrative centers" for self-coherence are found here.[103] We are now a cosmic creation, namely, a lyrical harmonic note.

This is the place in our brain where nature and nurture first meet. Panksepp and Northoff identify a place where this linking takes place: the periaqueductal gray (PAG) area of the brain. In this part of the *limbic system* of the brain our emotions and sensations converge. Panksepp and Northoff call it "a basic-emotion 'epicenter.'" It relates to "higher midline cortical regions" as well as to "the lowest midbrain integrator for emotionality."[104]

This epicenter creates our sense of self as a "me." This self *is a process that makes things cohere as "my" experiences with other events, persons, and things.* Raw affects, Panksepp and Northoff suggest, make up the lowest aspects of this network of events. Here, the co-occurrence of raw perceptual and affective levels of phenomenal consciousness is sustained. The higher aspects of this system allow these co-occurring processes "to become molded to fit cultural and ecological environments."[105]

The self is thus always a socially-embedded creation. But it is also more than this. It is, as Panksepp puts it, the ineffable feeling of being an active agent in the perceived world of events.

This domain, for Schleiermacher, is the way the interior and exterior domains get linked together into a unitive experience of cosmic consciousness. Peace of mind is achieved, Schleiermacher tells us, only with the acceptance of this unconditional, intimate (*innigsten*) union of the inner and outer domains. This self-relational process is the content of our character, the realm where the individual is born as a self with agency, coherence, unity, and an embedded relationship to others and the wider world. It is the place of the consummate, the accomplished, the perfected (*des in sich Vollendeten*), namely, the place where everything that is art in nature and in the works of humans is found.[106] Here we experience our original unity. Here we experience "the original relation of feeling and intuition from which alone their unity (*ihr Einsein*) and their separation (*ihre Trennung*) is to be understood."[107]

In contemporary terms, Schleiermacher's delineation of the original relation between feeling and sensations/perceptions is the co-occurrence of raw perceptual and affective levels of human experience. Schleiermacher's analysis of all three domains of human consciousness is reaffirmed.

Spirituality, namely, cosmic consciousness is the experience of unity. The extended, infinite moment of peace. This experience is not a cultural creation. The attempt to explain it, however, is the cultural creation called religion. Religion explains the universal human experience in concrete cultural terms. This is why there is no such thing as a universal religion. Religion, by definition, is a cultural creation. But the human experience to which it originally refers is not a cultural creation. It's a feeling of being aligned with and supported by life itself. The dancing priest called this feeling "God."

The link between self-processes and emotional-affective states also makes religion invariably social. Religion always has an objective, external reference to a particular culture and tradition. The linkage occurs because the affective processes and the valuation entailed therein are (1) fundamentally self-related processing[108] and they are, at the same time, (2) embedded within a social world.

Schleiermacher's argument, thanks to our translation project, can now be laid out as a series of propositional claims.

First, the original task of religion, Schleiermacher argues, is to trigger affective states of exaltation, to stir up emotions in their highest direction.

Second, this means that pious feeling, according to Schleiermacher, entails within it a sweep of emotions from debasement to exaltation. This is the case because pious feeling affirms its opposite feeling as a beginning or endpoint. Contrition, for example, is changed to joyful self-sufficiency because religion stirs up and exalts human emotions.[109]

Third, since the purpose of the *Speeches*, according to Schleiermacher, is to show his readers how piety can be found in all human sentiments that unite humans for a higher or even a more sensuous enjoyment of life,[110] Schleiermacher now focuses his reader's attention on the ways

  i. human affections are triggered and moderated as internal states of human consciousness, and
  ii. raw emotions are changed into the social impulse (*der gesellige Trieb*) that Schleiermacher refers to as religion. As he notes in his Fourth *Speech*, "If there is religion at all, it must be social, for it is the nature of man, and it is quite peculiarly the nature of religion."[111] Moreover, as Schleiermacher notes in the Introduction to *Christian Faith*, pious communities create what they feel together affectively and become a shared community of these embodied states as a "consciousness of kind [*Gattungsbewußtsein*]."[112] Shared affect piously valenced, for Schleiermacher, is thus foundational to the creation of religious community.

Fourth, these pious feelings described by Schleiermacher are, in Panksepp's terms, our brain's neurological-affective responses to the impact of environmental facts upon our bodies. As neuro-psychologist Darcia Narvaez reminds us, "humans are born with 75 percent of the brain yet to develop. As a result of the rapid brain development after birth, children's initial brain and body formation is highly influenced by those who care for them, especially in the first five years of life. The foundations of the brain develop in concert with care-giver treatment."[113] So how the baby is nurtured quite literally helps or hinders brain development. Panksepp calls these "environmentally-constructed neurological responses to the way we are nurtured secondary (memory and conditioning) and tertiary (cognitive-type) emotions."[114] They are created "entities," actual occasions of experience in which nature (primal affects) and nurture (the caretaking environment) meet. Our emotions, simply put, are autobiographical. And each chapter of this autobiography can be thought of as a particular passage of our life, a "distinct entity" that gives us the content of our socialized character. We are conditioned; we are socially-constructed beings whose memories and ideas are linked to the way we learned to affirm, set aside, and/or deny our feelings.

These "distinct entities"—discrete personal experiences—emerge, Panksepp argues, "largely from social-labeling processes, whereby we experience slightly differing patterns of primary feelings [like anger, fear, playfulness and care in various social contexts] and come to accept them as distinct entities." This work must go on in our brains, Panksepp concludes, because at the beginning of our lives "we are utterly dependent creatures whose survival is founded on the quality of social bonds."[115] The hand that rocks the cradle shapes the brain.

Our primary social bonding experiences go hand-in-hand with our ability to experience loneliness, grief, and other feelings of social loss. Accordingly, the way our brain links together our disparate experiences is of critical importance. It establishes and re-establishes our impulse equilibrium. The lowermost, interfacing structure of the emotional brain is thus "absolutely essential for spontaneous engagement with the world."[116]

Damage to this integrative center for the coherent display of feeling creates sluggish behavior. If the damage is excessive, Panksepp concludes, the result is a semi-comatose (vegetative) state. Neuropsychologist Darcia Narvaez gives us a vivid picture of what this damage entails:

> Good caregiving and social support foster the positive social emotions (care, play, joy in relationship, empathy) and the regular and deep social pleasures found among hunter-gatherers would facilitate the right brain and the engagement ethic.
>
> Many modern Western societies have eliminated the supports for virtue development that our ancestors experienced at all ages.... In the USA, social supports have been decreasing among all age groups for over 50 years.[117] With neglectful

or harmful child care now common in USA practices, the right brain and the social emotions are not cultivated with much intensity or are thwarted entirely. So the view presented here is that the USA is more likely to raise people with dispositions toward detached and vicious imagination among the privileged and wallflower or bunker mindset among the poor. These are conclusions I have drawn from looking at a range of data and findings from across disciplines. The culture influences not only childrearing practices but also moral functioning generally.[118]

In workshops that Narvaez and I conduct together, we characterized this damaging of the brains of our children in the following way: dominant child rearing practices harm our kids' social development, blunt their capacity to care for the natural world, and impair their emotional development and sensate intelligence. And when many of these children grow up, their damaged feelings become rooted in distrust, fear, and self-protection.

Fifth, in line with Panksepp's observations, we can conclude that the overarching content and creation of distinct entities—personal characteristics—by the periaqueductal gray (PAG) area of the brain differ among human societies. This is the case because we are born in a particular time and place, and within a particular social context. Each social context has its own respective "intermixture" of secondary and tertiary cognitive-type emotions that characterize the ethnic or social group as, for example, impassioned or restrained. Each intermixture thereby constitutes a cultural/psychological matrix, a complex of actual entities bound together affectively and "coded" linguistically to create the emotional ethos or "distinct [psychological] entity" of a particular people. Each culture, if you will, puts its own particular spin on its members' emotional development and thus on the content of their character.

Eighth Step
The King's Letter to Schleiermacher

On September 27, 1817, Schleiermacher received a letter from Friedrich Wilhelm III, the King of Prussia. Wilhelm III was also the highest bishop of Schleiermacher's Reformed Church tradition, which followed the Protestant teachings of the Reformation Reformer John Calvin. The king wanted to celebrate the Lord's Supper with his wife, who was Lutheran. And thus the king's query: Why should these denominational differences prevent them from celebrating the Holy Sacrament together as Christians? Since Schleiermacher was president of the United Synod of Lutheran and Reformed minsters and also dean of the theological faculty at the University of Berlin, the king ordered him to set things right. He must construct a service the couple could participate in together without violating their own respective Protestant traditions, doctrines, and beliefs.

In response, Schleiermacher and the other members of the synod created a United Evangelical worship service and celebration of the Lord's Supper for the King and his wife. The service took place with sixty-three heads of state and ministers present. Five years later, the full union of the Lutheran and Reformed churches took place. On Palm Sunday in 1822, the Evangelical Church of Prussia was born.[119]

Both church traditions, Schleiermacher reasoned, triggered affect, namely, turned the raw and ravaged emotions of their folk into the socially-constructed pious feelings of their flock. As noted earlier, triggered affect, for Schleiermacher, is thus foundational to the creation of religious community. Pious communities are created by the reproduction of affective states "by means of facial expression, gesture, tone of voice, and indirectly by means of the spoken word." These expressions are "contagious."

This pious way triggered feelings are handled, Schleiermacher concluded, is the defining work of every religious community. Churches attend to affective consciousness in order to create pious feelings in their individual members and in their wider religious community.[120]

Thanks to the King of Prussia, Schleiermacher was given the prompt he needed to explain his new affective theological system to his religious world in nondenominational terms.

Thanks to Panksepp and Northoff, we can track his nondenominational explanation of religious experience as the co-occurrence of sensations, concepts, *and* emotions.

And thanks to Panksepp, Northoff, *and* Schleiermacher, we need no longer talk about religion as, at base, a set of good or bad ideas because the foundation of Schleiermacher's theological system is personal, affective experience. The unitive content of this experience is called cosmic consciousness.

Schleiermacher, however, lost the affective access point to cosmic consciousness, he affirmed. To retrieve it, we now have to read Schleiermacher against himself.

Chapter Two

Schleiermacher's Split Self

As is illustrated by my story in chapter one about the worship service my colleague and I attended in Roxbury, Massachusetts, mainline liberal church services tend to shortchange feelings, while Evangelical churches cash in on them.

This affect-deficiency problem in liberal churches today is part of the legacy of Schleiermacher's own failed attempt to make triggered and transformed affections a core factor in liberal theology. His own gender biases also got in the way. As a consequence, he toppled the emotional openness and inclusion he spent his life trying to affirm.

This chapter shows how Schleiermacher, at one and the same time, affirmed the emotional unity and also the sundered condition of the self. The proof-text for both claims was his own life. But appeals to personal experience, of course, aren't normally generalized to all people's experience. Schleiermacher did this and then acknowledged his mistake to a friend. [1]

Here's a bullet summary of his predicament.

- Schleiermacher, as noted in chapter one, felt both joy and a ceaseless pain when Eleanore Grunow—his "soul mate"—ended their seven-year relationship.
- He drew on gender-coded, nineteenth-century Prussian ideas and concepts of affect to explain this sundered state of his soul.

- He also affirmed the ongoing integrity of his soul by drawing on his experience of music and his notion of a primary,
  non-gendered soul.

Two results followed. Schleiermacher's analysis of personal
experience is more nuanced than his own gender-based, male and
female affective constructions and images of the human soul. So
his work can be used to prove opposing claims, namely, that he
is both a progressive supporter and also a retrograde despiser of
women's rights.

In this chapter, I sort through the plethora of conflicting claims
about Schleiermacher's views of women in order to reaffirm what
Schleiermacher failed to affirm in his actual life: equal rights for
men and women.

The sorting process undertaken here is not an academic exer-
cise. Rather, it is a human rights concern. But it is also a spiritual
concern because his gender biases blocked access to affective experiences of emotional transformations. In short, it walled off the
access point to cosmic consciousness.

Schleiermacher reaffirmed theology as an academic field for
men. Thanks to the professionalism of theology in the nineteenth
century spearheaded by Schleiermacher, "scientific" theology assumed the nature of an academic guild that excluded women[2]
and analyzed the human condition from the standpoint of men.[3]

Moreover, he now used his affect theology to biologize wom-
en's subservient social position. The educational and civil restric-
tions on women's activities must be maintained, he insisted, so
that the "natural," "female disposition" of the woman to attend to
her household, her marriage, her children, and her religious feelings would not be "damaged."[4]

This twofold assault on women's rights by Schleiermacher's
impaired, affective theological system created clergy who began
to write texts against it. Modern feminist theology arose as "advocacy theology"[5] for the liberation of women from the vested
androcentric interests of the liberal theology spearheaded by
Schleiermacher. So, too, did racial, ethnic, class, and gender theo-

logical enclaves create phalanxes against the entrenched self-serving interests of the original academic guild.

Schleiermacher, of course, is not solely responsible for the demise of liberal Christian ministry and the tanking of liberal seminaries and mainline congregations. But he must be held accountable for the systemic inability of his heirs to find and affirm a shared, affective foundation for their disparate beliefs and academic strategies today. His theological enterprise, after all, did not show them how to explore the space between thoughts, but instead taught them how to close off insights into this human state of cosmic consciousness that is the human foundation of spiritual experience and the first reference for religious beliefs.

This chapter focuses attention on a major conceptual source of Schleiermacher's gender biases, namely, the divisive linguistic terms he used to describe the non-divisive, affective state of cosmic consciousness. More precisely, I track how he used the same *male and female terms to describe the schism in human consciousness and to define its original wholeness.*

A simple way to understand this complex linguistic problem is to think of the *New Yorker* cartoon in which an unreconstructed patriarch introduces his wife to friends saying, "I want you to meet the little woman, a person in her own right." The words stripped the wife of the personhood her husband ostensibly set out to affirm.

Similarly, Schleiermacher's use of male and female terms had a paternalistic linguistic turn that elevated the stature of women dismissively as his use of male/female gender terms became prescriptive rather than descriptive.

The problem I focus on here begins with his linguistic shift from a genderless state of wholeness—cosmic consciousness—to a gendered state of split consciousness. To resolve this linguist problem, I then read Schleiermacher against himself to reconfirm the state of wholeness his experiences affirmed and his words denied.

Consider his *Christmas Eve* dialogue,[6] which demeans what he promotes: women.

I

The structure of Schleiermacher's peace of mind is linked to the female images in his *Christmas Eve* narrative. To this end, he made the images of women definitive, concrete facts of human consciousness rather than expressive descriptors of his own imaginatively improvised world as he grappled with the loss of Eleanore Grunow.

Christmas Eve consists, predominantly, of mental constructions linked to the determination of pious affections that are displayed (images) from multiple perspectives. It is an improvisational orchestration of the vast array of Schleiermacher's own religious affections ordered and sustained as images. The human soul is displayed here as the back-and-forth movement of human consciousness between pious affections (female) and pious rational reflections (male). We get to watch, simply put, Schleiermacher gender-caricature the human soul.

The "plotline" spins around a wager by the dinner party guests at a Christmas Eve celebration in one of their homes. Who can best explain what Christmas is really all about? The dominant image throughout the stories and comments by the women is that they are closer to Christ than men because women have never broken the continuity of childhood within them. Like Christ, they are not in need of conversion because they never broke away from the divine human nature. Their affections, we would say, have not been split.

The first level of the narrative is the music. Friedericke plays the piano, sings lyrics from the poems of Romantic poets, and improvises melodies to accompany or as interlude to the conversation among the friends. Sophie, a spritely child, also plays and sings. The host explains the link between music and religious feeling, saying "every fine feeling comes completely to the fore only when we have found the right musical expression for it." And further, "it is precisely to religious feeling that music is most closely related.... What the word has declared the tones of music must make alive, in harmony conveying it to the whole inner being of its hearers and holding it fast there."[7]

The second level of the play is the images, which for Schleiermacher are the first mental expression of human affections religiously configured. Accordingly, Schleiermacher's women provide the group with the definitive content of the imagination: pious feelings.

Ernestine describes a lady, seated on a church pew, as she and a small child peer into each other's eyes, transfixed. Although Ernestine could see the disposition of the mother shift, what was communicated throughout was "a sense of affable serenity."[8]

Agnes describes the image of an infant who was not interested in his Christmas gifts because he was "still completely oriented toward his mother.... His consciousness [was] still united to hers." Only she "could cherish and gladden it."[9]

Karoline describes an infant who lay dying in his mother arms but gains new life after all had lost hope. The mother thus feels blessed twice because a special gift of grace had given her two heavenly children: her son and the Christ child.

The third level of the narrative presents the concepts. Leonhardt, the rationalist, affirms Christianity as a "vigorous social force," locates its meaning in symbolic expressions of God's eternal decree rather than in a historical Jesus, and deems the main object of Christmas celebration to be children.[10]

Ernst believes that Christmas represents the mood that the festival is designed to incite: joy.[11] The cause of this joy is the Redeemer, because "there is no other principle of joy than redemption." The festival thus makes persons conscious of "an inner ground out of which a new, untrammeled life emerges."[12]

The final speaker is Josef, who arrived while the men were speaking. He pronounces the men's speeches tedious, cold, and joyless: in short, affection-less.

Women, in this overall scenario, are raised up to their biological height as mothers who bear and care for children. This uplift lowers women to feeling and raises men to reason.

II

Three results follow from this facile male and female gender stereotyping in *Christmas Eve*.

1. Schleiermacher's analyses and discussions of male and female affective states express only a part of the human experience of wholeness.
2. In Schleiermacher's conceptual scheme, it is impossible to be a male or female human being and be complete without reference to the opposite gender.
3. Male and female experiences are both sundered or split states of affective consciousness.

Accordingly, the way Schleiermacher's work gets assessed as advocacy for women's rights is based on whether the investigators focus on

i. the equality of functions Schleiermacher establishes between the male and female genders,
ii. the unitive experience of affective consciousness (and the female as closer to this unitive experience than the male), or
iii. his reification of these gendered distinctions as a split consciousness that reduces the other (female) to terms that complement and complete male deficiencies.

Scholars who emphasize Schleiermacher's high valuation of women's moral and religious character in his 1798 essay "Idea for a Catechism of Reason for Noble Women" correctly deem him to be a friend of contemporary feminist issues.[13] And scholars who point to his stands against the political, educational, and social liberation of women rightly call him an opponent of women's civil rights.[14] Most accurately, those scholars who realize that his "feminine impulses" and "anti-feminist exclusion of women from public life" are not easily separated wisely call for more research because something seems amiss.[15]

We can now sort through, order, and explain these disparate conclusions and judgments by using the above threefold key to Schleiermacher's work on women.

Two examples illustrate the point.

1. Marilyn Chapin Massey's book *The Feminine Soul*

Massey assesses Schleiermacher's use of gendered images and concepts and his ideas about women's civil rights from the standpoint of principle (iii): his reification of gendered distinctions for male benefit. Massey thus concludes that Schleiermacher granted women a special function in religion for the benefit of male autonomy.[16] She carefully identifies the nineteenth-century gender coding Schleiermacher uses to describe the women in his *Christmas Eve* narrative. Massey draws on ample evidence from Schleiermacher's own views to support her claims.

Massey's own standpoint is clear. She seeks to give women the special status possessing the superior soul. She thus rejects Schleiermacher's fundamental claim that humanity, when whole, is one gender.

The major problem with Massey's critique of Schleiermacher is her own agenda: she strives to prove the feminine soul superior to the male soul. She has written her book to affirm "the unique spiritual qualities" of women as superior to those of the male soul and salvific for the world.[17] Massey thus commits the same crime for which she indicts Schleiermacher: gender superiority. The core level of the error for both Massey and Schleiermacher, however, is not gendered arrogance but a constricted cultural imagination. Their work displays "a presumed natural law of dimorphism, encoded in cultural reasoning, that assigns all things sexual to biological types, male and female."[18]

Anthropologist Gilbert Herdt, when defining this problem of a presumed ontologically two-valued determination of sexual identity as either male or female, vividly identifies the central problem: both Massey and Schleiermacher are biologizing culturally-defined gender traits.

2. Ruth Drucilla Richardson's groundbreaking book *The Role of Women in the Life and Thought of the Early Schleiermacher (1768–1804): An Historical Overview*

Richardson focuses on principles (i) and (ii): the complementary equality of the male and female, and the unitive experience of wholeness in Schleiermacher's work. As Richardson notes in the introduction to her book, her work is the "first monograph-length study in any language on gender relations and the role of women in the life and thought of the early Schleiermacher."

Richardson trenchantly demonstrates Schleiermacher's consistent use of gender images and concepts in works written during the same general period in which he wrote *Christmas Eve*: his *Monologen*, *Confidential letters on Friedrich Schlegel's "Lucinde,"* and his *Brouillon on Ethics*.[19] Throughout all of these works, Richardson argues, Schleiermacher

> ardently professes the limitations of gender and the importance of the fusion of the male and female *Geschlechtscharaktere* [gender-based characteristics] (and even their eventual extinction as separate entities), it also would seem that any interpretation of *Christmas Eve* that focuses on the women's stories or solely on the men's discourses would be working at variance with Schleiermacher's own intent.[20]

Richardson thus affirms principle (ii) of our key: discussions of male or female human beings are not complete without reference to their opposite gender.

Richardson's review of two centuries of scholarship on Schleiermacher's *Christmas Eve* also reveals a basic but overlooked fact: leading Schleiermacher scholars have failed to understand the importance of the co-determinate relationship between male and female gender terms in Schleiermacher's work. As Richardson notes, a restrictive focus on either the male or female experiences "has characterized the entire history of the interpretation of *Christmas Eve*, an interpretation that has covered two centuries and included lengthy analyzes by scholars such as Friedrich Wilhelm Joseph von Schelling, David Friedrich Strauss, Wilhelm Dilthey, Emmanuel Hirsh, and Karl Barth."[21]

Richardson, emphasizing the nonconceptual, "one" gender aspects of Schleiermacher's work, coins the term "psychological androgyny" to refer to the unitive human experience. Richardson's choice of the term *androgyny* is, however, unfortunate because it refers to someone with both male and female sexual organs. Schleiermacher, however, refers to the one gender, "artist," as someone who is not defined by a split (male and female) consciousness. Thus Schleiermacher does not use male and female terms to define this one gender because creativity in its own terms is neither male nor female, nor both. Schleiermacher's doctrine of human affections moves beyond the gender dimorphism that informs his more pervasive, prescriptive use of gender images and concepts.

Richardson concludes that Schleiermacher is someone who actively embraced and affirmed the full humanity of self and others. Richardson can reach this conclusion because she does not emphasize principle (iii): Schleiermacher's reification of his gendered distinctions as a split consciousness that reduces the other (female) to terms that complement and complete male emotional deficiencies. Massey, as we saw, paid pointed attention to this latter aspect of his work and dismissed the part of Schleiermacher's work that Richardson admires: his affirmation of human experience as a state beyond the isolated male or female soul.

Richardson and Massey can **reach mutually contradictory conclusions** about Schleiermacher's views of women because he used gender terms to lead reader's minds to their genderless soul.

III

Schleiermacher believed that the human soul is genderless. But he could not prove it linguistically. He simply experienced this affective state of consciousness musically because of the way he listened to music, described by one of his friends as "sinking" into the musical tones.

An illustration of what happens in the brain when music is experienced is presented by affective neuroscientist Jaak Panksepp and his co-author Günther Bernatzky in their essay "Emotional sounds and the brain: the neuro-affective foundations of musical appreciation." They undertook an experiment to test their hypothesis that affects are neurological patterning principles, and as such, they are formulaic and can be translated into mathematical and functional relationships.[22]

Panksepp and Bernatzky hypothesized that if modulation of sound by music has the same molecular modulation patterns as a particular emotional operating system of the brain, then they could be akin.[23] To test their hypothesis, they piped into the cages of baby chicks a certain kind of music that was structurally similar to the patterning principles within the brains of the chicks for reducing separation distress. The separation distress was reduced.

Panksepp and Bernatzky drew two initial conclusions as sources for further investigation. First, the mathematical schemes common to music and to affect can reveal the link between "acoustic dynamics and emotional dynamics." Second, music can evoke chills and a "wistful sense of loss blended with the possibility of reunion" in humans because the affective pattern, "may be so well represented in the dynamics of sound that we become deeply moved." The affective power of music might work at the molecular, generative level of human emotions. As the two scientists put it: "Such musical experiences speak to us of our profound humanness and our relatedness to other people and the rest of nature. The musical experience may communicate to us the possibility of redemption, the joy of being found and nurtured if one is lost."[24]

The use of liturgies "thick" with affective resonance through music can transform congregants by the very act of performing (singing or chanting) or simply hearing and thus resonating with the timbre and tones of these worship protocols. The fundamental nature of the "liturgical act itself," as liturgical theologian Aidan Kavanagh notes, is thus a concrete event that creates a shift in temperament within the participants.[25]

Schleiermacher's experience of sinking into music was, for him, an access point to what happens between thoughts when a person hears the music as emotional attunement to life itself: cosmic consciousness.

Schleiermacher would then "awaken" during the breaks in the musical performance and describe his affective experience of music rather than offer "learned discourse" about music.[26] When in this state, he described his feelings rather than critiqued them. And he felt himself to be an artistic creation at the moment of its birth. He had entered his cosmic interior self.

In the first edition of his *Speeches on Religion,* Schleiermacher did try to describe this life-sustaining and creative moment he felt when listening to music as the "natal hour of everything living in religion."[27] The unity of mind and body, understanding and affections, were quite literally for Schleiermacher the "holy essence" of the universe: cosmic consciousness. Here Schleiermacher used male/female, dimorphic gender images to describe rather than define the unitive state of the one human gender. He used male and female images of sexual play and intercourse to describe the experience of the one, artistic gender of creativity at the moment of its creation. This moment, however, is fleeting:

> With the slightest trembling the holy embrace is dispersed, and now for the first time the intuition [*Anschauung*] stands before me as a separate form; I survey it, and it mirrors itself in my open soul like the image of the vanishing beloved in the awakened eye of a youth; now for the first time the feeling [*Gefühl*] works its way up from inside and diffuses itself like the blush of shame and desire on his cheek. This moment is the highest flowering of religion.[28]

When the original unity is sundered, the access point to cosmic consciousness is split in two, and a purely mental form of awareness (*Anschauung*) and a purely internal feeling of awareness (*Gefühl*) appear. The human spirit is now divided into a mental form and an affective form. The content of the unitive experience is originally empty of thoughts and images (*Anschauung*) and filled with a cosmic sweep of feeling that is the receptivity of the self to life itself without any affective determination defined (*Gefühl*). But this moment splinters into (1) a mental form distinct from the entirety of its affective, feeling-based content and (2) a moment of raised affect, which must be determined, ordered, and arranged by pious feelings.

From this sundered former unity, a blush or some other facial expression or body gesture necessarily appears as the organic, external, affect-based expression of the prior moment of union. A mental form also must appear. The initial content of this form is images and then concepts emerge as the re-presentation (*Vorstellung*)[29] of a unitive event that has just occurred but is now gone.

Schleiermacher now uses reason (images and concepts) to define the content of the male and female gender terms of split consciousness. Reason replaces affect. And the embodied, emotional, and sensate experiential content of the gender experiences he describes are gone. The original gender of self-consciousness is lost. The space of genuine difference between male and female split consciousness—genderlessness—is omitted. His use of male/female gender terms is now prescriptive rather than descriptive.

Here's how this shift happened.

IV

The shift from description to prescription marks Schleiermacher's mature theological enterprise. Schleiermacher's Christology, as explained in *Christian Faith,* is the most abstract aspect of his doctrine of the human soul, and is generally known and studied as his theology of redemption wrought by Christ. Christ, in this scenario, is the only human being who was always whole and never suffered from a split state of consciousness.

Concepts, definitions, and logic are used here. Schleiermacher's affect theology has been replaced with a rational theology that tracks religious ideas shorn of feelings. Gender terms do not define his theology. Rather, they simply exemplify what the male split in consciousness (from Schleiermacher's perspective) does when left to its own structures: it reasons.

Schleiermacher's Christology thus consists of propositions and claims rationally presented and argued. Schleiermacher readily acknowledges the impossibility of proving experientially that his theological claims are correct. In this realm of human experience, he says, there is no mathematical proof to demonstrate that things must be so and not otherwise.[30] The only test, Schleiermacher concludes, is personal experience. And so he calls upon his readers to examine the structure of their own piety, that is, their own "self-consciousness." They must use this self-evidence, Schleiermacher insists, to determine the veracity of his claims. They must find the affective (female) side of pious experience in order to complete through description, his (male) definitional claims.

Accordingly, in his *Christian Faith,* logical arguments are used to affirm the penetrating presence of Christ in human nature as a creative act. The most concrete context for his analysis of Christ's activity as creative activity and its relationship to human affections is his doctrine of human affections. Affective context is absent in this theological work because feeling's native expression is movement and gesture, rather than speech.[31] Schleiermacher elaborates, conceptually, the affective experiences the concepts presuppose: Christian pious affections.

An example of his use of logic to make his points about the redemptive activity of Christ can be reconstructed into the following propositional argument:

Premise One: If in the formation of the Redeemer's Person the only active power was the creative divine activity, which established itself as the being of God in Him, then also His every activity may be regarded as a continuation of that person-forming divine influence upon human nature.

Premise Two: The only active principle in Christ is the creative divine activity.

Conclusion: Christ's every activity may be regarded as a continuation of this person-forming divine activity.

As a correlate to this argument, Schleiermacher can claim that the "penetrating" activity of Christ cannot establish itself in an individual without becoming person-forming in the person.[32] This means that all of the activities of Christ are first determined in and as human affections. Thus when Christ has penetrated human affections and become its vitality principle "all impressions are differently received (*alle Eindrücke anders aufgenommen warden*)—which means also that personal self-consciousness becomes different."[33]

Christ's activity is thus known within the self as human dispositions. Christ, Schleiermacher concludes, reconciles the disparate parts of a person so that they act in tandem as one harmonious whole. Christ is the condition of the union, this higher state of consciousness. Cosmic consciousness is now Christ consciousness for Schleiermacher. Christ, according to Schleiermacher, is the perfected ground of human consciousness. How is His presence known? It is felt as the wholeness of the self. His presence is known through the sustained feeling of wholeness that is expressed and experienced as the music, facial expressions, gestures and tones of a religious community.[34]

V

The rational complement to Schleiermacher's theological reasoning are his theological imaginative improvisations. This is the case because imaginative improvisation *(Fantasie)*—the first cognitive expression of the way in which the cosmic sweep of human affection has been altered—is concrete thinking, a schematization of human consciousness.[35] Imaginative expressions are movements of sustained human consciousness, measured, ordered, and displayed. They are, in sum, the closest mental expressions to the experience of altered human affections sustained. They are affect-near. Concepts, by contrast, are affect-distant.

In Schleiermacher's scheme of things, theological fantasies will thus be closer to female rather than male gender-defined images. Why? Imaginativeness is always accompanied by affection. Schleiermacher called this link between feeling and imaginativeness their "living association" *(lebendigen Zusammenhang)*. The link itself is their attunement one to the other.

We can now spotlight the original genderless state of the self using Schleiermacher's two musical terms: attunement and harmony.

Attunement: an orchestrated movement of the self in the universe felt as a resounding moment of one's birth anew into life itself: a cosmic suite of orchestrated feeling. Schleiermacher's analysis of music begins by tracking the affective disarray he feels as the performance begins. When the sounds are first heard, Schleiermacher explains, they are not measured movements, but rather the sheer agitation of altered affect.[36] Music making, according to Schleiermacher, transforms this agitated state of human affect into art, as a conscious act of creation.[37] The difference between the original impress of sound on the ear and the subsequent experience of musical notes, he concludes, is the space created by the human spirit. It's the soul's mental act of understanding and gaining control of the shift in affect that has just occurred within it.

Spirit and affect, Schleiermacher argues, are linked by our act of trying to make sense of the sound, namely, the rhythmic vibrations that have internally altered our affective state of consciousness. This link between the act of understanding and the shift in the affect is the creation of a conscious moment of awareness.

Human consciousness *is* this lived experience of coherence, Schleiermacher insists. It is the human experience of coherence, of wholeness as a being who both thinks and feels.[38] This coherence is our attunement, our feeling of being part of the great all of life. The link *is* the self. Musically, it's our experience of harmony.

Harmony. Schleiermacher uses gendered and non-gendered terms to explain the human experience of harmony. The basis for harmony, Schleiermacher argues, is the reflective awareness of the difference in tone between male and female voices, for example, when men and women sing the same note. Our awareness of this difference is, for Schleiermacher, the foundational self-reflective stage of harmony.[39]

The actual difference between the male and female voices, however, is neither male nor female. Nor can the difference between them be characterized as harmonic or disharmonic because the distinction is not a determinative fact of consciousness. Rather, the distinction is the space of difference between the two voices that links them together as a unitive experience. This link, as noted above, is the self, the soul, the wholeness of human consciousness.

Accordingly, Schleiermacher's reference to a twofold division of human genders into male and female terms is insufficient to grasp the most elemental structure of the state of the soul that precedes the human awareness of gender division and harmony.

The experience of harmony presupposes our awareness of difference or division, which is achieved by comparison. Harmony, in sum, is a *reflective act* of understanding. This comparative difference, however, is not the same as the transition point between the two because the shift itself is a *state* of self-consciousness. But this state is not self-reflective. It's sheer presence. The natal hour of everything living in religion.

The Genderless Self. Schleiermacher thus gives this shift in consciousness—this felt state of consciousness that constitutes the difference that binds a sundered soul together—a genderless identity described as the "one gender" called the "artist." "Artists are an acutely sensitive gender" (*die Künstler überhaupt, ein reizbares Geschlecht sind*).[40] They respond immediately to what is going on around them. This one gender, Schleiermacher argued, is the original state of the self (psyche or soul) before it is split into male and female genders. Schleiermacher is drawing here on his own experiences of cosmic consciousness when, for instance, he listened to music.

Music enables each person to become whole again through an experience of the person's original gender, which is neither male nor female or androgynous. Men and women are whole souls when in the genderless, primordial state of regeneration and renewal. In this state, a person is neither male nor female, Greek nor Jew, citizen nor slave. Schleiermacher found this place through music and affirmed it in musical terms that exceeded his rational, theological reflections and gender biases.

Schleiermacher thus created a doctrine of human nature that both affirmed and denied the fundamental equality of man and woman. They both *have* whole, genderless souls, but they are also sundered souls. As soulful pure presence they are equals. As fully present human selves, they are not. And this is just fine with Schleiermacher because biology is destiny for him. Women are designed to bare and care for children and their husbands. Women cuddle. Men cogitate.

This role-codified, gendered-defined way of handling affect can be avoided when Schleiermacher's primordial musical experiences and analysis are reaffirmed. This reaffirmation takes place when Schleiermacher's affective music experiences are read against his gendered theological reflections on the differences between the affective dispositions of men and women.

Accordingly, when we read Schleiermacher against himself, we affirm what he experientially found and linguistically lost: the personal experience of wholeness that occurs in between reason and feelings, in between ideas and emotions. In between thoughts. Here the human soul resounds with all of life as a cosmic suite of the infinite affective resonance of life itself.

Paul also described this place of affective wholeness and mapped it as the "law of Christ" (Gal 6:2) and the "law of Spirit" (Rom 8:2), which has also been called the law of love that leads Christians to bear one another's burdens.[41] In short, to love beyond belief.

But Paul must be read against himself in order to reaffirm his law of love because his references to the gentile conscience got in his way.

Part Two

Jewish and Gentile
Affect-Strategies

Chapter Three

The Jewish Paul

Introduction

Paul invented the conscience as a discrete category of Christian experience.[1] This invention, namely, this new way of thinking about, gathering together, categorizing, and judging internal affective states of consciousness was designed by Paul to help Gentiles understand how they could become—inwardly—a Jew (*en tō kryptō Ioudaios*, Rom 2:29), but instead it shows them how Paul became—inwardly—a Gentile.

Paul and Pauline scholarship must be read against the grain to tell this story as a design problem of Paul's own invention. Such is the task at hand. I interrogate a linguistic historical fact and read three of its narrative consequences against the grain to achieve this end.[2] This narrative is a story about incommensurable affective states of consciousness defined and explained by mutually contradictory Hebrew and Greek terms.

The historical fact highlighted in this narrative is Paul's linguistic innovation. Paul is the first New Testament writer to use the Greek word συνείδησις (*syneidesis*), which today is often translated as "conscience." Moreover, he used the term and others associated with its linguistic word group more often than any other New Testament writer—fourteen times in the "authentic" Pauline letters[3] out of the thirty times the words appear in the Christian scriptures.[4]

Three consequences followed. First, originality. Paul created a biblical word not derived from the Septuagint or colored by the Hebrew experience.[5] More precisely, the word appears only once in the Septuagint (Eccl 10:20), and the underlying term (מַדָּע *madda'*) is translated in the Revised Standard Version of the Bible as "thought."[6] Thus the new story: Paul invented something for his work with Gentiles that was not Jewish in origin.[7]

Second, normativity. Paul's use of the term *syneidesis* became normative for Christianity's explanations of personal internal strife,[8] thanks in no small part—centuries later—to the work of Augustine and then Martin Luther. Paul is also "hailed as the hero of the introspective conscience,"[9] in the words of Krister Stendahl, thanks to this genealogy.

Finally, expediency. Paul used the term, so the scholarly narrative goes, because his Corinthian followers apparently used the Greek word in their correspondence with him about food.[10] Paul, from the perspective of this scholarship, responded in kind, expediently using the Gentiles' term to explain a new way for them to think about (1) their conscience, (2) their behavior during table fellowship, and (3) their faithfulness to Christ.

The major argument developed in this chapter can now be easily summarized. If Paul used the term *syneidesis* to show Gentiles how to become inwardly a spiritual Jew, then his use of this term is of critical importance in understanding how Paul tried to turn Gentiles inwardly into Jews without drawing on traditional external Jewish rites and practices like circumcision.

Paul, I argue in this chapter, did indeed use the term for this purpose. He strove to teach Gentiles a new way to understand their triggered affective states of consciousness, namely, their passions. This account produces the following narrative line: I can track how the consequences linked to Paul's use of this term not only produced Gentiles who thought of themselves as the "real Jews,"[11] but also how the results help explain how Paul inadvertently "provided the theological structure"[12] for almost two thousand years of Christian tyranny against Jews. The results also help explain how in the tradition Paul became, linguistically, a self-despising Jew with a sundered gentile soul. He made the gentile conscience the access point to Christ. As a result, the distinction between (1) cosmic consciousness as a spiritual but not religious state of consciousness and (2) religious consciousness as a cultur-ally-constructed pious state was lost.

By constructing the Pauline origin story of Christian tyranny against Jews in this new way, I affirm the claim by New Testament scholar Lloyd Gaston that Paul's work created a conceptual im-passe for liberal Christians today because Paul's work "occupies more than one-half of the Christian Bible."[13] Nevertheless, Gaston argues, a "Christian Church with an anti-Semitic New Testament is abominable, [but] a Christian Church without a New Testament is inconceivable."[14] The church and its traditions, Gaston insists, must not be abandoned but redeemed. The question here, of course, is how is this Pauline tradition to be redeemed?

One way contemporary scholars have attempted to "redeem" Paul's anti-Judaic legacy is by "re-Judaizing" Paul, as John G. Gager puts it, namely to relocate Paul "within the religious and social world of Graeco-Roman Judaism."[15] Such attempts, how-ever, have not redeemed Paul, but rather have provided more in-culpatory evidence against him.

Several examples from Jewish scholars who track Christian claims about a "re-Judaized" Paul illustrate this critically impor-tant point.

Daniel Boyarin—a Talmudist, postmodern Jewish cultural critic who is a leading practitioner of the new perspective re-Ju-daizing scholarship on Paul—concludes that Paul, although he intended to introduce a discourse of radical reform to his own culture, instead ended up gutting the Jewish tradition of its own people by turning the fulfillment of its promises to God over to the Gentiles.[16] Boyarin calls this unintended result of Paul's strategies an example of "ethnocide."[17] Paul has claimed, Boyarin argues, that "anyone at all can be Jewish, and those who call themselves Jewish are not necessarily Jewish at all. This utterance of Paul has had fateful consequences for the Jews in the Christian West." There is no longer a need for genealogy, history, and practice now to be a "true Jew" because all you now need is the right inner disposition.[18]

Similarly, the Jewish New Testament scholar Amy-Jill Levine notes that Paul's teachings erased the ethnic identity of Jews in his famous declaration that "there is no longer Jew or Greek ... in Christ Jesus" (Gal 3:28).[19] Moreover, his belief that Israel's failure to be a "light to the nations" as called for in Isa 49:6 is interpreted by Paul as a hardening of the heart of Jews by God (Rom 9:18; 11:25) so that Gentiles as well as Jews could experience God's mercy and be saved (Rom 11:32). Two thousand years later, as Levine points out, "It is scant comfort for Jews to be told that they are 'enemies of God' for the sake of the church (Rom 11:28)."[20] And even if Paul's declaration in 1 Thess 2:14–16—that Jews (Ἰουδαῖοι) killed Jesus and the prophets and that God's wrath had overtaken them at last—is not intended to be anti-Jewish, his gentile audience then and now might nevertheless receive it as such because "what one intends and what another hears are not necessarily the same thing."[21]

Finally, Jacob Neusner and Bruce Chilton in their book *The Intellectual Foundations of Christian and Jewish Discourse: The Philosophy of Religion Argument*, argue that when Paul claims in Gal 3:13 that Christ has redeemed "us" from the curse of the law, he not only included himself (as a Jew), but also by extension, all religious Jews along with him.[22]

Whether this cancellation by Paul of the Laws of the Torah for all Jews is meant literally or is simply a rhetorical device is not relevant to the point Neusner and Chilton make here. Paul, they argue, betrayed his own Jewish tradition by publicly rejecting a bedrock Judaic claim about the means to salvation for the Jewish people. Whatever Paul intended, the history of the tradition reveals how it was heard.

Granted, as Neusner and Chilton point out, many faithful Jews have interpreted the meaning of Torah, the Jewish teachings of Mosaic law, using nonbiblical sources. The Pharisees, for example, used the tradition of the sages—the unwritten traditions handed down from master to disciples and students in supposedly unbroken succession back to biblical times; the Essenes used the guidelines of the Righteous Teacher; the Sadducees referred to customary Temple practice; Philo drew on Plato.

Unlike Paul, however, the extra-biblical strategies used by these faithful Jews did not abandon Torah, nor did they claim it had ceased to have relevance for Jewish life. In making such a claim, Paul moved beyond "the range of permissible disagreement" within the various forms of Judaism.[23] Paul's Judaism, write Neusner and Chilton, was thus on the way to becoming something other than Judaism.[24]

Jacob Neusner (1932–2016)—one of the world's foremost scholars on Jewish rabbinical texts, who published more than nine hundred books in this field—goes even further, concluding that Christianity and Judaism have no continuity, connection, or shared background.[25] Christianity, says Neusner, "is not a kind of Judaism," nor is it a continuation of "the Judaeo-Christian tradition." Indeed, he writes, Judaism is unrelated to Christianity: "Each one is wholly other."[26]

Daniel Boyarin has skillfully refined Neusner's claim, noting that "Judaism and Christianity were invented in order to explain the fact that there were Jews and Christians."[27] Thus it does not make historical sense to argue that one emerged from the other. Rather they emerged together: "The transformation of both nascent Christianity and nascent Judaism from groups of sects—to collections of philosophical schools [of thought] would be seen on this reading as part of the same sociocultural process and practice.... [Indeed,] there are no grounds for believing that the rabbinic developments are earlier than the Christian ones, indeed, the opposite may have frequently been the case."[28] Boyarin's research and arguments laid out in *Border Lines* are not only compelling, but also deeply informative for my own work with Paul among first-century Gentiles and Jews.

If Christian scholars like John G. Gager[29] and Lloyd Gaston, then, have not erased the regnant narrative of Paul as an apostate Jew, it is because Paul—by intention or otherwise as the above-cited Jewish scholars have pointed out—was indeed an apostate Jew. Scholars who thus place Paul, as Apostle to the Gentiles, back into his Pharisaic first-century contexts to "re-Judaize" him, embolden rather than diminish his apostasy.

Accordingly, my work undertakes a re-Judaizing reading of Paul against himself. The goal here is not to redeem Paul. Such a project is impossible to achieve because Paul's work to create

Gentiles as inwardly the "real Jews"[30] had catastrophic consequences for Jews. Rather, the goal here is to provide liberal and
progressive Christians with a New Testament Pauline narrative
that affirms the emotional foundation for faithfulness (the law of
Christ to carry the other's burdens, Gal 6:2, namely the "law of
love"[31]) that Paul tried but failed to create internally in Gentiles.

The work in this chapter thus affirms and interrogates Paul's
own account of his mission-driven expediency principle, namely,
his claim in Gal 4:12: "I beseech you, become as I am, for I also
have become as you are." So, too, his claim in 1 Cor 9:20: "And to
the Jews I became as a Jew, that I might win Jews; to those who are
under the Law, as under the Law, though not being myself under
the Law, that I might win those who are under the Law." He acted,
in sum, like a Jew among Jews and a Gentile among Gentiles. Paul
the missionary here cloaks himself as a gentile sinner in order to
save gentile sinners.[32] I thus affirm the insight by New Testament
scholar Lloyd Gaston that Paul intentionally "put himself into the
same status as his followers [in order to] identify with those with
whom he was commissioned to preach."[33] To this end, Paul low-
ered himself in order to lift up his followers. He put on the mantle
of a Gentile and, as a consequence, became one with them.[34]

My narrative, however, adds another dimension to Gaston's
claim by tracking the differences between Paul's disposition as
a Pharisee and that of his gentile converts.[35] By so doing, I can
affirm with Gaston, that "Rom 7 is not autobiographical,"[36] and
show at the same time how this text became autobiographical
for Paul thanks to the expediency principle entailed in his flawed
invention of the gentile conscience. Paul, simply put, slew his
Jewish self and gave others permission to do the same thing using
his own expedient invention.

Two kinds of narratives give me permission to read Paul
against the grain of his own invention: contemporary neuroscience and Paul's own autobiographical claims.

Contemporary Neuroscience

Affective and cultural neuroscience and also neuroimaging studies give me permission to postulate that a mapping of Paul's

emotional life as a Pharisee would probably have revealed neuro-patterning principles in his brain that differed from those of his gentile converts. More precisely, the embedded liturgical and cultic disciplines Paul experienced as a Pharisee, I argue, can be theorized in neuro-conceptual terms because brain science research has shown, for example, that the same word lights up different parts of the brain in persons from different religious traditions.[37] Accordingly, the emotional brain mapping of a charismatic Christian, for example, differs from the emotional mapping of a Quaker when both are asked to think about the term "religion."

This approach of differentiating the brains of Jews and Gentiles neuro-conceptually, however, does not require me to deny the numerous distinctions among and within the various Jewish sects and schools of Paul's own era (e.g., the Essenes, the school of Hillel, the school of Shammai).

Nor does this approach to Paul's brain development require me to deny individual dispositional differences between Paul and other Jews, such as Philo of Alexandria.

Finally, my claim does not blur the differences among the enormous variety of Graeco-Roman traditions from Plato and Aristotle to Epicurus and the Stoics that instructed adepts to direct their thoughts and behavior in specific ways in order to attain, for example, peace of mind and inner tranquility.

Rather, I simply affirm—with the help of neuroscientific insights—that Pharisees like Paul probably achieved their internal peace of mind and tranquility through cultic practices and cultural beliefs that encoded their mental and emotional life as observant Jews rather than as Graeco-Roman Gentiles performing cultic rites and rituals to the gods of the Roman Empire.[38]

Most helpful here is the way Daniel Boyarin describes, in personal terms, his own internal discernment process of becoming an observant Jew. Boyarin here reminds readers that he, as an observant Jewish man, draws upon his own experiences of "Jewishness" when trying to make sense of Paul as an observant Jew.

Boyarin's claims are of particular interest here because "Jewishness," for him is not a club, namely, an affective association of individuals. Jews in general, Boyarin suggests, feel that Jewishness is not something they have freely chosen but rather an essence that has been inscribed or even imposed on them by birth.[39] A baby, Boyarin argues, is not born with Jewish DNA that turns him into an observant Jew. The baby born of a Jewish mother, can, for example, be baptized or christened and raised Christian. Or the baby can be raised without a religious disposition at all. Religious identity, in short, is an inculcated emotional disposition and mentality. One typically becomes Jewish by birthright (bloodline) and through culturally-inscribed traditional practices.

Accordingly, Boyarin concludes that the baby's Judaic identity and dispositions are cultural creations, a kind of learning how to be Jewish through hegemonic cultic practices.[40]

Using Boyarin's own claims about his Jewish experiences, I can say that Paul, when talking about being inwardly a Jew to Gentiles (Rom 2:29), probably had firsthand experiences himself, being inwardly a Jew. Moreover, these inward experiences would probably have a different brain scan pattern than those of a Gentile who tried to learn how to become and to feel inwardly like a Jew.

Paul's Autobiographical Claims

Paul, by self-proclamation, was not only proficient but also advanced in the Pharisaic tradition (Gal 1:14; Phil 3:4–6). He was a Hebrew born of Hebrews, circumcised on the eighth day, a member of the people of Israel and the tribe of Benjamin, a Pharisee who followed Mosaic law, and a righteous blameless man who had persecuted those of his fellow Jews who gathered together in the name of Christ.[41]

This self-description can tell us several things about Paul's life as a faithful Pharisee.

First, Paul, like other Pharisees, would have been a lay Jewish man who strove to live every aspect of his life as if he were a Temple priest.[42]

Second, Paul, as a Second Temple Pharisee, did not belong to the Pharisaic-Rabbinic tradition, whose formulators redacted the Second Temple Pharisaic traditions of Paul's era. These redactions occurred after Paul's death in the mid to late 60s CE, after the destruction of the Jerusalem Temple by the Romans in 70 CE, and after the defeat of the Bar Kokhba Revolt against Rome sixty-five years later. The redacted tradition of teachings and practices of the Pharisaic sages of Paul's era (e.g., the schools or "Houses" of Hillel and Shammai and their disciples) as well as the redacted traditions of other teachers, sages, elders, and fathers identified as part of an unbroken line of succession going back to Moses at Sinai, became the exegetical tradition and system for teaching of Oral Torah, also known as the Mishnah, a "philosophic law code that reached closure at the end of the second century."[43] These strategies resulted in the struggle of fifth- and sixth-century rabbis to establish themselves as having sole control using the institution of Torah as they interpreted it as proof-text for this authority.[44] The Mishnah; the commentaries and supplementary materials concerning it called the Tosefta, which reached closure a century later; the two sustained and systematic commentaries on the Mishnah called the Jerusalem (ca. 400) and Babylonian (ca. 600) Talmuds; and Jewish Scripture ("the written Torah") collectively became the canonical foundation of Rabbinic Judaism.[45] Or more precisely, Pharisaic-Rabbinic Judaism.

Paul was neither a predecessor nor a member of this Pharisaic-Rabbinic tradition invented by the rabbis.

Third, Paul, as Apostle to the Gentiles, tried to bridge the difference between the inward dispositions of spiritual Jews and gentile faithfulness to Christ by identifying a common interior ground (Rom 2:28–29). This claim by Paul gives us permission to pay attention not only to the inner lives of Jews and Gentiles, but also to try to track his own inner life as well.[46]

Hellenistic Jews like Paul, after all, were "cultural negotiators." They socially and culturally maintained their Jewish identity and yet remained embedded in the Hellenistic way in a wholly unproblematic way (e.g., Philo of Alexandria).[47] Moreover, a binary opposition between Hellenism and Judaism, as Boyarin notes based on his own research, needs major rethinking,[48] because Judaism "is itself a species of Hellenism."[49] Pharisaic Jews like Paul both "used and refused Hellenistic culture, neither adopting it uncritically nor rejecting it outright."[50] They were part and parcel of the Hellenistic scene.

Paul, by his own testimony, knew that he lived in two emotionally distinct worlds and he also knew the differences could be bridged as Hellenes who were children of the God of Israel *and* the nations. In a sense, he was capitalizing on this identity rhetorically. His testimony grants us some latitude to construct a narrative of how Paul's disposition might have been created Pharisaic, without relying on the Pharisaic-Rabbinic tradition to which he did not belong. This narrative can be constructed by focusing on (1) discourse on the *yetzer ha-ra'* (יֵצֶר הָרָע)—the evil inclination and how the term itself, which predated the rabbinic discourse, might have helped inform Paul's own first-century era and theorizing about (2) Pharisaic rationales for table fellowship.

Did the notion and the cultic practices together help create the personal and collective resources for handling personal dispositions and experiences as Jews in the first century?

Best to consider the scholarly arguments and analyze the textual evidence.

Part One
Paul and the *Yetzer ha-ra'* (יֵצֶר הָרָע), the Evil Inclination

During Paul's era there were evidently two different schools of discourse about the meaning of this term.[51] One view is identified with the school of Rabbi Akiva,[52] a second-century rabbi (died ca. 135) who played a central role in the formulation of Mishnah and the Midrash Halakah.[53] Two of the three texts by writers from this school in which the term is found refer to the *yetzer* as the source of fears that can be calmed by the teachings of the Torah.[54]

Ishay Rosen-Zvi presents the commentary on Exod 34:24 found in *Mekhilta de-Rabbi Simeon bar Yohai* to make the point:

> I will drive out nations from your path … no one will covet your land—the Torah spoke regarding the *yetzer*, so that Israel would not say, How can we leave our land, our homes, our fields, and our vineyard and make pilgrimage, lest others

will come and dwell in our places. Consequently, the Holy One, blessed be He, warrants them: "no one will covet your land when you come up to be seen [to make pilgrimage to the Temple]."[55]

This text, as Rosen-Zvi points out, provides reassurance. It addresses the *yetzer* as something natural to man: fear.[56] Rosen-Zvi discovered, however, that the idea of the *yetzer* as a natural impulse to man was supplanted by a new, very different one, making the former claims the exception rather than the rule in rabbinic literature.[57] Homilies from the school of Rabbi Ishmael (90–135 CE), who was Rabbi Akiva's contemporary, take this new view of the *yetzer*. Writes Rosen-Zvi:

> In both schools the *yetzer's* objections [to following the teachings of the Torah] are linked to the observance of the commandments, but while, for the school of R. Akiva, [as noted in the above citation] the *yetzer* fears the subsequent loss of its property ..., for the school of R. Ishmael, the *yetzer* seeks to negate the very existence of the commandments (by seeking permission to engage in idolatry, or by preferring foreign laws to 'ours'). The Torah's response to this claim changes accordingly: for the school of R. Akiva the response (that is, the verse expounded) is a promise [to the *yetzer* that the man's property will not be lost], while the school of R. Ishmael doubles and strengthens the prohibition [against the *yetzer*]. In other words, in one the Torah gives the *yetzer* a positive answer, and in the other a stark negative one.[58]

The evil *yetzer* for the school of R. Ishmael is no longer a natural disposition or embodiment of human desires, Rosen-Zvi concludes; it is now "an antinomian entity residing within men and inciting them against the Torah."[59]

This new image of the *yetzer* turns it not only into a demonic enemy, but also into "a (the?) central component of [rabbinic] anthropology ... as the explanation of the human tendency to sin."[60] The *yetzer* in the new interpretation tries to argue, cajole, and persuade man to sin, arguing as if in a court of law. And thus, according to the new interpretation, "the dangers lurking for man are within him, and not outside."[61]

Both views of the *yetzer* agree on one thing, however: that the *yetzer* prevents man from loving God with all his heart and from treating his fellow man with lovingkindness.

It is important to note here that the rabbis altered the meaning of the *yetzer*, but they did not invent the Hebrew term.

The Biblical Context. The root of the Hebrew term *yetzer*— *ytzr* (יצר)—is found in three verses of Genesis, as Jonathan Schofer notes in his essay "The Redaction of Desire: Structure and Editing of Rabbinic Teachings Concerning *Yetzer* (Inclination)."[62]

1. Gen 6:5. The "bad" *yetzer*, as Schofer observes, first appears in the story of the flood in Gen 6:5. God, seeing that "every *yetzer* of the thoughts of [man's] heart, is only bad (*ra'*) all of the time," decides to destroy humankind.
2. Gen 8:21. In Gen 8:21, God vows never to curse the earth again on account of its people because "the *yetzer* of the heart of the human is bad (*ra'*) from his youth."
3. Gen 2:7. The idea of two inclinations, a good *yetzer* and a bad *yetzer*, Schofer suggests, probably arises from "midrashic reflection upon God's formation of Adam in Gen 2:7." Rabbinic commentators believed two forces of the heart were described there, which they characterized through the category of *yetzer*—you should love God "with good *yetzer* as well as bad *yetzer*."[63]

By the second century BCE, the figurative and secondary meaning of the term had "become 'disposition' or 'possibility to choose.' In the texts of the Dead Sea Scrolls the emphasis in the understanding of the word is that it implies human 'creatureliness,' primarily in the sense of corporeality, while also in one case it got the imprint of 'desire.'"[64]

The redactors of the Pharisaic-Rabbinic tradition used the Hebrew term *yetzer ha-ra'* to talk about innate human emotional impulses and inclinations including lust, greed, and jealousy that if not properly instructed by Torah, prayer, and with direct assistance from God, lead humans to do harmful things and thus to suffer.

Although the meaning of the term as it evolved in this tradition invariably pertained to a strictly human condition,[65] the tradition also made it clear that the *yetzer ha-ra'* cannot be wisely regulated by man alone.

This discourse on the bad *yetzer*, however, had little in common, as the Jewish theologian Solomon Schechter notes, with "the evil principle of [Christian] theology." The Pharisaic-Rabbinic notions refer to human passions "without which neither the propagation of species nor the building up of proper civilization would be thinkable. They only become bad by the improper use man makes of them."[66] This early concept of "bad," then, differs from the Christian notion of sin in that it refers to "the abuse of those passions which are in themselves a necessity."[67]

Thus, unlike sin, the bad *yetzer* is not essentially an evil human characteristic. Without it, as Schechter notes, humanity would not proliferate. The impulse is located not only in the heart but also in other body parts, including man's sex organ,[68] which according to the Babylonian Talmud, makes man "if one starves him, he feels sated, and if one sates him, he feels hungry."[69]

The Literary Context. Thanks to the post-Second Temple writers who redacted the Second Temple traditions, contemporary readers know that some of the discourse in Paul's era might have centered on ideas about a bad or evil inclination in the human heart.[70]

The *Tractate Abot* or *The Tractate Fathers*, meaning fathers of the traditional or oral law rather than of the written Mosaic law of Hebrew Scriptures, is one such text. It is a small book of five chapters compiled around 250 CE, the ninth Tractate of Nezikin (Damages) found in the Fourth of Six Orders or divisions of the Mishnah.[71] A second tractate, called *The Program of the Fathers according to Rabbi Nathan*, in two parts (A and B), serves, at times, as a non-canonical commentary within Rabbinic Judaism on *Tractate Abot*.[72] This text, also containing collections of the sages' maxims, probably developed parallel to the *Abot* in competing (and also non-competing) post-Second Temple rabbinic circles.[73]

The *Abot*, however, entails the "invention of rabbinic orthodoxy,"[74] namely, the presentation of an unbroken line of teachings by master to disciple, beginning with Moses, who received unwritten as well as written laws from God and is seen as the first rabbi, and ending with the third-century rabbis of the Common Era.

So I cannot argue that the narratives found in this text give me insight into the original meaning and use of the terms in Paul's first-century era. But they do give me permission to focus on the internal life of observant Jews, namely, to pay attention to their emotions and how they are explained and handled through Jewish conventions or, perhaps better, inventions.

The rabbis, as Schofer argues, laid out and explained ideal motivations and emotions formed in relation to God.[75] To this end, various texts focus attention on the disciplining of raw human impulses that prompt persons to act. Attention is paid, says Schofer, to the way "rabbinic practice transforms intellect, emotion, desire, and action in accord with specific values."[76] Jacob Neusner elaborates on this important point:

> If the position of sages is that feelings, as much as deeds, can
> be restrained, disciplined, moderated, and controlled, then
> feelings, as much as deeds, are important for a holy way of
> life. Emotions, no less than opinions, play a role in the drama
> of salvation. From the simple commandment to love God,
> much else flows. Once the importance of love is established,
> other virtues that fall into the same classification as love also
> take on significance for the religious life. Hence, affections
> become subject to the evaluation, including the restraints, of
> the Torah. That is, they become matters of religious experience
> because they can be made holy.[77]

A case in point here is the *yetzer ha-ra'*, the evil inclination in paragraph 2:16 of the *Abot*. Found here is the first mention in this text of the notion of an innate inclination in man[78] called "the evil impulse." The text reads as follows: *Rabbi Joshua said: The evil eye, the evil impulse, and hatred of mankind put a man out of this world.* The evil eye, as the editor and translator of the Hebrew text notes, refers to "envy," and the evil impulse "to one's instincts without control."[79]

The text itself leaves little doubt, as the translator Ronald W. Pies observes, that the evil impulse is negative. Nevertheless, Pies continues, Talmudic commentaries sometimes depict it favorably. According to one passage, "The greater the man, the more powerful his impulses" (*Sukkah* 52a). As Pies goes on to note,

> in the Midrash (*Genesis Rabbah* 9:7), the question is if all that God created is "very good" (Genesis 1:31), "Is the evil impulse very good?" The answer given by the rabbis is yes: "Were it not for that [evil] impulse, a man would not build a house, marry a wife, beget children, or conduct business affairs."[80]

In short, such rabbinic texts reveal, as G. H. Cohen Stuart points out, that the evil inclination is indispensable to human life.[81] So these inclinations must not be ignored; they must be monitored and controlled.

Rabbinic studies scholar Jonathan Schofer puts it this way: "What people are at origin or by nature—concerns the starting point of ethical transformation." And faith traditions define this starting point, as Schofer notes, by identifying and defining primal emotions, desires, and motivations. A crucial category for this religious and ethical discourse, Schofer concludes, is *yetzer*.[82]

This challenge by the *yetzer* raises the following question for the rabbis: Who or what will have "power over the body"?[83] The answer: prayer, Torah study, and the good *yetzer*—all of which are empowered by God.

Torah Study

The most popular tool for battling the *yetzer*, as Rosen-Zvi points out, is Torah study: "'The school of R. Ishmael taught: If this repulsive one assails you—lead him to the study hall' (*b. Qidd.* 30b; *b. Sukhah* 52b)." Or, as Rosen-Zvi goes on to note, *Sif. Deut* 45 (103–4) offers greater detail about how Torah study can help:

> Be occupied with words of Torah and [the *yetzer*] will not reign over you. But if you abandon words of Torah, then [your evil *yetzer*] will gain mastery over you … as it is said [Gen 4:7]: "sin crouches at the door, its urge is toward you"—it has no business other than with you.[84]

Rosen-Zvi lifts three main points from this text: (1) The *yetzer* was given by God—Genesis 4:7—and has a single inclination: evil. (2) Men and their *yetzer* are in constant battle since its goal is to dominate men and ensnare them to sin. (3) Torah study will ultimately defeat the evil *yetzer*.[85]

Prayer

Although man can counter the *yetzer* by studying the Torah,[86] even Torah study can be fraught with peril. According to the rabbis, "David said, 'Master of the world, when I am occupied in Thy Law, allow not the *Evil Yezer* to divide me … but make my heart one, so that I be occupied in the Torah with soundness (perfection or fullness).'" Even the Torah, then, is not by itself enough to defeat the evil *yetzer*, as Schechter repeatedly asserts. "The conquest," he writes, "comes in the end from God. We are thus brought to the necessity of grace.… Hence, the various prayers for the removal or the subjugation of the *Evil Yezer*."[87] One such prayer is repeated several times on the Day of Atonement:

> Our God and God of our fathers, forgive and pardon our iniquities on this Day of Atonement.… Subdue our heart to serve thee, and bend our *Yezer* to turn unto thee; renew our reins to observe thy precepts, and circumcise our hearts to love and revere thy Name, as it is written in the Law: And the Lord thy God will circumcise thy heart and the heart of thy seed, to love the Lord thy God with all thy soul, that thou mayest live.[88]

The *Yetzer ha-tov* (יֵצֶר הַטּוֹב), the Good Inclination

The good *yetzer* is formed at age thirteen, suggests *The Fathers according to Rabbi Nathan A*. At this age, if a person:

> desecrates Sabbaths, it says to him "You idiot! Look," it says, "The one who desecrates it will surely die!" (Exod 31:14). He kills people, and it says to him, "You idiot! Look," it says, "If a man spills blood of another man, his blood will be spilled" (Gen 9:6). He goes to do an act of sexual transgression, and it

says to him, "You idiot! Look," it says, "the adulterer and the adulteress will surely die" (Lev 20:10).[89]

Unlike the bad *yetzer*, the good *yetzer* is not innate to man. Rather, it arises from instruction that cultivates in the student a disposition to monitor his own impulses in order to encourage holy feelings and behavior. In short, it arises from Torah study. So starting at thirteen (i.e., puberty), a boy can use the teachings of the Torah to control his physical passions, drives, appetites, and impulses—in other words, his bad *yetzer*.[90]

As Abot 3:21 notes, "If there is no [study of] the Torah, there is no proper behavior."[91] This is why rabbis claim that in God's eyes, "little children commit no sin."[92] Children, after all, have not yet begun to wrestle with their passions. Even the new voice to which the thirteen-year-old harkens—the voice of the good *yetzer*—"does not pop into a person's head."[93] Rather, he hears the voice only after an acculturation process, albeit one that is treated by the rabbinic literature as if it is a natural rather than a cultural happening.[94] The good *yetzer*, then, entails a twofold faculty in that it denotes (1) the human capacity to internalize the Torah and (2) an inner monitoring faculty that registers, observes, and adjudicates the drives of the bad *yetzer*.

The Scholarly Debate

Did Paul, as a Second Temple Pharisee, know the Pharisaic notions of the bad or evil *yetzer* that pervaded the discourse on the inward life of Jews during his own first-century era and use insights from it as Apostle to the Gentiles? Scholars have not reached agreement on this twofold question. A sampling of the debate illustrates the point.

Second Temple Judaism and Early Christianity scholar David Flusser argues that Paul's command in Rom 12:14—"Bless those who persecute you; bless and do not curse them"—counts as evidence of an "attitude ... prone to develop into a more humanistic position." This position, as Flusser demonstrates, was in keeping with the "vectors towards a genuine humanism"[95]—an altruistic, social love, as he puts it—that "achieved the highest value index by being considered the very essence of Judaism during the days of the Second Temple."[96] From this perspective, Paul can be counted as part of this emerging Pharisaic humanism, which was precedent for "rabbinic humanism."[97]

W. D. Davies, on the other hand, argues that Paul's conception of flesh as the sinful opposite of the spirit is nowhere to be found in Rabbinic Judaism.[98] In this Judaic tradition, Davies reminds us, evil and good impulses both reside in the same place, the human heart.

Like Davies, Frank Chamberlin Porter, in his seminal work "The Yeçer Hara: A Study in the Jewish Doctrine of Sin," argues that any parallel between Paul's spirit-flesh dichotomy and the rabbinic discourse on the good and bad impulses of the heart is negligible to the point of irrelevancy. "Of course Paul in Romans 7 is describing the same experiences of struggle between two opposing forces in man upon which the Jewish doctrine also rests," Porter writes, "but his way of expressing the struggle as a war between the law (of sin) in his members, and the law of his mind (νοῦς), or between that which he possesses and does in his flesh and in his mind, is widely different from the Jewish conception, and seems to rest on a different view of the world and of man."[99]

Paul's concept of the spirit, Porter insists, has nothing in common with the rabbinic idea of the good *yetzer*. The good *yetzer*, for these rabbis, entailed a twofold capacity of religious Jews to internalize Torah study and thus gain the capacity—with the help of God—to monitor and control their bad impulses and expel the evil forces residing within them.[100] The resemblance between Paul's spirit-flesh dichotomy and the "Jewish conception of the Law as the divinely given remedy for the evil nature of man," Porter concludes, is—at best—remote.[101]

I highlight several claims made in this debate in order to explain my own hypothesis based on reading these texts with and against their grain.

First, as Porter rightly suggests, the Pharisaic doctrine and Paul's explanation of it in Romans 7—as a war between the sinful law of his body and the spiritual law of his mind—describe the same experience of struggle between two opposing forces in man, but they seem "to rest on a different view of the world and man": one Pharisaic, the other gentile idolatry.

Second, as Flusser points out, Paul takes a Pharisaic humanist view of human affections in Rom 12:14 when he says: "Bless those who persecute you; bless and do not curse them." Taken together, Rom 7 and Rom 12:14 seem to illustrate Paul's own self-contradiction in both affirming and contradicting Pharisaic humanism.

Third, as W. D. Davies notes in *Paul and Rabbinic Judaism: Some Rabbinic Elements in Pauline Theology*, Paul was in all likelihood familiar with these Pharisaic concepts—and related discussions about human sin.[102] The Pauline scholar Krister Stendahl makes a similar point in his seminal 1976 book *Paul Among Jews and Gentiles and Other Essays*.[103] Unlike popular gentile discourse about human emotions, impulses, and desires, a kind of man-on-the-street theology that explained emotional discord to the "popular mind" as a divine punishment for violating an oath to the gods,[104] the Pharisaic Sages of Paul's era evaluated and explained such discord in a totally different—Jewish—way.

My standpoint in this debate affirms, with Flusser, that Paul's project of getting the Gentile to experience the world in the manner of an inwardly spiritual Jew (Rom 2:25–29) seems informed by the psychologically sophisticated Jewish perspective on human emotions emerging during his own era.

This new Jewish discourse on man's interior life—which emerged in the wake of "the Maccabean revolt (166–160 BCE); the capture of Jerusalem by Pompeius in 63 BCE; the destruction of the Temple by Titus in 70 CE; and the crashing defeat of the last revolt of Bar Kokhba"[105]—espoused empathy and introspective solidarity with, rather than automatic condemnation of, those who give in to temptation. In the Second Temple era, the dictum "Love your fellow man as yourself" was, says Flusser, "singled out of the Pentateuch to serve as the matrix and foundation for the entire Mosaic law." The injunction to love one's neighbor, in turn, fostered egalitarianism, including as it did the notion that the self and the neighbor were alike in having done both good and bad deeds,[106] certainly a novel idea in those times.[107]

The new discourse, as Flusser notes, replaced the "gallant' simplicity" of earlier Hebrew Scriptures with a "more profound and complex understanding of human nature and religious rationale, a more sophisticated relationship between the divine and the human aspects produced [by this new kind of engagement]."[108]

The "psychological sophistication," as Flusser puts it, led to a "refined sensitivity" in the Judaic discussions about "bad" human impulses and "evil" inclinations in the Pharisaic age of which Paul was a part.[109] Arguments for service to God and man were no longer tied to compensation for good works or to fear of God, but rather to love of God and man. Awe—with its links to fear, compensation, and retribution—was superseded by love as the human motivation for right action.[110] Rabbinic tradition subsequently understood the awe of God to be synonymous with the love of God, and eventually the latter came to be seen as superior to the former.[111]

Furthermore, Flusser claims: as Hanina, deputy to the priests, argued in the Second Temple era, self and neighbor had done good and bad deeds and thus were one alike.[112] Wrath and anger against others were "abominations" clung to only by sinful men.[113] We all have our weakness, as a Ben Sira text points out, and "incline towards evil."[114] Having recognized this, one will not readily condemn one's neighbor for weaknesses both may share. Indeed, personal awareness of one's own internal instability will foster "sympathy and solidarity with those who yielded to temptation and sin" in their ongoing combat with their evil impulses.

I affirm, with Flusser, that Paul seems to have been part of this emerging Pharisaic humanism.

I also affirm that this new Jewish narrative, as scholar of rabbinic literature Jonathan Schofer argues, entailed a "psychological dualism" that pertained to "innate tendencies to transgress and the guidance of the traditional discourse" to prevent such transgressions. Schofer rightfully contrasts this Judaic psychological dualism with the body versus spirit dichotomy found in much of Christian thinking.[115] In the rabbinic texts, Schofer convincingly argues, we do not see such familiar equations as "animal = body = bad desires" and "divine = soul = good desires." Nor does the soul, as understood by the writers of these rabbinic texts, "necessarily denote a 'superior controlling center' or an overarching dimension of the self that includes desires and emotions." Such notions, he concludes, more likely have their roots in Plato than in the rabbinic use of binaries.[116]

Finally, I am persuaded by Hebrew cultural studies scholar Ishay Rosen-Zvi's masterful study of the variegated rabbinic discourse on *yetzer* that it pertains "by and large [to] a highly sophisticated entity, struggling to drag man to sin.... It is evil, not base."[117] The rabbis, in other words, are usually talking about a demon,[118] an entity "independent and distinct from people [and yet] residing within their body."[119] It is an internal entity dragging man to sin. Man's religious task is thus to struggle against this entity within him[120] because:

> the evil yetzer creates a duality and division with the human heart, thus preventing the singularity that is necessary for serving God. One cannot serve the Lord with all his heart when the evil yetzer resides in it. The yetzer must therefore be extirpated in order to attain the desired unity.[121]

From this perspective, a duality in the heart shows that the evil *yetzer* is present.[122]

Rosen-Zvi's research leads me to treat the term *yetzer* as referring to both an "entity" believed to be distinct from man and also believed by some to refer to primal human emotions like lust, anger, jealousy, and fear. And like Porter, I argue that Paul, by affirming a body-spirit duality, adopted a perspective at odds with both Pharisaic standpoints.

Thus, these are my three conclusions. First, the Pharisees' teachings in Paul's era probably included instructions about how to prevent an evil entity from dividing man's heart and thereby his attention so that his will and God's will are no longer aligned. Second, Paul the Pharisee, thanks to this discourse on the *yetzer* in his own era, would *not* have believed that he was innately tarnished or damaged because of the evil inclination within him. Third, there is no equivalent term for *syneidesis* in Hebrew because *the Pharisees did not contend with a bad conscience but rather with a bad or evil inclination that, unlike the gentile conscience, did not tell them that they had committed a moral or religious infraction.* Quite the contrary. It urged them to sin and tried to compel them to do so. The Pharisee's bad *yetzer*/evil inclination, in sum, would not have been the equivalent to the Gentile's *syneidesis*, but, as will be demonstrated in the next chapter, its opposite!

Part Two
Table Fellowship of Paul and Other Pharisees

Pharisees engaged in table fellowship to transform their internal lives by disciplining their emotions.[123] Accounts of Pharisees like Paul found in the rabbinic literature about this Second Temple period, from this standpoint, "stress the same concerns," as Jacob Neusner notes:

> first, eating secular food in a state of ritual purity; second, careful tithing and giving of agricultural offerings to the priests, and obedience to the biblical rules and taboos concerning raising crops; third, to a lesser degree, some special laws on keeping the Sabbaths and festivals; and finally, still less commonly, rules on family affairs ... as a cult-centered piety, which proposes to replicate the cult in the home, and thus to effect the Temple's purity laws at the table of the ordinary Jew, and quite literally to turn Israel into a "kingdom of priests and a holy nation."[124]

Neusner here is not denying that the transition from Pharisaism to rabbinism, or their union, was complex.[125] Rather, he is affirming that the changes the rabbis made to the pre-70 practices cannot be discerned by modern readers because not only are we often reading second-century discussions, but also we may be learning only second-century theory rather than first-century perspectives.[126]

The table fellowship of Pharisees, nevertheless, was one cultic way of inculcating their mindset by disciplining their emotions ritualistically to create lovingkindness dispositions towards others and devotion to God.[127] The continuity of cultic attention to the disciplining of emotions practice is what Neusner wants to affirm.

Neusner thus highlights what he deems to be the most strik-
ing pattern of Pharisaic behavior: its "ordinary, everyday character." It was "wholly routine." Every meal was quotidian. Fasting
seemed to play no significant part in the Pharisees, according to
the rabbinic traditions that recounted them. Rather, the Pharisees
acted as "common folk, eating everyday meals, in an everyday
way ... that set them apart from the people among whom they
constantly lived."

The table fellowship was guided by their observances of
Jewish law: "Keeping the laws included few articulate statements,
for example, blessings. The setting for observance was the field
and the kitchen, the bed, and the street."[128] Their way of life was
practiced rather than preached.

These group practices as well as other kinds of Jewish cultic
gatherings, however, were not simply a strategy for exclusivity,
separation, and overcoming tension within the broader society.[129]
Rather, they also provided positive dimensions for group-society
interactions that enabled Jews to thoroughly interact and integrate with Graeco-Roman civic society.[130] The emphasis here is
thus not on conflicts between Jews and polis and empire,[131] but
rather on an inner way in which Jews enabled themselves to integrate with non-Jews while maintaining emotionally-enabling and
transformed feelings as Jews.

Table fellowship was also a survival strategy for living victori-
ously, boldly, and interactively rather than simply reactively as a
politically vanquished people.[132] The handling of emotions plays
a critically important role here. To this end, "religion," as Gerd
Theissen wisely notes in *Psychological Aspects of Pauline Theology,*
"constantly attempts to restructure even extreme situations with
high tensions into meaningful challenges." These tensions can
then be experienced as motivating impulses in a more meaningful way.[133]

Jacob Neusner's insights affirm this function of cultic practices,
when noting that for the Jews to survive and flourish as a politically defeated people, their feelings must not only be handled but
also transformed. The following passage from Neusner's book,

Vanquished Nation, Broken Spirit, makes this evident with remarkable clarity and soaring power:

> In politics and culture, in matters of the sacred and convic-
> tions about the holy, a construction took shape that would
> stand firm through storm and change.... Individuals, seeing
> themselves as private individuals, were *taught to feel for them-
> selves all of those emotions* to which, in the way of life and world
> view of the larger society, the [religious] system as a whole
> gave full expression. In consequence, *how individuals felt in
> their hearts*, their virtuous attitudes, turned out to correspond
> exactly to how the nation lived as a whole, in its politics and
> social culture.
>
> In a word, the vanquished nation, meant to endure in sub-
> jugation, able to go forward only by accepting its condition of
> weakness, educated the individual to the virtues of the broken
> heart. Teaching restraint and not rebellion, genial acceptance
> and not defiance, concern for the feelings of others and not
> unrestrained self-expression, above all humility and not ar-
> rogance, the nation translated its politics into prerequisites for
> the virtuous affective life. These expressed in terms of emo-
> tions what in fact conformed to the unchanging contingencies
> of national political existence....
>
> *No space remained for the full expression of impulses* to strike
> out or to follow brute instincts, at least none for Israel. The
> instinct to do evil, as much as the instinct to do good, must
> pass through the crucible so as to emerge purified in God's
> service....
>
> In consequence, the nation lived. True, it was a life favor-
> ing restraint and accommodation, *discouraging immoderate
> affect*, on the one side, rebellious spirit, on the other. The *ap-
> proved repertoire of feelings* may strike some as one suitable for
> slaves. It assuredly conformed to the condition of weakness. A
> system that taught, for example, that strength lies in winning
> over one's enemy,[134] riches in accepting what one has, well
> served to reconcile the weak to weakness, leaving strength to
> others. But Israel *was* vanquished. The hearts of the people

(so we surmise, and the evidence is strong) were broken. Teaching the virtue of what had to be accepted, training the heart to feel what the mind acknowledged, the system drew remarkable resilience precisely because *it educated feeing and disciplined the heart's emotions.*[135] (Emphasis added.)

This narrative by Neusner illuminates the mindset of second-century Jews after the destruction of the Second Temple and after the defeat of the Bar Kokhba Revolt.

Such disciplined emotional restraint, however, was also necessary during Paul's own first-century era. During that era, Jews were forbidden public outbursts of emotions, except in sanctioned ways (e.g., state-sponsored public games or other events designed to provoke and immediately satiate the public's emotions). Rome, in short, monitored the way Jews in Paul's era expressed their feelings.

Rome, after all, ruled Palestine not as an occupier but as a permanent overlord, as late antiquity scholar Paula Fredriksen reminds us. Rome thus took an interest in major Jewish festivals. Josephus—the Jewish Pharisee who deserted his own people, became a Roman citizen, and as a historian for Imperial Rome preached accommodation to Roman rules[136]—explains the Roman concern: "it is on these festive occasions that sedition is most apt to break out."[137]

And thus the consequences were torture and terror. "The [Roman] prefect," writes Fredriksen, "together with his troops would march in to reinforce the contingent" of permanently stationed forces. The issue here was crowd control. More precisely, the monitoring and control of the Jews' emotions. Inflamed emotions, after all, had led to incendiary acts, which in turn led to bloody Roman campaigns of reprisal. To bring home this point, Fredriksen offers details of the Roman campaigns against incensed, out-of-control Jews by torturing and thus terrorizing them:

Varus, the Roman legate of Syria, crucified two thousand rebels as part of his effort to pacify the rebellious Jewish countryside.... James and Simon, sons of the Galilean rebel

Judah, were crucified c. 46–48 CE by the procurator Tiberius
Alexander.... Under Cumanus, a later Judean governor (48-
c. 52), a murderous skirmish between Samaritans and some
Galilean pilgrims passing through Samaria on their way to
Jerusalem for a festival escalated into a round of crucifixions
once the tumult threatened to spread.... The Roman historian
Tacitus, who speaks of this event, mentions specifically the
fear that the initial incident might have ignited armed rebellion engulfing all of the Galilee and Samaria.... Finally, in
the violent convulsions just preceding the war in 66 CE, the
procurator Florus responded to provocations in Jerusalem by
rounding up many citizens, even those of high rank, and first
scourging and then crucifying them.... Titus's soldiers nailed
captured Jews to crosses visible to those watching from the
city, "hoping that the sight would terrify the rest into surren-
der."[138]

The Romans used terror, in sum, as an instrument of *first*
resort. The public spectacle of crucifixion—or more broadly
the "punishment of suspension" as the New Testament scholar
Gunnar Samuelsson calls it—was a terror campaign. Suspensions
were designed to affect the maximum possible humiliation of a
perceived enemy of the Empire.[139] According to Samuelsson, the
ordeal entailed

1. A public suspension on a pole, a plank, a city wall, a house,
   the rosta, a statue, or nearly anything else.
2. The victim was forced to do a shameful walk attached to
   the torture tool.

The agony caused by such torture, unimaginable to anyone other
than the victim, put the person, as Elaine Scarry notes in her book
The Body in Pain, "entirely outside the boundaries of an external,
shareable world."[140] Facing this sanction for the slightest disobedience to Rome, the Jews of Paul's era had somehow to find resilience and strength.

We can think of Pharisaic strategies that emerged during Paul's
Second Temple era as a narrative invention to grab hold of terri-

fied private emotions and uplift them into timeless feelings, feelings that depended on normalizing routines like table fellowship that put Jews in right relationship with man and God by monitoring and controlling every aspect of man's appetites.

The Pharisees, however, were not the only Jews to follow these prescriptions. The Essenes—self-enclosed isolated communities of celibate men who cultivated the land and raised livestock—also strove to live righteously in all their daily endeavors, considering their own sacrifices even purer than those performed in the Jerusalem Temple.[141] But unlike the Essenes, the Pharisees lived among the people, though in a distinct and separate way.[142]

The normalized practices of the Pharisee's table fellowship, I contend, helped to create Paul's inner, affective disposition as a spiritual Jew. Paul's inner disposition, in my reading of Rom 2:28–29, means that one is not a Jew who is outwardly a Jew, nor is circumcision something external and physical. Rather, one is a Jew who is inwardly a Jew, and circumcision is a matter of the heart. It is spiritual not literal.

Paul set out to teach Gentiles to become inwardly spiritual Jews, just like himself. His failure produced catastrophic results.

Chapter Four

Paul's Gentile Conscience

Introduction

Paul taught Gentiles to link judgments of their affections to Christ. To this end, Paul told Gentiles their *syneidesis/conscience* serves as a guarantee of the truth of such judgments, but only together with Christ and the Holy Spirit (Rom 9:1).[1] Accordingly, Gentiles must now do two new things: (1) revise the way they think about their conscience and (2) avoid affective behavior that troubles the conscience of others and thus is a sin against Christ (1 Cor 8:12).

This chapter shows how these two lessons by Paul launched his daunting legacy as one of the most polarizing and controversial figures in Western history.[2] Few figures in Western history, as John G. Gager aptly notes, "have been the subject of greater controversy than Saint Paul. Few have caused more dissension and hatred. None has suffered more misunderstanding at the hands of both friends and enemies. None has produced more animosity between Jews and Christians."[3]

Paul began this legacy, I argue, when he tried but failed to revamp the gentile discourse (i.e., invent a new narrative) about the way the gentile conscience judges human affections. In short, triggered affect.

First, Paul was probably aware of the difference between the following things:

1. Pharisaic discourse—*yetzer ha-ra'*, *the evil inclination*—used
   to assess and explain bad affective desires, inclinations,
   and demonic forces in Jews;
2. Gentile discourse—*syneidesis*, the conscience—used to assess and explain bad desires, inclinations, and demonic
   forces in Gentiles.

Second, Paul tried but failed to meld the differences between
these two narratives. The failed attempt, I conclude, reduced his
lessons to a series of self-contradictory, non-cancelable propositions that when posited together as premises rendered every
conclusion false (because it could be countered by an opposite
conclusion deduced from the same evidence/premises).

This chapter reads Paul's lessons against their affective grain.
The goal of this contemporary affect theology strategy is to encourage Christians (scholars, laity, and clergy) today to stop repli-
cating and re-affirming Paul's failures in their own lives and work.

Best to begin with the obvious. Paul was deeply interested in
how table fellowship was conducted by his Corinthian followers.[4]
And his interest, thanks to the Corinthians' apparent reference
of the term *syneidesis* in a letter, led him to talk about their conscience.

Paul's Link Between Table Fellowship and the Gentile Conscience

Background

Paul's lessons about table fellowship and the way his followers
should handle their *syneidesis*/conscience were a big deal because
communal meals played a critically important role during the
Graeco-Roman era in which Paul lived.[5] The meals "were a social
institution of the first order," as Richard S. Ascough notes, that
"pervaded all levels of ancient life [and] played a crucial role as
alternative space for political, social and religious networking."[6]
The various types of these associations were part of the urban
structure of Roman society and, collectively, were encoded social
units of communal identities that ensured allegiance to and identity maintenance aligned with the pax Romana.[7]

These occasions, as Matthias Klinghardt notes, were thus a
kind of "utopian counter image" to the pervasive deficiencies de-

spoiling daily life. "The values of community, quietness and peace attributed to the communal meal mark its ability to provide utopian perfection." Or at least a taste of it. Paul knew, as Klinghardt convincingly demonstrates, that if everything happened during these occasions "decently and in order" (1 Cor 14:40), there would be "peace" rather than "disorder."[8]

Paul took special interest in the protocols for table fellowship among Gentiles because banquets, communal meals, "civic order and table fellowship" went hand-in-hand, as demonstrated in the research of Dennis E. Smith. The importance of dining together thus turned the dining group into a community "whose identity was defined internally by means of social bonding and externally by means of social boundaries."[9]

The Setting

Corinth was a Roman city built in 44 BCE on the site of a Greek city-state the Romans had burned to the ground a century earlier (146 BCE).[10] This major political and mercantile center of the Roman Empire—with a population (perhaps one hundred thousand) that included both Romans and Greeks—was organized according to Roman customs that included cultic loyalties to Isis, Demeter, and Persephone, and temples dedicated to Asklepios, Poseidon, Apollo, and Hermes.[11]

Paul's First Corinthians epistle is the only surviving literary piece that tells us anything of substance about the Corinthians' life and ethos during the mid-first century.[12] New Testament scholar Raymond F. Collins enumerates things we know about the Corinthians' lives thanks to Paul:

> The city had a social mix (1:26); dinners were part of its social life (10:27; 11:20–21, 34). Paul's references to the coming and goings of Christians (1:11; 4:17–21; 16:1–12, 17–18) and the market (10:25) suggest the hustle and bustle of a busy commercial center with easy access to trade routes. Mention of the games (9:24–27) and of the theater (4:9) says something about the size and importance of the city. His references to the city's many gods and lords (8:5, 10; 12:2) are an indication of the various cults that were celebrated.[13]

This specificity of detail with its many allusions to the social ethos of the city tells us that Paul's letter "was written to people caught up in the ebb and flow of day-to-day existence in an important metropolitan center in the Hellenistic world."[14]

The Query

The Corinthians gave Paul the venue for talk about table fellowship when they reminded him, apparently in a letter, that his orders not to eat meat sacrificed to the gods contradicted another of his teachings. All food dedicated to idols could be eaten without hesitation, Paul had told them (1 Cor 8: 5–6), because gods did not exist.[15] So which teaching was right: eat or do not eat sacrificial meat?

They also gave Paul permission to talk about their conscience because the Corinthians, so it seems, used the term *syneidesis* in their correspondence with Paul about food.[16] An account of Paul's lessons in table fellowship and its link to the gentile conscience thus begins not simply with his advice about what they should eat, but also with his advice about how they should act so that the conscience of others would not be harmed.

Thus Paul's advice: Eat what you purchased in the marketplace without worrying that its origins might trouble your *consciences* (10:25). And if an unbeliever invites you to dinner and you wish to go, eat the meat he serves you, again without worrying about the response of your *conscience* (10:27). But, if he says the meat you are served has been offered in sacrifice (10:28), then you must inquire about the conscience of the others present (10:29). And if your consumption of the meat would encourage a weak brother to do the same—and thus result in his feeling defiled—you must not eat the meat.[17]

Paul here focuses attention on affective states of consciousness, namely, inner dispositions and feelings rather than on beliefs and ideas. He spotlights the vanity of the so-called stronger brothers, whose insensitivity to their weaker brothers indicates to Paul that their own vanity has not yet been yoked by the love of Christ.[18] For Paul, as Collins pointedly notes: "The 'law of Christ' (*ho nomos tou Christou*; Gal 6:2; cf. Rom 8:2) is the law of love. It leads

Christians to bear one another's burdens. Those who love their neighbors have fulfilled 'the law' (see Rom 8:2). Paul's thought is that Gentile Christians, subject to Christ whom they recognize as Lord, fulfill and must fulfill the demands of the law of God."[19]

The stronger brothers, from the perspective of the law of Christ, which is love, did not act with lovingkindness toward their weaker brothers. Rather, they took pride in their knowledge (8:1) that idols are not gods and touted their ability to eat the sacrificial meat with impunity. They condemned the others as weak. Paul acts, as Dennis Smith notes, on the principle of "building up" the community rather than "breaking up the [meal] through actions that serve the individual over the community."[20]

The kind of arrogant condemnation of persons perceived as weak, however, was in keeping with the popular Graeco-Roman philosophical writers of Paul's era, most especially the Stoics, who used the term "weak" for those prone to make false judgments or fall short when it came to the demands of virtue.[21] Arguing against this gentile view, Paul judged the knowledgeable, stronger brothers morally culpable because of their hubris and their indifference to the plight of their weaker counterparts.[22] Vanity, as Collins notes, is an attribute of the bad *yetzer*.[23]

Thus our first question is: Was Paul attempting to explain table fellowship using this Pharisaic concept of the evil inclination, now expressed in terms of the Gentiles' talk about their conscience?

Several factors must be taken into account to answer this question. First, Paul's linguistic strategy regarding discourse about the *syneidesis* was revisionist.

Paul's Changes

Background

A brief review of two major stages in the linguistic history of *syneidesis* helps explain why Paul tried to redefine rather than simply set aside the term.

First stage: intuitive knowledge. The term *syneidesis* was first employed in writing by the pre-Socratic philosopher Democritus (ca. 460 BCE—ca. 370 BCE) and the Stoic philosopher Chrysippus (ca. 279 BCE—ca. 206 BCE), neither of whom used the term in its later ethics-related meaning.[24] Rather, both philosophers used the term to refer to knowledge gained intuitively, instead of through reasoning.[25]

Democritus observes, for example, that "some people, ignorant of the decomposition of their moral nature and because of the [*syneidesis*] of detestable behavior in life, spend their time being anxious and fearful. This is the case, Democritus argues, because of what they imagine will happen to them after they die." This anxiety is caused not by the fact that their transgressions are known by others or by the gods, but rather by their fear of what the gods will do to them after death, as noted by Philip Bosman.[26] So the term's primary meaning at this stage of its development is self-reflexively acquired knowledge and its personal emotional import.

The word then dropped out of sight, reemerging just before the Christian era.[27]

Second stage: moral consciousness. Hellenism (336 BCE to 30 BCE) brought back the term *syneidesis* and the two other noun forms (*synesis* and *syneidos*) and the various verb forms derived from the verb *oida*, which refers to intuitive knowledge; and from the prefix *syn*, which refers to a kind of knowledge gained by witnessing.

In the more specialized Hellenistic meaning, the compound term *synoida* still denotes a kind of self-knowledge, an awareness or "consciousness" of one's own evil deeds,[28] but now *syneidesis* also refers to "an important but little analyzed experience of the ordinary man,"[29] namely, the permanent governing faculty dwelling in man's soul.[30] As Bosman notes, "'Consciousness' became an inner monitor, the so-called retrospective conscience [that is consistently used] by Paul."[31]

This phase was a reflection of what antiquities scholar Don E. Marietta, Jr., calls the "Hellenistic concern for ethics and the individual's inner attitudes."[32] The term now gained currency with the common people, with a street meaning denoting a kind of moral consciousness.[33] It now had a street currency and was used as if it were a repository of universal values.

Paul's First Revision: The Judgments
Are Cultural Not Universal

Paul's discourse changed the gentile conscience from an agent of universal moral truth claims and value judgments about human affections to an artifact of particular cultural values and biases. But he didn't try to make this gentile entity disappear. Why? The term *syneidesis*/conscience and other words from the *synoida* word group were used by his followers to refer to something real, namely, "an inner entity"[34] that assesses a person's private dispositions and intentions preceding and accompanying a particular behavior.

The gentile conscience, in short, is an actual occasion of experience, namely, a real event. In other words, any judgment made by it about the personal meaning and value of something, from this perspective, was a personal experience—even if the claims made are wrong. This notion or "entity"—the conscience—was thus thought of as an "*Instanz*,"[35] or an inner human court of law as witness, spectator, accuser, and executioner.[36]

This special kind of inner awareness tracked affective states of being that were moral and religious violations of which only the transgressors themselves are aware. It did so by identifying discrepancies between a person's knowledge of the good and the person's actual affective motivation for action. Accordingly, actions that might appear upright to others might not appear that way to the actor's conscience, which would know about any hidden motivations such as deceit or flattery.[37]

Paul puts forth a new explanation of the term, claiming that reports from the Gentile's conscience on hidden motivations are never absolutely reliable. A case in point is its ability to roil some of Paul's converts because they had eaten sacrificial meat. Nor does the absence of such negative responses mean that one had been justified and acquitted of bad motivations by the Lord (1 Cor 4:4). Paul concludes that simply because he, himself, is not conscious of something—the *syneidesis*—within him, this *lack of awareness* of the conscience does not mean that he has not, in fact, sinned.

It is not the conscience, he argues in Rom 2:15–16, but God, through Jesus Christ, who will judge the secrets of the human heart. By itself, Paul insists, judgments of the conscience are unreliable. Its judgments have been customized and habituated (*sunetheia*) by culturally-constructed gentile, idolatrous beliefs (1 Cor 8:7).

Paul concludes that conscience is a tool for creating feelings of chastisement for wrongdoing[38] rather than an instrument for displaying a transcultural, universal human faculty, or as Bosman puts it, "a common human experience."[39]

Paul's Second Revision: Attentive Care

The gentile conscience must be attended to with care rather than harsh judgment because the term *syneidesis* refers to something that had extraordinary power: human affections. The person who violates his conscience, for example, could become hopelessly ensnared and stumble (1 Cor 8:13). Injuring another person's conscience thus constitutes a sin against Christ (1 Cor 8:12).

The gentile conscience Paul refers to in these passages thus seems to name a faculty that in addition to its cultural component also has an originating power beyond its semantically based social constructions. It can be trained, for example, either to prevent a person from eating sacrificial meat to avoid feeling bad or to enable the person to eat it without feeling defiled. In other words, the Gentile's conscience entails an acculturated habit of thought. Accordingly, knowledge gained from the conscience entails a tentative rather than absolute knowledge of God's judgment and will, but the faculty itself must be handled as something beyond its cultural inscriptions.

Paul thus reaffirmed the notion of the conscience as a universal capacity of Gentiles, while—at the same time—undermining the efficacy of this internal monitor of affective states to make sound judgments. The universal nature of the gentile conscience was thus affirmed (the structure) and also undermined (the content) at the same time.

These complex revisions made by Paul to the meaning of terms from the *synoida* word group, however, were not enough.

He wanted to change not just the way Gentiles *think* about the judgments of their conscience, but also the way the actual *syneidesis functions* within his converts' gentile lives. To this end, Paul mimed how the *syneidesis* made them feel, namely, how it acted in the life of a Gentile. A case in point is Rom 7:24.

Romans 7:24

When Paul cries out in Rom 7:24, "Wretched man that am I, who will rescue me from the body of death?" the Greek phrase — *sōmatos tou thanatou*/the body of death — does not refer to the way in which Pharisees experienced or thought about the *yetzer ha-ra'*. As noted in chapter three, the Hebrew term refers to either (1) a natural impulse to man or (2) a demonic enemy of "[rabbinic] anthropology ... as the explanation of the human tendency to sin."[40] Discourse about the *yetzer* that took place during Paul's own era drew on (1) Jewish experiences of the evil inclination and how it is moderated and/or expelled, rather than on (2) gentile experiences of the gentile conscience that condemned Gentiles for violating their oaths to the gods.

Paul's strategy here can be summarized in three steps.

First, Paul speaks *as if* he is a Gentile struggling with a sundered self that cannot do what his mind commands, but rather succumbs to the passions, interests, and desires of his body. The faculty that makes Gentiles aware of this wretched immoral condition within them is their *syneidesis*/conscience. So Paul mimes a Gentile laid low by a chastising conscience, which seems closest, according to Gaston, "to the Jewish concept of the 'evil impulse.'"[41] Close, I would add, but not close enough to conflate them. Paul kept distance between them by referring to what Gentiles feel rather than what Pharisees experience and believe about their bodies.

To reiterate, the bad *yetzer* is not the same as "the evil principle of [Christian] theology," as Jewish theologian Solomon Schechter notes.[42] Unlike Christian sin, the bad *yetzer* does not refer to a fallen, evil human characteristic that traps man within his body, but rather to something that must be controlled. Man's body is not condemned as a tomb from which he must escape, but rather is affirmed as a place in which he can live joyously with the help of God.

Second, Paul cries out in Rom 7:24 to show empathy with his gentile followers. Their conscience tells them they are governed by the law of sin that rules over the members (i.e., limbs) of their body and wars against the law of "the inward man" (Rom 7:22–23). The new inward Gentile will be the Gentile who has become—inwardly—a spiritual Jew (Rom 2:28–29).

Paul thus differentiates the affectively trapped inner Gentile (Rom 7:24) and the affectively liberated new inner gentile Jew (Rom 2:28–29). The former has a gentile conscience that Paul mimes, while the latter has access to consciousness as a *spiritual* Jew, which Paul celebrates. He does so because this new state does not require Gentiles to rely on cultic Jewish rituals and practices in order to achieve this spiritual internal state of being a "real Jew."

Third, Paul mirrors their wretched gentile condition because he is not a Gentile. His inner life was not inculcated with a Gentile's *syneidesis*. Rather, as noted in chapter three, faithful Pharisees like Paul had a prayer life, Torah study, and a covenantal relationship with God who, as their father, would intervene on their behalf. So the awareness of their own evil inclinations did not entail a gentile-style agony wrought by a gentile conscience, but rather a Jewish experience wrapped in joy.

Thus my conclusion again, first stated in chapter three, is that there is no equivalent term for *syneidesis* in Hebrew because *the Pharisees did not contend with a bad conscience but rather with a bad or evil inclination.* Unlike the gentile conscience, this inclination did not warn them that they had committed a moral or religious infraction. Quite the contrary. It urged them to sin and tried to compel them to do so. In sum, the Pharisee's evil inclination was the very opposite of the Gentile's syneidesis![43]

For Jews like Paul, the discourse was about a natural impulse that must be controlled or a demonic force that must be expunged. For Gentiles, the discourse was about a body of painful feelings they could not control that instead must be escaped.

So when Paul mimed gentile wretchedness (Rom 7:24) as a state that Christ himself must rectify by delivering Paul from his earthly body—which warred against his mind and left him captive to the law of sin (Rom 7:23) and ultimately death—such a view of the human body was not Pharisaic but Gentile. And Paul himself, when in this state, was not Jewish but Gentile. Paul, in short, was *acting* like what he wasn't: a Gentile.

Paul also puts on this gentile persona in Phil 3:7, where he appears to set aside all he has gained through his Jewish relationship with God and counts it as "loss because of Christ." So, too, when he says Christ came "in order that he might redeem those under the law" (Gal 4:4–5), or "this is the law from whose curse (Gal 3:10) Christ has redeemed the Gentiles" (3:13–14).[44] Dressing up in the Gentile's moral attire (i.e., their *syneidesis*), he ministers to them as if he, too, is a Gentile saved through faithfulness to Christ.

Paul, from this contemporary affective theological standpoint, is not damning himself as a Jew when he claims to be a miserable sinner who needs to be redeemed from the curse of the law. Rather, he is condemning a posed gentile self. Readers, I am arguing here, can identity when Paul is posturing as a Gentile rather than speaking for himself as a Jew, whenever he condemns the Jewish way of life he has praised. These contradictions, simply put, indicate Paul's two-ness as a posed Gentile and an authentic Jew.

Nor has he contradicted himself when he praises his Pharisaic background. Rather, he has split himself into Paul the Gentile and Paul the Jew, Paul the wretched and Paul the blessed. He has set up incommensurable, side-by-side states of consciousness, neither of which cancels nor denies the other.[45] He is not, however, a split self. Rather, Paul, by choice, is a culturally bifurcated missionary.

Paul's Bi-Focal Self-Consciousness

Paul is not the kind of split self as explained in contemporary psychological discourse. Rather, he is a missionary practicing radical empathy, the law of love, namely, love beyond religious belief; he mirrors the feelings of his flock as an act of ultimate care.

People with split selves, as Arnold Goldberg notes in *Being of Two Minds*, are aware of the existence of disparate personalities within themselves that despise the values and actions of each other.[46]

The emotional principle behind splitting in this technical sense of the term involves both pain and pleasure:[47] like binging on food. It is pleasurable because of a deeply gratifying bodily experience of satiation. It is also punishing because the binging self that has a pleasurable emotional experience is then condemned as bad and wrong by a judging self that arises from inculcated social values.

In contrast, Paul's inculcated values—as a Second Temple Pharisee—did not require him to split his personality into the warring factions of a sundered self. So while Paul mimed gentile agony, he did not have to mime Jewish joy because he already had it culturally inscribed within him as a Pharisee.

Paul the Pharisee, to reiterate, would thus have called the evil impulses within him to act against God the bad or evil *yetzer*, and he would have known that with Torah study, prayer, and God's assistance he could harness his passions and expel demonic forces.

Faithfulness to Christ linked to the Gentile's *syneidesis*, as Paul explains it, is now set up to function in the same way as the religious Jew's experience of being yoked to God. This link is the law of unconditional love—love beyond belief—in which no one is a stranger, no one is Gentile or Jew, male or female. Perfection has been felt because we bear one another's burdens and thus fulfill the law of Christ (Gal 6:2), which is love beyond belief.

But Paul's new moral and religious internal evaluative system for Gentiles that yokes their *syneidesis* to Christ consciousness couldn't give Gentiles the Jewish experience of being yoked to God through Torah study, prayer, and table fellowship. Why? The gentile *syneidesis* cultic system was founded on negative emotions, namely, "crippling fear,"[48] "shame,"[49] "guilt,"[50] "tribulation,"[51] and "pain."[52]

In contrast, Pharisees like Paul had a prayer life, Torah study, and a covenantal relationship with a God who, as their father, would intervene on their behalf. So the awareness of the evil inclinations by Pharisees like Paul did not entail a gentile-style cultic agony but rather a Jewish cultic joy.

Accordingly, the pain and suffering wrought by the conscience, according to popular reason among Gentiles, was brought on by fear of divine wrath and retribution for moral violations.[53] The gentile conscience, in sum, had a cultural history that turned it into an artifact of non-Jewish cultic beliefs and practices.

Paul's revisionist and missionary strategy thus combined contrasting affective venues. And thus the problem: Paul's joyous Pharisaic perspective on handling untoward impulses and inclinations—and expelling evil forces—might have been too unfamiliar for Gentiles to absorb. Solomon Schechter makes this point when noting that those who have not experienced the Jewish sense of blamelessness and chosenness cannot understand it.[54] So when Paul used the gentile term *syneidesis* to extend the Jewish temperament of love beyond belief and unbounded joy to his converts, did he unintentionally re-establish faithfulness to God based on the experience of gentile pain? So it seems.

A New Religious Identity for Gentiles

If Paul failed to give Gentiles a new affective foundation for determining faithfulness to the God of Israel, he nevertheless did succeed in giving his converts a new lineage through Abraham, as New Testament scholar Caroline Johnson Hodge notes in her book *If Sons, Then Heirs*. Through baptism, Paul insisted, Gentiles belonged to Christ and thus became descendants of Abraham and heirs to God's promise to Abraham (Gal 3:29).[55]

His converts' new religious identity, however, did not alter their ethnic identity. They were still Gentiles. But now, as Hodge pointedly argues, they self-identified as Jews—not only because of baptism, but also, I add, because they tried to judge their inner life (feelings) like spiritual Jews.

Accordingly, they now had a "mixed or 'hybrid' identity."[56] They were Gentiles who thought they were, as Boyarin puts it, the "real Jews." From this "hybridity,"[57] Hodge argues, emerged a new race, one that, I would add, both did and did not include Paul, whose Jewish identity remained intact. Thoroughly and utterly Jewish by birthright, by cultural and cultic rites, and by self-proclamation (Gal 3:11; Rom 3:1), Paul nevertheless presented himself as a gentile convert (which, of course, he was not) as well as one who followed Christ. In short, he invented himself—emotionally—as a gentile member of his own gentile flock.

Paul's hybrid gentile identity, however, entailed a twofold structural difficulty.

First, he undermined his Pharisaic emotional foundation for faithfulness to God, while at the same time keeping it intact. According to Hodge, adoption by the God of Israel for first-century Jews like Paul occurred through the experience of ethnic—and I would add here emotional—continuity with the faithfulness of their ancestors' cultural origin with Abraham. But by portraying his internal life *as if* it were the inner life of a Gentile, Paul defeated his own purpose. To Jews, he had betrayed the Pharisaic tradition. To Gentiles, he had become a Gentile, with a gentile *syneidesis*.

Second, as Hodge points out, the Gentiles adopted the God of Israel through the "ethnic disruption and rearranging" of their ancestry, the rejection of their former "gods, religious practices, myths of origin, epic stories of their ancestors and origins," and thus through the construction of new identities as adopted sons and daughters of Israel through faithfulness in Christ.[58] But did this disruption penetrate to the Gentiles' innermost emotional life?

The emotional life of Paul's converts probably remained undisturbed thanks to Paul's use of their term *syneidesis* and his miming of their conditions as if he also had a gentile conscience. Rather than transforming their internal moral and religious valuation system, Gentiles simply learned to call it by a new name: the inner Jew (Rom 2:28–29). Their awareness of painful emotions through their *syneidesis/conscience* was now, thanks to Paul, linked to their consciousness of themselves as Jews.

Thus the consequence was that, thanks to Paul, Gentiles could now *think* of themselves internally as good, spiritually faithful Jews. But they continued to *feel* the pain of tumultuous, out-of-control, and conflicted triggered emotions monitored and made evident by their unreconstructed gentile *syneidesis*. As a result, they would have felt like the bad Jew, someone who had broken God's law and was now being punished for his sins.

Paul's program for securing gentile faithfulness to Christ, I conclude, was probably based on gentile pain rather than on Jewish joy. And as hard as he tried to change the cultural meaning of the term *syneidesis*, the term itself with its weighted cultic history retained its emotional content of pain and suffering.

This conclusion is based on probability. It gains a more definitive explanatory power because of what happened next: Augustine made the negative emotional content of the gentile conscience autobiographically self-evident. Luther then laid out its dire consequences for the rebellious Other.

Both men could give Paul credit for their insights about the emotional content and meaning of the Christian conscience because they paid attention to Paul's gentile conscience. Based on the principle of self-contradiction, however, Paul's strategies also undermined their claims because he made mutually contradictory statements to accomplish his missionary work. Thus their conclusions (based on Paul's self-contradictory premises) end up falsifying themselves. Self-contradictory claims and arguments, in short, contradict themselves.

When we re-Judaize Paul as a contemporary affect theological strategy, we affirm the self-contradictions. We thus reconfirm affective states foundational to Paul's work—love beyond belief—and also show, at the same time, how Paul established the opposite: the Christian basis for hate beyond belief toward anyone who troubles the Christian conscience, which, thanks to Paul, became the Gentile's link to Christ.

Part Three

Impaired Affect
Theology

Chapter Five

Augustine's Invention

Introduction

Augustine invented the gentile, affective content of Paul's character. Thanks to Augustine, Paul no longer simply sounded and acted like a Gentile. He actually felt like one. More precisely, Paul's inmost self, his personality traits and gut-wrenching struggles, his core beliefs and signature feelings were now those of the fifth-century North African bishop and revered Catholic Church Father himself: Augustine.

This chapter first shows how Augustine accomplished his remarkable feat. He generalized his own emotional[1] struggles as a split self and a sundered soul in his autobiographical *Confessions*.[2]

Then he made these generalizations the universal rules and foundational principles for the Catholic Church's first official doctrine of human nature,[3] which deemed all souls fallen and broken.[4] And by applying Paul's teachings to baptized Christians *only*, as Elaine Pagels rightly notes in her book *Adam, Eve, and the Serpent*, "Augustine effectively invented this interpretation of Paul's words."[5] This present chapter goes one step further and argues that Augustine affectively invented Paul the Gentile.

Thanks to Augustine, Christians learned to think about Paul, others, and themselves guided by the church's low estimate of the human body and its "carnal" affections, claims which cannot be adequately understood apart from Augustine's own rational theological terms.[6]

Augustine, in effect, created in Christians an assurance, promised them an end to pain, and thus provided them comfort by claiming, as Elaine Pagels puts it, "'You *personally* are not to blame for what has come upon you; the blame goes back to our father, Adam, and our mother, Eve.' Augustine assures the sufferer that pain is unnatural, death an enemy, alien intruders upon normal human existence, and thus he addresses the deep human longing to be free of pain."[7]

Neither Pagels nor I can prove that this kind of assurance was Augustine's intended goal. We can, however, examine the consequences and offer a theory that explains the behavioral results. The usefulness of the theory is its ability to explain inner states and reliably predict human behavior prompted by triggered and transformed feelings. Such is the goal of contemporary affect theology.

Next, this chapter reads Augustine's *Confessions*[8] against the grain of the received tradition of reading Paul's inner life as if it is gentile. I do so by replacing the rational theological terms Augustine uses to explain Paul's self-declaration of internal discord (Rom 7:22–23), with nomenclature and insights from contemporary affective neuroscience and related fields.

Three results follow from this contemporary affect theological strategy. First, Augustine's inchoate affect theology, if you will, is found, which affirms his body and its affections as foundational to human life. Second, this lost Augustinian affective theological strategy reveals what both Paul and Augustine together affirmed: the experience of Christ as a love beyond mistaken religious beliefs. In short, an experience of cosmic consciousness. Third, this affirmation shows how the inner life of Paul became an Augustinian biographical invention: Augustine projected his own cultural biases and personal conflicts onto Paul.

This contemporary affect theology way of reading Augustine's *Confessions* from the bottom up (feelings) as well as from the top down (reason) is divided into three basic parts.

Part one tracks how Augustine created a rational theology and an affect theology. He did so by (1) illustrating the ruptured condition of the human soul in personal terms. He then (2) named its two broken parts (*animus* and *anima*); (3) developed concepts to describe what these two discrete parts of the human soul respectively do (think and feel); and in his *Confessions*, he (4) gave both parts their own respective rational and affective theological conversion stories: the former for his rational soul whose vision is unveiled by God, the latter for his emotional soul whose feelings are taken hold of by Christ.

Part two shows how Augustine's rational theology affirmed his conscience's rebukes against him.[9] Some of the charges against Augustine by his conscience, however, were the product of its mistaken judgments, the source of which were the cultural biases of Augustine's own caretaking community and era. As a consequence, Augustine not only misinterpreted Paul's miming behavior of Gentiles, but he also misunderstood Paul's explanation of the link between the gentile conscience and Christ. I correct Augustine's mistaken judgments by placing them back in their social contexts.

Part three retrieves the lost emotional foundation for Christian faith that Augustine's affect theology and Paul affirmed, namely, love beyond belief. To this end, I show how a collusion principle functions in Augustine's *Confessions* that keeps his disembodied mind and his body's passions in conflict. Revealed here is the paradigmatic role Augustine's mother and his readers play in maintaining Augustine's narrative as a sundered soul. When we step back from this support structure it collapses, revealing the lost Pauline foundation for Christian faith: the love of Christ for persons not because they are sinners, but because they are suffering.

A conclusion reached by master Augustinian scholar Peter Brown frames my entire project. Brown, after reading the late twentieth-century discovery of new sermons and letters by Augustine, now claimed that his own "one-sided attention" to the inner rationally-constructed life of Augustine "subtly diminished the man."[10]

Peter Brown already knew a great deal about the tumultuous times in which Augustine lived. During Augustine's lifetime, for example, five different emperors held the throne. There were tax rebellions and riots. A peonage system was pervasive and cruel.

And Germanic tribes sacked Rome and the North African prov-
inces. But Brown now discovered that in 404, Augustine was
shouted down from the pulpit for refusing to obey the demands
of the crowd as to where he should stand when he preached. Nor
did Brown know that in 422, Augustine watched fellow North
Africans—Roman citizens—illegally sold into slavery through
government collusion. When he tried to intervene he was sued.[11]
Brown had ignored the little man hidden behind the magisterial
curtain of Augustine's rational, theological mind.

Brown now offers advice to correct ahistorical readings of
Augustine: "never read Augustine as if he is contemporary with
ourselves." Augustine's body, Brown insists, must be relocated in
its actual times.[12]

I follow Brown's advice in this chapter by (1) spotlighting
Augustine's social and cultural contexts, (2) lifting up his descrip-
tions of his own emotions in this social environment, and then by
(3) tracking his emotions interoceptively, namely, as externally induced, internally triggered, and experienced feelings. Augustine's
rational theological reflections, in sum, are separated from his embodied emotional experiences.

I also follow the advice of Margaret Miles in her book *Desire
and Delight: A New Reading of Augustine's Confessions* to become
"disobedient" rather than "obedient" readers.[13] She urges readers
to hold onto that which Augustine tried to get rid of: his impassioned emotional life. I am a very disobedient reader.

This chapter thus tells the story of two Augustines. One
Augustine affirmed the efficacy and agency of his emotions,
which the other Augustine denied.[14] I hold onto the affective intelligence Augustine let go of not only for the sake of our own emotional integrity, but also for the sake of the lost Pauline emotional
foundational requisite for a viable liberal faith today.

I begin with the obvious.

Part One

Augustine's Broken Soul

Augustine's soul was sundered and he knew it. Evidence for this
kind of self-knowledge by Augustine is found in his *Confessions*

when he describes himself as broken, shattered asunder, and dis-integrated (II.1.1). So, too, when he says in Book VIII: "I was at odds with myself, and fragmenting myself. This disintegration was occurring without my consent" (VIII.10.22). His soul was in battle with itself. It waged a ceaseless self civil war that he was powerless to end on his own because he himself was the problem: he was quarrelling with himself (VIII.8.19). Powerless to end the battle, he felt shame (VIII.10.22).

Readers can follow the blow-by-blow accounts of Augustine's embattled soul because he gives the two contenders their own respective names: *anima* and *animus*. I make this claim while acknowledging that Augustine does not use the two terms in a rigidly systematic fashion. Nevertheless their use by him has suffi-cient patterning principles for my general classification of the two terms in the following way.[15] As a consequence, I argue, two dis-crete conversion narratives are found in Augustine's *Confessions*: one for *animus*, the other for *anima*.

Anima. The term *anima*, in Augustine's *Confessions*, tends to refer to the source of the life of the body. It refers to his body's animating principle, namely, its vitality by means of which his whole frame is filled with life and he is united to his body (X.7.11). Accordingly, Augustine believes he cannot by this faculty find God because the horse and mule have this faculty, too, but they have no understanding of God (X.7.11). The term thus refers to the motions, dispositions, and carnal feelings we share with other animals (IV.14.22). *Anima* thus pertains to affective states of con-sciousness.

Animus. The term *animus,* in Augustine's lexicon, usually refers to the purely rational part of the soul. According to Augustine, this aspect of his soul is his essential, inmost self, namely, his mind (X.7.11). It is the place of memory and recollection (X.8.14). The place where things are known in themselves as thought, cog-nition, intellection unaided by sensations (X.10.17–12.19). *Animus* is one thing and the body an entirely different thing, Augustine tells us (X.14.21). *Animus* thus tends to refer to Augustine's intel-lection: his ability to reason. *Animus*, writes Augustine, "is noth-ing other than my very self" (X.17.26). His soul, however, is not in its entirety a disembodied faculty; rather it has a disembodied aspect (*animus*), which is his purely mental, reasoning capacity.[16]

Augustine invented the word "*soliloquies*" to describe what *animus*—the part of the human soul defined purely as a thinking thing—can do by itself. It can soliloquize, namely, it can reason with itself as if it were two.

Augustine created this new word and strategy at the very beginning of his life as a Catholic Christian (386–87).[17] According to Augustine, here's an explanation of how this kind of thinking works, which he recounted in his *Retractationes* (427 CE), written toward the end of his life:

> I asked myself questions and I replied to myself, as if we were two, reason and I, whereas I was of course one. As a result I called the work *Soliloquies*.[18]

His text (*Soliloquies*) remained unfinished, but during the same year, 387, he began another writing project: his *Confessions*.

Augustine now used his new form of thinking to write his autobiographical reflections. He thus wrote his *Confessions* as a man of two minds. But he himself, as he said, is not two but one. So Augustine's strategy as writer is akin to playing a game of chess with oneself. The basic back-and-forth moves advance the player's ability to play a stronger game. Similarly, Augustine strengthens his reason by reasoning, logically, as his mind moves back and forth as a play of ideas.

Animus, when enlightened, ascends toward God. *Animus* thus does not need either the sensate data of the body or its carnal affections to know God. When freed from the distractions triggered by the carnal affections of *anima*, this purely mental capacity of his soul can find glory, wealth, and salvation in God.

Since Augustine's soul, by his own linguistic definitions, has these two discreet parts, each must be converted in its own terms. Augustine, I conclude, presents two discrete conversion narratives for *animus* and *anima*. Both accounts are required, in sum, because Augustine by his own self-definition is a fragmented and disintegrated soul. So each part must be addressed separately.

The Conversion of *Animus*

The conversion of Augustine's mind, namely his rational soul — *animus* — to God is perhaps the most famous story in his *Confessions*. Often called Augustine's mystical experience, it is recounted in Book VII.

This conversion story begins as Augustine, with God's help, turns his attention inward and enters therein guided by the eyes of his soul (*oculum animae meae*). This kind of vision is pure intellection and thus categorically different from the carnal vision man shares with mules, horses, and other animals. His mental vision now sees above itself the unchangeable light of God (VII.10.16), who is incorruptible, inviolable, and the supreme, sovereign and only true God (VII.1.1). Augustine now trembles with love and dread (VII.10.16). Freed from the distractions that stimulate his carnal, lustful desires, Augustine's mind (*animus* VII.5.7) watches the madness of his carnal soul (*anima*) waste away like a spider's web (VII.10.16).

Flooded with a purely mental, non-sensate inspirational love, Augustine cries out: "O eternal Truth! And true Charity [*caritas*]! and dear Eternity! Thou art my God, to thee do I sigh day and night" (VII.10.16). As a consequence, Augustine, a professor of rhetoric "steeped in the intellectual heritage of antiquity,"[19] and who had always been a Christian, now becomes a *Catholic* Christian.[20]

Augustine's mental vision, in sum, consists of his mind's conversion to the Catholic tradition, which is in no way derived from the flesh (VIII.14.20). Rather, the conversion of this part of his soul takes place in his essential, inmost self, namely his mind, his very self (*hoc ego ipse sum*). In short, in *animus* (X.17.26). His intellect is now free at last from the gnawing needs of *anima* to seek advancement and riches, and to wallow in the filth of his lust (IX.1.1).

Augustine now turns to the writings of Paul, which previously had seemed filled with self-contradictions and in conflict with the law and the prophets. These problems now melted away because of what had just happened to his mind (VII.21.27). Augustine now realizes that Paul (Rom 7:22–23) is just like him, someone who has to contend with the law in his bodily members that strive against the law of his mind (VII.21.27).

As we saw in chapter four, Paul mimed these gentile movements and spoke the words of a Gentile with a sundered soul and a tormented conscience. Augustine, in contrast, lived the experience and thus filled out Paul's gentile impersonations with the content of Augustine's own character.

Augustine now thinks he is just like Paul. In truth, Paul is now Augustine manqué, namely, the Gentile Paul with a personal history not of his own making. More precisely, Augustine has projected his own inner struggle as a Gentile onto Paul. The inner conflict raging in Augustine's life is now the content of Paul's inner life. I return to this immensely important point in parts two and three of this chapter.

Meanwhile, Augustine's out-of-body mystical experience and his pure mental pleasure derived from it do not last. So his mind, once again, is weighted down by his self-designated loathsome carnal affections and desires.

Clearly, a second conversion experience is now requisite to entrain his carnal affections. Only then can Augustine's mind focus solely on God.

The Conversion of *Anima*

The setting for this second conversion narrative is the Milan garden scene in Book VIII of the *Confessions*. More precisely, the first conversion story was not given a site-specific physical locale because all of the action takes place within Augustine's mind. The second story, in contrast to the first, takes place in Augustine's physical body and so it must have a physical locale, namely, the determinate place in which his body is actually situated. Here his body gestures, movements, and facial expressions must be described and transformed in physical terms.

I capture the power of this second conversion story by presenting it as if he is speaking directly to us today in simple, direct terms we can immediately understand. To this end, I also make the implicit dramatic details of his narrative explicit. The goal here is to use these additions to help us better track Augustine's impassioned story.[21]

> I will give you the barest of facts. My attempts to find steadfast comfort and peace with my parents, my friends, and with women had failed. I knew that I could not find the peace I sought in the child who would become my bride. I would be her master; she would be my slave. My heart was dulled by despair and loss. And yet I still longed for the companionship of women and friends knowing that they too would fail me as the source of permanent peace. My body still craved the sexual company of women. I wished to give up this desire but I could not do so because the very vitality of my life was enslaved by its sexual desires. And I still had worldly ambition. How could I renounce the desires that had brought me such pleasures and that had been a source of such pride? It is as if I were saying to God, "Grant me chastity and self-control, but please not yet." But now I was set naked before my own eyes and my conscience upbraided me. I had said I would cast off these illusions when I was certain of God's nature. Now I was. He is Light. I was caught. I was wasting away. I scourged my soul to follow my command to be chaste and have self-control as I tried to follow God. But to no avail. All my arguments, all my reasoning, all my intellect counted for naught.
>
> This violent conflict raged on within me, this quarrel with my soul. I blushed, my brow, cheeks, and eyes were flushed. The accent, the cadence of my voice expressed my mental disposition more so than did the words I uttered. The tumult in my breast swept me into the garden of the house in Milan. I was going mad. I tore at myself; I groaned; I was shaken by violent anger; I was pulled this way and that. While this vacillation was at its most intense many of my bodily gestures were of the kind that people sometimes want to perform but cannot, either because the requisite limbs are missing, or because they are bound and restricted, or paralyzed by some

illness, or in some way impeded. I was at strife with my self and fragmenting my self. This disintegration was occurring without the consent of my own intellect.

Oh such misery, such agony, such sickness as I waged a merciless war against myself, twisting and turning this way and that to break the slender tie that still bound me, less it thicken again and constrict me more tightly. I redoubled the lashes of fear and shame. And I was bitterly ashamed, because I could still hear the murmurs of those frivolities. I was still hanging back. I couldn't let go. The argument raged on in my heart and I was swept away in a storm of tears. I rose and left my friend Alypius, who had been by my side. I needed solitude for the business of weeping. How long, O Lord, how long? I went on weeping and talking like this in the intense bitterness of my broken heart.

But suddenly, I heard a voice from a house nearby—perhaps a voice of some boy or girl, I do not know—singing over and over again, "Pick up and read, pick up and read." My expression was immediately altered. I realized that this was not a child's ditty. I stemmed the flood of my tears and rose to my feet, believing that this could be nothing other than a divine command to open the Book and read the first passage I came upon. I did this. It was from Paul, Romans 13:13–14: *Not in dissipation and drunkenness; nor in debauchery and lewdness, nor in arguing and jealousy; but put on the Lord Jesus Christ, and make no provision for the flesh or the gratification of your desires.* I had no wish to read further.

I was free. The light of certainty flooded my heart and all dark shades of doubt fled away. My face was peaceful. My friend Alypius read the next verse after I told him what had happened to me, and he too made the vow of chastity. We went in the house and told my mother what had happened. She was overjoyed (VIII.8:19–12:30).

What happened? Augustine's emotional soul (*anima*) and his rational soul (*animus*) had been at war until Christ stepped in and parsed Augustine's carnal affections with the Divine Word. The Divine Word made flesh enters Augustine's carnal appetites and takes control. Augustine thus has a mystical, physically affective, emotional encounter with Christ, flesh to flesh.

Christ: the Bridegroom of *Anima*

Augustine explains the conversion of his emotional soul by Christ Jesus as his Savior in the opening chapter of Book IX:

> O Christ Jesus, my helper and redeemer? How sweet did it suddenly seem to me to shrug off those sweet frivolities, and how glad I now was to get rid of them—I who had been loath to let them go! For it was you who cast them out and entered yourself to take their place, you who are lovelier than any pleasure, though not to flesh and blood, more lustrous than any light, yet more inward than is any secret intimacy, loftier than all honor, yet not to those who look for loftiness in themselves. My mind [*animus*] was free at last from the gnawing need to seek advancement and riches, to welter in filth and scratch my itching lust. Childlike, I chattered away to you, my glory, my wealth, my salvation, and my Lord and God.

Christ, in this above scenario, does not heal Augustine's inordinate desires. Rather, Christ puts Himself in their stead and thus becomes the re-ordering principle for Augustine's carnal feelings. Christ and not Augustine now rules his physical affections. Christ has full agency here. Emotionally hamstrung Augustine has none. As Augustine tells us in Book IX, Christ—his helper and redeemer—drains the cesspit of corruption of his heart and plumbs the depths of his death.

Christ now resides in Augustine's *anima* as its Bridegroom (XI.8.10; VII.21.27). Christ is thus positioned by Augustine's account as the mediator between God and man. Christ mediates *anima* thereby setting *animus* free from its slavery to corporeal desires. Writes Augustine:

> A mediator, now betwixt God and man, must have something like unto God, and something like unto men [i.e., flesh]; lest,

that being like unto man in both natures, he should be too
far unlike God: or if like unto God in both natures, he should
be too far unlike to men: and so be a mediator in neither way
(X.42.67).

What Christ and Augustine now have in common is affective
consciousness, namely, the deeply personal and immediate emotional experiences of feeling alive. And this affective consciousness of Augustine's physical desires—his carnal affections—does
not trigger licentious pleasures but rather makes Augustine feel
the presence of Christ in him.

Why Augustine's Carnal Affections Disappear

Augustine's explanation of this disappearing act can be summarized as follows. When Christ, who is the Divine Word made
flesh, enters Augustine's *anima*, his carnal affections disappear
because his feelings are now parsed by Christ. The Divine Word
made flesh in Augustine's carnal desires vacates what it analyzes
because it is divine awareness, which is always aware of itself.
Augustine thus feels within himself God contemplating Himself
and thus the Logos unfolding itself in Augustine's carnal soul.

In this Augustinian scenario, the presence of the Divine
Mediator is thus always required to rightly order Augustine's disordered *anima*. Christ, however, does not *repair* Augustine's carnal emotions, but *replaces* them with Himself. Christ rather than
Augustine casts out his libidinous desires and enters therein flesh
for flesh to take their place (IX.1:1).

The affective link between Augustine's physical affections and
his reasoning capacity is always in dis-repair. But when Christ
is present the disrepair is not triggered because the determining
agency is now Christ.

As a result of this divine work by Christ, Augustine's soul, so
he tells us, can now attend to its inmost capacity as a purified intellect without carnal distractions. Writes Augustine:

I will soar beyond that faculty of mine [*anima*], by which I am
united unto my body.... But another faculty there is, not that

only by which I give life, but that too by which I give sense unto my flesh ..., commanding the eye not to hear, and the ear not to see, but the eye for me to see by, and this for me to hear withal; assigning what is proper to the other senses severally, in their own seats and offices; which being diverse through every sense, yet I the soul [*animus*] being but one, do activate and govern (X.7).

Anima, in the above citation, is explained and affirmed as the link between the body and the inmost aspect of Augustine's soul, *animus*. This link is the lynchpin of Augustine's theological enterprise. It's the place where his affective theological interests (Christ) become aligned with his rational theological designer (God).

Augustine's rational theology thus explains this event from the standpoint of his transformed mind. His affect theology, on the other hand, explains the same event from the standpoint of his transformed feelings. These contrasting perspectives meet in-between the two, which is *felt* as the love of Christ and *thought* as the purely mental awareness of God's awesome light.

This link is the place where the two discreet parts of his soul meet. It is thus a state of cosmic consciousness, but a state immediately reduced to Christian religious terms. The Word made flesh by God is now the carnal words of Augustine's affections replaced by the Word of God, which is Christ. And since God = Christ, the union of the two parts of Augustine's soul is God himself. This is why Augustine's heart cannot be quieted until it rests in God (I.1.1). And this is also why Augustine believes he is in God, rather than claims that God is in him (I.3.2). The union, unity, and rightful alignment of the two parts of his soul are God's work on Augustine in God's being. Augustine's self, aligned with both God and Christ, is now wholeheartedly in God.

The last three chapters of Augustine's *Confessions* are, fittingly, the confessions of the preacher rather than of a penitent who has not yet found God. Augustine's carnal affections now ordered by Christ enable him to explore the laws of God without physical and emotional distraction. Augustine, by his own account, can now speak solely as someone who has been led to "preach the word and administer the sacrament" (XI.2.2). His mind is now free to contemplate time and eternity (Book XI), heaven and earth (Book XII), and the days of the church and the prophecy of the church (Book XIII) because his dispassionate mental disposition is now filled with spiritual affection: *caritas*. He can now write and speak as a purely rational soul, in sum, for three basic reasons.

1. *The agitation.* Augustine's agitated affections, once they are united to Christ, no longer weigh down his mind and cause affliction. When Christ is in his heart as its Bridegroom (XI.8.10), Augustine's mental state is thus calm, ordered, and free to ascend by degrees toward God.

2. *The stillness.* Freed by Christ of deranged carnal affections, Augustine can be the preacher. He is free to meditate in keeping with God's law, and by so doing, find chaste delights in God's Scriptures (XI.2.2). His affections are now disposed toward Christ rather than carnal desire. His disposition is that of *caritas*, spiritual affection toward God.

3. *The ascent.* Augustine's intellect now illuminated by God's light (XI.11.13), his attention no longer disturbed (XI.2.2.), his intellect thus pure (*mentem puram*; XII.11.13), his newly ordered *anima* (*intellegat anima*) set right, Augustine's mind (*animus*) can now begin its pilgrimage back to God as the true source of its delight.

So why does Augustine, much to his consternation, continue to have wet dreams, indulge in fine food, and still find great pleasure in song? Why, in short, haven't the carnal affections of his *anima* completely gone away?

Augustine gives us two contradictory answers to these two queries: (1) Augustine is still being punished as a sinner for being a split, conflicted soul who hurts himself and others and (2) he is an innocent soul trying to escape a punishing world that hurt his feelings and broke his soul.

Both contradictory answers are right. But the second answer is not self-evident to Augustine or easily found in his work. His rational theology, in effect, obscures insights from his affect theology that affirm what *animus* condemns: his carnal emotions. Augustine, however, gives us the linguistic tools needed to free him, Paul, and ourselves from his rational theological biases.

Part Two
Affects—The Body's Native Tongue

Augustine created an affective theological system in his *Confessions* that explains the communication system of his body and affirms the affective work of Christ as love that extends beyond mistaken religious beliefs. The construction of this system begins in Book I of his *Confessions,* when Augustine introduces readers to the universal language of the human body, namely, affective displays.

Augustine, so we discover, used this universal communication system to learn the language his caretakers spoke: Latin (I.8.13). Here's what he did.

He first studied the facial expressions of his caretakers, the glances of their eyes, and also the movements of other parts of their bodies. Next, by means of these facial expressions and bodily gestures—these so-called "natural words," as he put it—he watched and remembered the sounds his caretakers made when pointing to something. Finally, Augustine schooled his mouth to make those sounds and by so doing, he gradually learned to speak Latin.

Augustine was half wrong about the way in which he learned Latin. He mistakenly assumed that language is simply a way of labeling things. If this is the case, what physical thing does the word "the" indicate?[22] Clearly, he missed something about the purpose and function of human language.

But Augustine was also half right. His account of affective cues highlights a core fact of normal human development: babies and adults read each other's body gestures, voice timbre and rhythm, and facial expressions in order to know each other's needs, intentions, and desires.

Three examples reaffirm Augustine's insight in contemporary terms and lead us to question the adequacy of his rational theology's conclusions about his affective displays.

First, the work of Virginia Demos on affect's communicative and motivational function within an organism.[23] Augustine's "natural words" in the lexicon of Demos are affective "cues" Writes Demos:

These cues—a combination of facial expressions, vocaliza-
tions, and body movements—convey information primarily
about the infant's affective state and the infant's plans and
goals in relation to that state. Indeed, before the advent of language and other symbolic forms of representation, the infant's
affective expressive behaviors are probably the only reliable
and valid indication of the saliency of events for the infant;
they thereby constitute the primary medium of communication and meaning in the infant-mother system.[24]

The infant-mother system described by Demos is in keeping with
Augustine's core claim that he could read his caretakers' intentions
without understanding their spoken words. As Demos notes, the
affect-based system of communication between infant and mother
is a two-way street because both the infant and mother are in the
same situation. Each has to make inferences based on affective,
visceral displays of the intentions, needs, and feelings of the other.

How well infants are able to interpret adult behavior depends
in normal child development on how well the child is cared for.
If children are in a "playful, positive state—well-rested, well-fed,
and motivated by interest and enjoyment—they do not seem to
notice the mother's 'mistakes,' such as bad timing, inattentive-
ness, rough handling, or impatience.... If, however, infants are
fussy, tired, hungry, and generally irritable, then they seem to become much more discerning and demanding partners, containing
their irritation only if the mother is well tuned to their state."[25]

And thus our first query. Augustine, by his own reckoning,
was a fussy baby (I.6.8), who greedily beat on the breast of his
caretaker and tearfully begged for food (I.7.11). Was he acting sin-
fully or was the infant simply hungry?

Second, the work of affective neuroscientist Jaak Panksepp.
The "words" described by Augustine and the "cues" talked about
by Demos consist of what Panksepp calls "instinctual emotional
behaviors," which are normally displayed at birth.[26] Newborn
babies feel their way into the world. They cry when they need
food, make cooing sounds when their hunger is satiated, and

scream if left alone for too long. Each expression is an instinctual emotional behavior established to sort through, evaluate, and
respond to physical experiences of the body in the world. They
are genetically ingrained birthrights.[27] This sorting system of the
brain consists of a range of emotive expressions to denote satisfac-
tions and discomforts. The intensity of the experience, as I noted
in chapter one, is measured, registered, and felt as, for example,
pleasant or unpleasant, too intense or not intense enough. These
organic values are "intrinsically biological" values that are coded
expressions of positive and negative affect.[28] They alert us to the
"relevance" of an experience. Will it enhance or harm our life?[29]
Approach or retreat is based on these felt and thus experienced
affective emotional value codes.

And thus my second query. The first eight books of Augustine's
Confessions are stories about Augustine's intrinsically biological
values, which he refers to as his carnal affections. These carnal
desires and the behavior linked to them make Augustine's conscience gnaw away at him and rebuke him. Are these rebukes
sound or are they simply examples of the way Augustine has
turned the cultural values of the punitive system in which he was
raised into his own personal values?

Third, the work of neurobiologist and neuropsychologist
Darcia Narvaez. Narvaez gives a more detailed description to the
process Augustine affirms as the native language of the body: affective displays of physical desires and psychological states. Our
basic emotions, Narvaez argues, are formed early in life. They
emerge as affective microchips, if you will, namely, what Narvaez
calls elemental units of material—our body-neural experiences—
that accompany certain behavior patterns and make us cohere as
both a feeling and a physically animated being.[30] Accordingly,
childrearing practices play a crucial role in the way an infant,
child, and teenager not only feel, but also move and think.

In other words, the way we hold, treat, and care for infants
determines the emotional arc of their feelings, the type of intelli-
gences they develop, their capacities for friendship and intimacy,
and their orientation to the world. Writes Narvaez:

Caregiving practices affect the development of emotion systems, including the ability to regulate anxiety. Early care affects personality formation, for example, bringing about more or less agreeableness which is linked to prosocial behavior. Early care influences cognitive capabilities, including the ability to imagine. [Accordingly,] Parents who support an infant with a "good enough holding environment" assist the infant in maintaining "relational presence" with the care-giver, a factor related to later mental health and social functioning. Early experience forms "ideo-affective postures" (cognitive-emotional orientations) the child takes into adulthood. In adults, emotion systems interact with cognitive structures and physiological and motor outputs, powerfully influencing sensory, perceptual and cognitive processing.[31]

Thus, here is the telling result in Narvaez's account. When the infant, child, teen or adult is confronted constantly with the unfamiliar (people, actions, things) or when ongoing change keeps people in a state of alarm, it can become an uphill battle to calm the self down.[32]

Augustine lived in an unstable, punishing world akin to the kind of environment Narvaez described. Augustine concludes that he is the sinner. I wonder whether he was, instead, the victim.

Consider his social context.

The Roman Empire: A Punishing Regime

The Roman system of governance into which Augustine was born and reared was relentlessly pervasive. The bodies of men, women, and children, whether slave or free, Jew or Gentile, had to learn how to adjust to a pervasive and physically inescapable system of unrelenting institutional domination through the hands of family, state, and the so-called natural order of things. As a consequence, every *body* had to learn how to adjust to this system in order to survive.

The training began at birth. The upper-class Roman infant was bound tightly from head to foot for at least two months so that the infant could not move its limbs or head.

Food intake was restricted. Soranus, a Greek physician who practiced in Rome during the first half of the second century, believed that mother's milk was harmful to the child for the first twenty days.[33] The child, he argued, should be given nothing the first two days or, at most, goat's milk sweetened with honey. Furthermore, "babies should be fed according to a timetable: A baby should not be fed until he had completely digested the previous food, particularly at night.... He should be left to cry after his bath, for it would be harmful to feed him straight away.... Only if the child cried for a long time after a feed should his nurse comfort him by taking him in her arms, talking to him, and singing lullabies."[34]

Marriages were arranged and men wanted very young wives.[35] In Rome, girls' bodies "were groomed to serve their father's political maneuverings and their husbands' need for heirs."[36]

The ethical principle behind these strategies, as Aline Rousselle observes in her book *Porneia: On Desire and the Body in Antiquity*, "was, quite openly, one of obedience and docility."[37] The primary rationale for these reigning childrearing philosophies was pragmatic. "By oppressing the child from birth, society hoped to avoid having to repress him later on."[38]

Monica

Augustine's mother—Monica—was similarly raised. Monica's primary caretaker as a child was one of her family's servants. The nurse would not allow Monica to drink water whenever she was thirsty, but only at prescribed times. "It is water you are drinking now, because wine is not within your reach," she would say to the thirsty child, "but the day will come when you are married and find yourself in charge of storerooms and cellars, and the water will not seem good enough; yet the habit of tippling will be too strong for you" (IX.8.17).

Like many girls of the era, Monica was a child bride. Monica was compliant to her husband's every whim. When he was angry, she offered no resistance by deed or word. Augustine, in fact, described Patricius, his father, as an unfaithful and hot-tempered husband. So Monica stifled her own feelings in order to survive.[39]

Indeed, Monica apparently took on the role of reminding other wives of their legal status. They were bound by their legal marriage document to be slaves to their husbands. Obey, Monica counseled, and thereby avoid physical abuse (IX.9.19–20).

Monica did not rebel; she obeyed. The rule of her family's home, her husband's house, and the rule of the Roman Empire was the same: obedience. Obey or suffer physical assault.

And so we return to our first query. When Augustine as a baby beat on the breast for more milk, was he being greedy and thus a sinner as Augustine's rational theology claims (I.7.11)? Or was the kid simply hungry and left to wallow in his physical distress, as his affect theology discloses when shorn of its rational theological overlay? Augustine's carnal values, from the standpoint of his affect theology, were sidelined, gutted, or thrashed to create an obedience regime.

Two examples illustrate the punishing regime his affect theology narrated.

Education. Both Monica and her husband groomed Augustine for success. Thus by age sixteen, Augustine knew that he was in school for one reason: to get ahead. His parents shared the same goal even though their stated motivations diverged. According to Augustine, his father wanted his son to have personal glory as a Roman citizen. His mother, on the other hand, thought it would help him attain to the glory of God (I.10.14–16; II.3.8). Thus, when Augustine complained of the beatings he received at the hands of his teacher, *both* parents were amused rather than empathic. Augustine tells us that he suffered miserably and that the parental response was "Obey." "Be obedient!" "Obey me!" "Obey your teachers!" Thus, when he neglected his studies, he was severely beaten, and prayed to God for relief. His parents laughed, amused at his suffering.

Sexuality. Monica's negative reaction to the onset of puberty in Augustine was the opposite to her husband's joy. Patricius had seen him in the bath one day and began to look forward to grandchildren, gleefully announcing his discovery of the young *man* to Monica. Monica ordered Augustine to remain chaste. Not surprisingly, he condemned his mother's indifference to his suffering, calling her a distant resident in the Babylon she despised (II.3:8).

Monica wanted Augustine to marry well. Such a union, she reasoned, would help his rise in the class structure of late fourth-century Imperial Rome. So she delayed arranging a suitable marriage for him in order to make certain that he would not be distracted from his studies.

Augustine settled into a stable relationship with a concubine for fourteen years, an unnamed woman who became the mother of a son he adored. But when Monica decided Augustine should now marry and arranged for his betrothal to an eight-year-old child, Augustine submitted and consented to marry the girl in two years when she reached the legal age for marriage: ten.

Both of these stories show us an Augustine whose caretaking world repeatedly dashed his body's feelings. And yet by his own affective theological account, he could never completely silence his body's desires because they had, after all, their own native tongue. Accordingly, as long as he had a body, he would have emotions that could not be ruled solely by logic, the dictates of reason, and his rational will. His conscience exacted punishment whenever his body spoke its native tongue.

Paul and Augustine's Conscience

I draw three conclusions about the relationship of Augustine's rational theology to the content of Augustine's conscience and Paul from the above illustrations and narratives.

First, Augustine's rational theology sanctioned the way his conscience gnawed away at him and rebuked him (VIII.7.18). Augustine thus accepted the culturally-constructed judgments of his conscience against himself as if they were hallowed, inviolable, sacrosanct truths. They weren't.

He condemned himself, for example, because he wailed and flayed his arms as an infant who wanted food. And he condemned himself for not wanting to be chaste and for protesting the beatings by his teachers.

Today, we might simply call these various affective displays and presentments by Augustine signs of healthy protest against a punishing regime of affect strangulation. Augustine, after all, told his congregants that if they relied on the stability of the people and the world around them, they would surely perish.[40] He preached this gospel to people like himself, persons whose lives had been diminished, sundered, and betrayed by those upon whom they had to depend. So we do not normalize his era as a healthy environment in which human beings could have mentally and emotionally thrived.[41]

Second, Paul, as noted in chapter four, told his Corinthian followers that their consciences sometimes leveled mistaken judgments against themselves. The conscience of the Corinthian weaker brothers, for example, made errant judgments about eating meat dedicated to the idols, deeming the behavior idolatrous. Christ, Paul insisted, loved them not because they were sinners but because they were suffering. He loved them beyond their own mistaken, culturally-defined religious beliefs.

Augustine, so it seems, thinks like the weaker brothers in Corinth. He believes that his conscience got it right when making him feel guilt for his ostensible sins. Augustine thus missed the point of Paul's teachings: Christ entered into Augustine and saved him not because he was a sinner, but because he was suffering. Augustine's affect theology affirms this affective role of Christ, but cannot explain it in these terms. Rather, Augustine's rational, culturally-embedded condemnatory concepts take hold and cast Augustine as a sinner saved by Christ.

Third, Augustine's affect theology, when updated using insights from contemporary affective neuroscientific and related insights, frees him from the categorical judgments of his own rational theology. His emotional suffering can now be explained in empathic rather than condemnatory terms. I can thus affirm his suffering without, at the same time, rendering him a sinner. And my contemporary affect theology strategy of reading Augustine from the bottom up (affect) lets me do one more thing. I can explain Augustine's failure to recognize and affirm Paul's new emotional foundation for Christian faith: love beyond belief.

In Paul's own era, the failure of his followers to understand his new emotional foundation for gentile faith, as noted in chapter four, was a linguistic problem. It emerged from incommensurable cultural differences between Jewish and gentile views of human nature in religious terms.

Augustine's failure to understand Paul's teaching, in contrast, was based on the collusion principle.

Part Three
The Collusion Principle

Augustine did not become a split self and a sundered soul by himself. Monica helped him out. She created the requisite caretaking condition for a split self, namely, a structural gap in the parental caregiving affective system of the child. The gap consisted of the absence of adequate, nurturing care for the child.

Self psychologist Arnold Goldberg, in his groundbreaking book, *Being of Two Minds: The Vertical Split in Psychoanalysis and Psychotherapy*,[42] describes the collusion principle entailed in the creation of the above mentioned structural gap. This collusion principle can be summarized as follows: parent and child together split the child's self, and then both parent and child reward and punish the child for this splitting.[43]

I use Goldberg's study of this psychological condition to help explain how Augustine could simultaneously both affirm and deny Paul's intended emotional foundation for gentile faith. Augustine, by his own testament, was a split self. He is a paradigm for this way of being in the world. I thus use insights from Goldberg not to explain Augustine, but rather to illustrate in contemporary post-Freudian terms the kind of self-condition Augustine seemed to normalize.

I begin with a summary of Goldberg's major claims.

First, a split self is a person who *knowingly* takes up residence in two distinct and contradictory psychological worlds. Such people live as if they are two: they binge and then feel shame; they steal even though they could buy the item and then are demoralized by their action; they are grandiose and then feel diminished by their outrageous behavior; they lie and then feel morally demeaned by their deceit.

All of us, Goldberg argues, sometimes act against our highest, rational moral values. But when such actions reduce us to an internal battlefield that cannot be resolved, we have ventured onto the terrain of a split self.

Second, persons with split selves are conscious of the other part of themselves; persons with repressed selves are not. Split selves are aware of an alternative structure within themselves. The separation is vertical rather than horizontal. The term the "split self" thus refers to a "side-by-side" (i.e., vertical) existence of disparate personalities within the self that despise the values and actions of each other.

Third, the psyches of such persons seem to move back and forth between multiple realities. As long as this failure of reconciliation endures, there will be a heavy emotional price.[44] Unlike the "horizontal line called the repression barrier,"[45] which prevents conscious awareness of the repressed self, the vertical line does not stave off awareness of an alternative self structure.

Fourth, split selves cannot be achieved alone. The vertical split in a person's psychic life derives from parental collusion. Parent and child construct the split self together by separating affective experiences that must be attended to and thus *are* attended to, but then are punished for being attended to. In other words, the parent gives the child tacit permission for doing something that is deeply pleasurable and then punishes the child for having done it.

Fifth, the emotional principle behind splitting is thus one of both pain and pleasure.[46] It is pleasurable because the affective experience triggers a bodily experience of satiation that is deeply gratifying. It is punishing because the affective experience is then identified as bad and wrong. Persons in this conflicted environment must have the affective experience for the sake of their overall bodily integrity and then must condemn the experience for the sake of their learned social values. Writes Goldberg: "The parental directions given to the child, both explicitly and implicitly, demanded a division into these side-by-side sectors."[47]

Goldberg does not blame the parent for wrongdoing; rather he explains how both the child and the parent operate as split selves because human behavior—psychoanalytically considered—is an interaffective field of human engagement and disengagement. The child's "misbehaving" as a split self thus avoids a far more difficult and painful state, which the reintegration of the child's emotional life would reveal.[48] Revealed here would be the absence of a nurturing and life-enhancing, caretaking environment for the child.

This kind of awareness is too big for the child to take in. It's too big to know. The information cannot be taken in and synthesized as self-disclosing knowledge about the child's flawed parental care system. (Few of us as kids, after all, wanted to know that something was wrong with the caretaking strategies of our parents. Instead we often assumed that something must be wrong with us.)

Goldberg concludes that a "failure of synthesis [thus] characterizes this pathology." The child becomes, in effect, a being of two minds. The price for retaining this split "both saps the energy that would be available to an integrated person and demands an accounting for living in a real world."[49] Rather than experience the loss and disappointment of parental failure, the child engages in an affect-saturated action that is both pleasurable and punishing at the same time. The child, in sum, sets up a personal punishing regime that duplicates the world the child tries to escape.

The life of Augustine, as noted above, paradigmatically illustrates Goldberg's point regarding the failure of synthesis as core to the collusion principle. Both Augustine *and* Monica, in this context, can be viewed as victims who lived in a social environment that required them to sunder themselves from their native affective tongue in order to survive.

Monica, for example, allowed Augustine to engage in a fourteen-year sexual relationship with a concubine before betrothing him to an eight-year-old girl. Augustine, in effect, had filled in what was missing in his emotional life (a wife found by his mother) and now suffered the extraction: she is sent away so that he can marry the child. Augustine is thus rewarded and punished for the way he filled in an emotional need. We cannot speculate about the extent of the loss Augustine felt. He did, after all, immediately take up with another concubine. We can simply guess that the rupture wasn't pleasurable since affective habits of the heart tend to hurt.

And then there's Augustine's distress because his mother, when he reached puberty, expected him to remain chaste until he married. This narrative is immediately followed by his account of his theft of pears from a neighbor's tree (II.4.9). The act, he tells us, was pleasurable for its own sake. Afterwards he experiences guilt as the punishment for breaking the rules. Here we find the classic link between the pleasure of rebellion for its own sake and the punishment exacted upon himself for the deed. The victory that he had experienced in expressing an outlawed physical desire becomes the source of his experience of defeat when he severely chastises himself.

If my psychological analysis of the collusion principle at work in Augustine as a split self is reasonable (albeit speculative), I have here a viable way of explaining the common ground of Augustine's two theological systems today: us.

Self psychologist Volney P. Gay makes this point in his own analysis of Augustine as a split self. He includes us as part of Augustine's collusion principle. In his essay, "Augustine: The Reader as Selfobject,"[50] Gay argues that Augustine wrote his *Confessions* for an audience that can help him hold his split self together by paying attention to the grandiose bishop while ignoring the fragmented self of the actual historical man.[51] Augustine's readers, from this perspective, collude with Augustine to keep his split self in place.

The collusion principle, however, works both ways. I thus expand Gay's point. Readers also collude with Augustine to keep our own split selves in place. Augustine, after all, teaches us to do what he did: blame our own longings, feelings, and desires as evidence that we are sinners, rather than as evidence that there is a gap in our caretaking environment that we must bridge.

Readers thus collude in Augustine's own bridging terms.

Paul, as noted in chapter four, believed that Christ looked beyond the mistaken beliefs of the gentile conscience that caused suffering and instead attended to the suffering with a love beyond (the Gentile's) mistaken religious belief system.

Augustine also affirmed the Pauline role of Christ in his affect theology. He did so, however, without Paul's Jewish insight that the gentile conscience is a habituated cultural creation without access, on its own, to universal moral and religious truths. Augustine, instead, conflated his socially-constructed beliefs about sin with his body's native tongue.

And thus, here are the final conclusions. Augustine produced a split self that cannot be healed in Augustine's own rational theological terms. Quite the opposite. The socially-constructed theological values and categories expressed by his conscience when rebuking Augustine punished him for being broken by his caretaking environment; blamed him for being sundered beyond repair; and tormented him with incessant rebukes for being a shattered, conflicted soul. His rational theology, in sum, is designed as a punishing regime against his carnal feelings, which is the language of the body's native tongue.

This process described by Augustine is an unending punishing regime because (1) Augustine's body has a vitality principle, namely, affect; (2) its physical displays are ongoing life signs of his body, which (3) his conscience is culturally habituated to punish. And thus the never-ending loop of pleasure and pain is linked together as the normalized state of the Augustinian self.

Augustine's affect theology, however, affirms him as an embodied soul who needs to be comforted and sheltered from the abusive environment in which he must live. Requisite here is Christ as Paul's Law of Love, which I call love beyond belief. Augustine's affect theology affirms this kind of nonjudgmental love that exceeds his personal religious beliefs. But such affirmations are easily missed in his *Confessions* because his rational theology denies what his body and its affect theology affirm: the love of Christ reaches beyond a person's mistaken religious beliefs and comforts the sufferer.

Luther did not learn this lesson of love beyond belief from Paul or Augustine. Instead, he turned his Christianity into a "religion of conscience," namely, a crusade against everyone who troubled the Christian's conscience—most especially, rebellious peasants, Catholics, Muslims, and Jews.

Chapter Six

Luther's Troubled Conscience

Introduction

Martin Luther invented the affective content of Paul's gentile mind. More precisely, he re-invented the way Paul thought about the gentile's conscience and its relationship to Christ. Thanks to this Church Father of the Protestant Reformation, it now seemed as though Paul thought about, explained, and defended the Christian conscience all the time. And nowhere was this foundational patterning principle of Paul's thought more evident than in the *Letter to the Galatians* because Paul never used the Greek term *syneidesis* (conscience) once in this epistle. But in Luther's exegesis of this text,[1] he refers to the conscience more than seventy times in the first two chapters of his *Lectures on Galatians*.[2]

This chapter shows how Luther gave Paul's first-century mind its inordinate sixteenth-century interest in Luther's conscience. To this end, focused attention is given here to one of Luther's major works, his *Lectures on Galatians,* which reflects the work of the "mature Reformer."[3]

This chapter also shows how Luther linked his inordinate interest in the conscience, namely, inner Christian piety, to the exterior social order. Both of these domains must be given account here because neither domain alone is sufficient for Luther when explaining human experience.

The specific case chosen for this second focus is Luther's call to German rulers—in his treatise "Against the Robbing and Murdering Hordes of Peasants: 1525"[4]—to slaughter rebelling peasants in the name of God. According to Luther, German princes must "smite, slay, and stab, secretly or openly" kill rebellious peasants.[5] Nothing, Luther insisted, "can be more poisonous, hurtful, or devilish than a rebel. It is just as when one must kill a mad dog; if you do not strike him, he will strike you, and a whole land with you."[6]

Thanks to this chapter's twofold strategy a thematic question easily comes to the fore: How could Luther in good conscience goad authorities to engage in such brutal violence that caused the massacre of tens of thousands of peasants?

The answer given here is elementary. Luther split Christian consciousness into two domains: one ruled by Christ, the other by God. Luther's explanation of these two domains is easily summarized.

According to Luther, man's inner, affective domain is the source of Christian piety, and man's external domain is the source of civil peace, law, and order, which can only occur through the prevention of evil deeds. Neither domain is thus sufficient for man's wellbeing, Luther argues. Both domains are requisite to lead a Christian life.[7]

The present chapter thus argues that Luther didn't ignore the Christian conscience when he called for the slaughter of peasants who were in open revolt. Rather, he dissociated the conscience from civic rule by giving the conscience its own turf: piety. This turf was inviolate to rulers and if trespassed upon by them must produce Christian rebuke, resistance, and disobedience to civil rule gone mad.[8]

Luther thus espoused a theory of two kingdoms, which he delineated in his treatise "Secular Authority: To What Extent It Should Be Obeyed." Five basic points are made in his explanation.

First, secular authority keeps civil order.

Second, God gave rulers this authority to maintain civic peace, namely, law and order.

Third, this law-and-order-keeping authority of rulers, Luther reasoned, is not needed among Christians since they do much more than secular laws demand.[9]

Fourth, so rulers appointed by God must not set themselves in God's place and "lord it over men's conscience and faith, and put the Holy Spirit to school according to their mad minds."[10] Otherwise, Christians are obligated to "resist the emperor and disobey him."[11] Their inner affections are Christ's domain.

Fifth, the world and the masses, however, are and always will be unchristian even those who are baptized and are "nominally Christian."[12]

Luther's conclusion: "All who are not Christians belong to the kingdom of the world and are under the law," which is meted out by secular law and the sword of the ruler.[13] This is why rulers must be obeyed regarding secular law and the sword: they act in the world by God's will and ordinance for the sake of the unrighteous.[14]

Luther's theory of two kingdoms thus explains how one realm—Christian piety—is ruled by Christ,[15] who makes the Christian's conscience sacrosanct. The other realm is ruled by the secular rulers, appointed by God,[16] who make their civil authority sacrosanct. Christians thus live in two God-given domains: the conscience and civil society. And never the twain shall meet because worldly affairs, according to Luther, "are and always will be unchristian."

Luther could thus express his exasperation and righteous indignation against critics of his "harsh book" against the peasants by reaffirming his theory of the two kingdoms:

> There are two kingdoms, one the kingdom of God, the other the kingdom of the world. I have written this so often that I am surprised that there is anyone who does not know it or remember it. Anyone who knows how to distinguish rightly between these two kingdoms will certainly not be offended by my little book, and he will so properly understand the passages about mercy. God's kingdom is a kingdom of grace

and mercy, not of wrath and punishment. In it there is only forgiveness, consideration for one another, love, service, the doing of good, peace, joy, etc. But the kingdom of the world is a kingdom of wrath and severity. In it there is only punishment, repression, judgment, and condemnation to restrain the wicked and protect the good. For this reason it has the sword, and Scripture calls a prince or lord "God's wrath," or "God's rod" (Isa 14 [:5–6]).[17]

Rebellious peasants, by this two-kingdoms logic, are thus wrong twice. They, to reiterate, not only trouble the Christian conscience—and thus affront Christ, but they also disrupt the laws of civil society established by God and upheld by secular authority—and thus defame God. They rebel against Christ (in the Christian's conscience) and God (in the rulers' secular authority). Accordingly, they are "devils" that must be slain.[18]

This is the kind of reasoning by Luther in his two kingdoms theory with its link to the Christian conscience that overturned Paul's teachings. The goal in this chapter is to set things right again.

Three immediate results will follow. First, several points of contention within the scholarship on Luther's conscience are adjudicated and ways of resolving them are proffered. Second, his incipient affect theology for Protestant faith that explains emotional development in theological terms is found. The way it gets commandeered by Luther's own social prejudices and cultural biases is delineated. Finally, Luther's misreading of Paul's interest in the gentile conscience is identified and corrected. A case in point follows.

Luther's doctrinal explanation of the freedom of the Christian Conscience

Luther explained Paul's preaching freedom from the Law to his gentile followers as the freedom of the Christian conscience from the Law. Luther then claimed that when his doctrine, "which pacifies consciences, remains pure and intact, Christians are constituted as judges over all kinds of doctrine and become lords over all the laws of the entire world."[19] Luther could now explain doctrinally, for example, why persons who trouble the place where Christ resides—the Christian conscience—are "sent from the devil."[20]

Luther's emotional hubris. Luther arrogantly condemned rather than professed sympathy with the errant other. Paul, as has been seen, chastised the stronger brothers in Corinth for a similar kind of arrogance against their weaker brothers. The stronger brothers felt superior to rather than sympathy for their weaker brothers who suffered because of the mistaken religious judgments made by their conscience against them for eating meat dedicated to idols. Luther committed the sin of the stronger brothers, namely, an arrogant self-assurance that staunched empathy with suffering souls.

Luther's mental miscalculations. Luther conflated the culturally-created ideas, biases, and sentiments of his own era, on the one hand, with his ideas about God and his feelings about Christ, on the other. As a result, Luther made the same error as the weaker brothers in Corinth by accepting the errant judgments of conscience as if they are sacrosanct universal truths. They aren't.

This chapter revises and neuroscientifically updates Luther's doctrinal account of the Christian conscience and its link to his theory of the two kingdoms. The resulting contemporary affective theological system (laid out in chapter seven) shows how triggered emotions can be transformed into feelings of religious assurance without rendering the religious or rebellious other the antichrist.

The goal here is to reaffirm Paul's Law of Love, namely, love beyond belief as a viable foundation for a progressive faith today with an action profile of lovingkindness.

Part One
The Historical Contexts

Luther's invention of the affective content of Paul's gentile mind is difficult to fathom outside its linguistic contexts.[21] Accordingly, a brief history is presented here to show how Paul's interest in the gentile conscience morphed linguistically into a topic of central concern in medieval Christian theology.[22] Luther, as an Augustinian monk and then as a university-trained doctor of theology, adjudicated these debates increasingly in the personal terms of his own incessantly rebuking conscience.[23] Luther's own troubling life and times are thus part of this historical narrative.

The Linguistic Framework

> *Synteresis*. Noun. An aspect of one's conscience by which one can judge wrong from right and decide on what makes good conduct (as distinguished from *syneidesis*).[24]

From the *syneidesis* (Greek: conscience) to the *synteresis* (Latin: the divine spark of God in man). When Jerome began his Latin translation of the Bible in the fourth century, he used the Latin term *conscientia* instead of Paul's Greek term *syneidesis*.[25] The word *conscientia* was an obvious, but fatal choice, as C. A. Pierce rightly suggests in his book, *Conscience in the New Testament*,[26] because *conscientia* denoted more than did the Greek term used by Paul.

In Latin, *conscientia* could denote either a good or a bad conscience, and did not necessarily entail a moral judgment.[27] Not so with the Greek term. The popular usage of the Greek term *syneidesis*, which was apparently Paul's original referent for his own use of the term in his first letter to the Corinthians, referred to a bad conscience and always entailed a moral judgment of the person upon oneself. The Greek usage thus pertained to one's private moral judgments of one's own action.

Accordingly, attention to the etymology of the Latin word *conscientia* is necessary in order to track how the Christian conscience became a topic of major theological issue. In Latin, the root meaning of *conscientia* refers to knowledge, especially of a secret or private kind that was shared with another, and from which sharing came the possibility of public judgment, namely, of being testified against.[28] As such, the judgment of conscience was rendered objective and public in a way never intended in either first-century popular culture or by Paul himself.

Pierce highlights this point when noting that the use of *conscientia* in Jerome's translation "could not fail to reduce what was for the New Testament writers a precise, indeed somewhat narrow idea, into a conception so broad, vague, and formless as to confuse rather than clarify all ethical discussion from that moment forward."[29]

Jerome further altered the meaning of the original Greek term *syneidesis* in his gloss of Ezekiel's vision of four figures each having four faces: a man in front, a lion on the right side, an ox on the left side, and an eagle at the back (Ezek 1:10). The first three faces, Jerome explained, represent the threefold division of the human soul, namely, the rational soul, the irascible emotions, and the concupiscent desires. But, as Michael C. Baylor notes in his book *Action and Person: Conscience in Late Scholasticism and the Young Luther*,

> above these three elements and beyond them Jerome identified with the prophet's eagle a fourth element in man—the Greek "*synteresis….*" Jerome described the *synteresis* as "that spark of the conscience which was not quenched even in the heart of Cain when he was driven from paradise." Jerome argued that the *synteresis* is distinct from the other three elements of the soul and nobler, at least in the sense that it corrects the others: it makes us aware of our sinfulness when we are overcome by evil desires or rage or when we are occasionally deceived by reason itself. But Jerome concluded his gloss on the passage by arguing that in some men we see this conscience overthrown and displaced.[30]

Based on Jerome's gloss, which both affirms and denies the indestructible nature of the divine aspect of man's conscience, the meaning of the term *synteresis* was impossible to explain adequately.[31] More precisely, there was now confusion between the emotional and the rational soul of man and something that seemed to be rational but with an origin beyond human reason (namely, its divine spark—the *synteresis*). But rather than dismiss Jerome's gloss because of this confusion, the confusion enhanced its attractiveness. As Baylor aptly suggests, this gloss "determined the context and many of the problems in the medieval treatment of conscience."[32]

Accordingly, a new set of questions now came to the fore: Is conscience a faculty or power of the soul, and if so, what makes it distinct from the other powers? Can conscience be lost? What is the relation of the *synteresis* to *conscientia*?[33]

The irony here is that Jerome neither posed nor answered these questions. But nevertheless, his work gave birth to them.

The larger irony in this new set of concerns is that these questions are ones that Paul neither asked nor addressed. Such disembodied queries were not Paul's concerns. He was concerned about the ongoing nature of gentile congregants and how they are made one with Jews through the faithfulness of Christ (Gal 3:5 and 3:27–29). So Paul dealt with gentile bodies at risk. He believed that whether on earth or in heaven there would always be a body linked to the human soul.[34] Paul thus wanted the gentile soul to know the peace of a God that prevails beyond the end times of man's physical life on earth.

The new questions triggered by Jerome's work came of age in scholastic theology. Not only did the concern with the meaning of conscience have an especially prominent place in scholastic theology, as Emmanuel Hirsh notes in volume one of his work *Lutherstudien*, but also for the first time in the Catholic Church, it became the subject of rigorous theological treatment.[35]

This state of theological affairs is all the more remarkable because the Catholic Church during this period dominated and made objective the rules by means of which every aspect of a person's life should be ordered and lived.[36] Human emotions and human thoughts were now ordered, defined, reviewed, constricted, and controlled by the church. Moreover, there must not be a conflict between what the individual emotionally felt and what was thought. The role of the schoolmen was to establish the basis for this principle of coherence between man's rational and emotional soul while on earth.

A central question of scholastic theology was thus, "How should one understand a situation in which the conscience is in opposition with the corresponding rules and order of society?" This question, as Emmanuel Hirsch rightly notes, could be found in the work of every schoolman.[37]

The various investigations focused on the notion of the *synteresis* (namely, the divine spark in man) and attempted to ascertain the aspect of human nature to which it referred. Where did it reside? How did it link man's emotional soul to his rational soul, and his feelings to his ideas so that he cohered to the rule of the Christian Church *and* the Christian State? Where was this coherence principle between the two parts of man's soul to be found? The answer seemed to be man's *synteresis*, namely, that divine spark in man that could not be destroyed because it was God's absolute gift to man.

For Thomas Aquinas (1225–74), the *synteresis* refers to the universal moral principles assented to by all men by virtue of the fact that they possess a *synteresis*.[38] It is inborn, inextinguishable, and incapable of error.[39] The *synteresis*, for Thomas Aquinas, thus resides in the intellect.[40] *Conscientia*, on the other hand, although ontologically bound to the *synteresis* through reason, is nevertheless distinct from the *synteresis*.[41] Conscience refers to an act of judgment by practical reason.[42] It is subject to error.[43]

Bonaventura (1221–74) places the *synteresis* in the will and *conscientia* in the intellect.[44] According to Bonaventura, *conscientia* is moved by the *synteresis*. Duns Scotus (c. 1266–1308) identifies the *synteresis* with practical reason.[45] Johannes Gerson (1363–1429) deems it to be the first principle to morality and explains it as "an inexpressible power that animated the soul through the highest good" and brought spontaneous consent from the *conscientia*.[46]

For Gabriel Biel (c. 1420–95), the *synteresis* is "a vestige of man's pure nature [that enables] him to obey natural law thus to execute the will of God within the limits of his nature."[47] It is one of the natural ways in which a person can gain knowledge of God without a special revelation of God. The *synteresis* is thus a person's primordial gift from God. It is an embodiment of the laws of Scripture. As such, persons have within them innate and impeccable moral principles that can guide their actions. According to Biel, if humans simply *will* to do that which is naturally within them, they can lead morally upright and virtuous lives.[48]

For Biel and other *via moderni* schoolmen, the *synteresis*/the divine spark in man became the Law internalized. The *synteresis*, as such, refers to a gift from God to all so that persons on their own can know how to lead a virtuous, ethical life and do it.

Martin Luther was heir to this intense concern and investigation of the nature, role, and meaning of conscience in man. But he was racked by anguish from his punitive conscience for repeatedly breaking rather than following God's law. And he once compared the sores from the ulcerations of his body to stars in the sky, saying he had counted more than two hundred of them.[49] Why the sores? They were the visible sign of his private affections, desires, and impulses, namely, his sins. Try as he may, Luther always felt like a sinner rather than a man who on his own could honor and practice God's Laws.

So it is not difficult to understand why Christ, from Luther's anguished perspective, would become the Bridegroom of his conscience: Luther sought emotional relief from its punishing regime because he kept on breaking God's Laws. Nor is it difficult to understand why Luther eventually rendered the term *synteresis*/the divine spark in man meaningless in his lexicon.[50] On his own, the ongoing prompt he found inside himself for God's Laws was to break them.

The Social Contexts

If a man wishes to enjoy himself for once, says an old proverb, let him kill a fat fowl; if for a year, let him take a wife; but if he would live joyously all the days of his life, then let him turn priest.[51]

By the 1500s, the invisible church was quite visible. She seemed a grand dame of the night bedecked in jewels paid for by the day labor of her flock. Not only was her splendor not appreciated, but also many doubted her chastity, some being able to document their discontents by her promiscuity. A case in point follows.

On December 1, 1513, the College of Cardinals elected Leo X as pope. He was to bring with him reform and to honor the papal restraints the cardinals were trying to construct in order to do a bit of internal housecleaning. But Leo had other plans. His family interest demanded a continuous flow of money into its coffers,[52] so he induced the Lateran Council in March of 1517 to give him "a tenth of all church property throughout Christendom." And thus the result: three different commissions for the sale of indulgences traversed the German and northern states at the same time.[53]

One of the cardinals, Alfonso Petrucci, was so enraged by the pope's exploits that several times he entered the college with a dagger concealed within his robe. According to one church historian, Petrucci "would have assassinated the pope had it not been withheld by the consideration of the effect which the murder of the pope by a cardinal would have produced in the world."[54] And so he tried poison but was betrayed. Internal reform, to put it mildly, was having minimal success.

Externally, the church's exploits grew bolder and more audacious. "The churches were asylums for criminals, the monasteries the resort of dissolute youth," as one historian notes. "We find examples of monks who made use of their exemption from tolls to import goods for sale, or to open a tavern for the sale of beer. If any attempt were made to assail their privileges, they defended themselves with excommunication and interdict."[55] The sale of office (simony) was the rule, taxation the law. Plenary indulgences reigned. For the right price, so believers were told, they could leverage their souls or those of their deceased beloved ones into heaven.

Luther protested, but only to his colleagues. He penned in Latin the "Disputation on the Power and Efficacy of Indulgences," also known as "The Ninety-Five Theses."[56] In this text, he listed questions and propositions for scholarly discourse and theological debate among his peers. But instead of instituting a closed discourse among his peers, his theses were translated from Latin to German and published. The issues posed by Luther for debate were now open, public knowledge. And Luther was very quickly cast in the role of public reformer.

Events and public debates escalated and Luther soon found himself branded a heretic by the Catholic Church. Rome demanded that he recant. He would not, and in December of 1520, Luther burned the papal bull notifying him of the church's intention to excommunicate him. Four months later he stood before

Emperor Charles V at the Diet of Worms. Once again refusing to recant, Luther was banned by Charles, although the ban was never enforced.

After spending ten months at the castle at Wartburg, under Elector Frederick's protection, Luther returned to Wittenberg (in response to a request by the city council) to quell peasant riots inspired in part by his own rebellious defiance of church and state. In 1525, he denounced these peasants.

These peasants and serfs were in open revolt. They had grown tired of carrying on their backs the state, the church, the nobility, and the burgeoning middle class. And so they began to stand up for their rights. As early as 1493, German peasants held secret meetings vowing to pay no taxes that had not been levied on them with their own free consent, "to abolish tolls and duties, to curtail the privileges of the clergy, to put the Jews to death without ceremony, and to divide their possessions. They admitted new members with secret ceremonies, specially intended to appall traitors."[57]

Various princes, fearing rebellion, began to curb their tax demands, but to no avail, for the peasants' anger and rebellion spread until only the death of up to one hundred thousand in 1525, encouraged by Luther, could stem the tide.

In 1531, Luther also found himself caught up in a religious conflict that made him think of Paul. Wittenberg, from Luther's point-of-view, was being invaded by "false apostles," "the sectarians," "the Anabaptists, Sacramentarians, and other fanatics," who were winning converts from Luther's flock.[58] Luther deemed his crisis to be parallel to that of Paul in Galatia:

> Thus today the fanatics do pay us the compliment that we began the work of the Gospel correctly. But because we despise and condemn their blasphemous doctrine, they call us "neopapists," who are twice as bad as the old papists. Thus it is that thieves and robbers invade the Lord's sheepfold "to steal and kill and destroy" (John 10:10). First they confirm our doctrine, but then they correct us and claim to explain more clearly what we have understood incorrectly or only

partially. This was how the false apostles gained access to the Galatians.[59]

This strong awareness by Luther that his social and religious worlds were careening out of control created a framework of urgency for his 1531 *Lectures on Galatians*. His own life and times, in effect, had primed him for the work.

Luther was forty-nine years old. Protestantism was now firmly entrenched on German soil and Luther had accepted his role as a leading figure in the development of its central doctrines. Luther had been married to Katherine von Bora, an ex-nun, for six years; the Diet of Worms where he stood before Emperor Charles V and refused to recant his attacks against the teachings and practices of the Catholic Church was ten years behind him; and his Small and Large Catechisms for the new form of Christian faith he helped spearhead had been in circulation for two years. Luther's Lectures on Galatians are thus, to reiterate, the work of the "mature Reformer." And his fondness for this particular Pauline epistle was so great that he once said he was "betrothed" to it and called it his Katie von Bora.[60]

Luther's interest in the Christian conscience in his work on this epistle was essential to his doctrinal concerns as a church patriarch. He strove, in effect, to establish a sure foundation for Christian faith that was not dependent on human wiles, human institutions, and the human (in)ability to keep God's Laws. Rather, he now placed this foundation on the utter dependability of God as Father, Son, and Holy Ghost. And the human feeling born of this assurance of steadfast support took place, according to Luther, in the Christian conscience.

Part Two
The Scholarly Context

The importance of conscience in Martin Luther's affect theology has been widely noted as the following brief survey reveals. Highlighted here is an unresolved debate within this scholarship about the transmoral nature of Luther's conscience.

In part three of this chapter a resolution to the debate will be proffered based on an affective theological exegesis of (1) Luther's *Lectures on Galatians* regarding the Christian conscience and (2) the implications of his work when practiced toward the religious or rebellious other.

Five themes spotlighted by the scholarship are listed and briefly summarized below. Collectively, these five topics show how scholars have noted and analyzed Luther's paradigm-shifting work on the conscience, namely, his personal response to the theological and sociopolitical times in which he lived (summarized in part one of this chapter).

Luther's Religion of Conscience

Karl Holl rightly characterizes Luther's Christianity as "a religion of conscience."[61] Luther claims that "the way to heaven is the line of an indivisible point, namely of the conscience."[62] Holl identifies conscience as a central structural element in Luther's theology.

Luther as the Discoverer of Conscience

Bernhard Lohse agrees with Holl.[63] Lohse, in his essay, "Conscience and Authority in Luther," notes that Theodor Siegfried's objection to Holl's Kantian analysis of Luther is valid, but yet Siegfried himself nevertheless also agrees with Holl's emphasis upon the importance of conscience in Luther's work. Siegfried identifies Luther's use of conscience as the decisive turning point from the Middle Ages to the autonomous thinking of the Modern Age.[64] Lohse also notes other major scholars who have identified conscience as a central structural element in Luther's work, citing in particular, Rudolf Hermann's designation of Luther as practically the "discoverer of conscience."[65]

Luther's Conscience as the Place Where an Encounter with God Takes Place

Gerhard Ebeling, in his book *Luther: An Introduction to His Thought*, argues that the conscience is the place within the human being where the encounter with God takes place.[66] Conscience,

Ebeling suggests, is for Luther man's "most sensitive point, the very heart of his being, where the decision is made as to what his position should be ultimately—that is, in the sight of God."[67] Ebeling argues that Luther's use of conscience is not an "idealist interpretation of the conscience as an independent voice within man's own heart which gives him independence and is thus the basis for man's autonomy."[68] Rather, the term denotes the person's experience of and response to the overwhelming impact of the divine word upon that person.[69] The person's religious identity, Ebeling concludes, is thus autonomous from one's social setting and absolutely dependent upon Christ.

This principle of autonomy, for Ebeling, thus pertains to a religious state. So, too, for Lohse, who can rightly claim that Luther, in a strictly theological sense, identifies conscience with faith.[70] Conscience entails reliance not upon oneself but upon the divine promise.[71] As such, Lohse argues that "Luther's understanding of conscience agrees with all of the central themes of his reformatory theology, namely with the doctrine of justification, the distinction between Law and Gospel, the doctrine of the two kingdoms, or the distinction between the two governments of God."[72]

Luther's Conscience and the Divine Promise

According to Lohse's analysis, a good conscience, for Luther, refers to a person's proper reliance upon the divine promise. A bad conscience, on the other hand, refers to a person's improper reliance upon the Law, work, and so forth as the means to salvation. Luther, Lohse argues, places a good conscience and work in an antithetical relationship. Thus, Lohse finds it "astonishing that … Luther can still say occasionally that the good conscience, which the Christian obtains in faith, is important for his works, yes even for his certainty about his own call."[73]

Why is Lohse astonished? Is Lohse's astonishment born from something his analysis of the function of conscience in Luther's work might have overlooked? Has Lohse failed to understand Luther's notion of the inward religious experience, which then expresses itself outwardly as good-hearted willingness to duty?

Billing, after all, identifies the notion of duty as "Luther's idea of the call."[74] Has Lohse incorrectly characterized the work of Christians as "assigned"[75] because he has overlooked the transmoral role of conscience in Luther's work? These kinds of questions frame a debate in the scholarship that is summarized as follows in the final topic of discourse in my summary—to which I return after an exegesis of Luther's work on the conscience in his *Lectures on Galatians*.

Luther's Transmoral Conscience

Paul Tillich, in his book *Morality and Beyond,* suggests that Luther's justification by grace means the creation of a "transmoral conscience."[76] This transmoral conscience, Tillich argues, is one that participates "in a reality that transcends the sphere of moral commands."[77] Such a conscience makes judgments not "in obedience to a moral law, but according to its participation" in this transcendent reality.[78] According to Tillich, Luther is thus the discoverer of the *transmoral* concept of conscience. Tillich argues that Luther's concept thereby carries conscience beyond the confines of a moral agent and into the realm of participation in the divine.

Michael G. Baylor finds Tillich's notion of a transmoral conscience "somewhat ambiguously defined."[79] More precisely, Baylor, in his book, *Action and Person: Conscience in Late Scholasticism and the Young Luther*, takes issue with Tillich's use of the term *participation* in his definition of the transmoral conscience. Baylor prefers to use the term *appropriation*. Writes Baylor: "it is only through faith in the Word that conscience is able correctly to appropriate both the strict and merciful judgments of God which Scripture reveals about the person. Accordingly, if Luther developed an innovate, transmoral conception of conscience, he did not discover the transmoral nature of the conscience."[80] In a footnote appended to this last statement, Baylor suggests that "Unfortunately, Tillich himself is not always as clear on this difference as one would hope, for he also held that the conscience is naturally driven beyond morality '... by the unbearable tensions of the sphere of the law.'"[81] As will be seen, Baylor, not Tillich, seems to be in error here.

The Unresolved Debate Laid Out in More Detail

Baylor notes that Luther rejects "the conscience [as] a faculty with an inherent supernatural dimension."[82] For Luther, the conscience is not a human organ "intrinsically connected to the divine will."[83] But Baylor does not explain the way in which the divine will experienced as forgiveness enters the conscience and affects, from within, the behavior of a person. Does this oversight in Baylor's analysis cause him to consign Luther's understanding of conscience to the ethical sphere?[84]

Baylor acknowledges that Luther's concept of conscience "created a new bond between the conscience and faith."[85] Baylor notes that this "innovative link between conscience and the Word [is] based upon the idea that in faith the conscience judges as God judges."[86] Further, Baylor admits that "Luther held that a correct understanding of Scripture—which alone is to provide the positive content of theology—in its inner clarity and simplicity, is dependent upon the inspiration of the Holy Spirit in the reader, the same inspiring force which guided those who wrote it. But Luther also laid great stress upon the external clarity and intelligibility of the simple grammatical-historical sense of Scripture. And at Worms it was primarily to this objective and literal idea of Scripture that Luther was referring."[87]

Tillich disagrees. While Tillich agrees with Baylor that Luther's refusal to recant at Worms "is an expression of his conscientiousness as a doctor of theology,"[88] which was in line with other late medieval scholastics in "keeping the authority of conscience within the ethical sphere,"[89] Tillich nevertheless disputes Baylor's overall assessment of the role of conscience in Luther's work. Tillich's analysis is based on the work of the mature Luther who derived and developed his new concept of conscience from his experience of justification through faith. Baylor's analysis is based on the work of the young Luther. The subtitle of his book, *Conscience in Late Scholasticism and the Young Luther*, highlights this fact. Can this dispute be resolved if Baylor assesses Tillich's "ambiguous" definition of Luther's transmoral conscience by taking into account the mature Reformer's more developed understanding of conscience?

The following exegesis suggests that this debate can indeed be resolved when Luther, the mature Reformer, explains the conscience as the Bride of Christ in affective theological terms.

Part Three
Luther's Lectures on Galatians

Luther turned the Christian conscience into the Bride of Christ using a threefold strategy that has the markings of an incipient affective theological enterprise. This threefold strategy is first delineated. Then the affective theological system embedded within it is highlighted and analyzed.

The threefold strategy used here entails three major claims by Luther (emboldened below). The textual propositions he makes to support each major claim are respectively listed following each of the major claims.

First, Luther argues that Christ is not a cruel master (LW 26, 37). Accordingly, Christ can't be a lawgiver or a judge (LW 26, 178). Rather, "He is nothing but sheer, infinite mercy which gives and is given" (LW 26, 178). He is "the Lover of those who are in anguish, sin, and death, and the kind of Lover who gives Himself for us and becomes our High Priest, that is, the One who interposes Himself as Mediator between God and us miserable sinner" (LW 26, 178–79). Without this interposition, the sinner, according to Luther, knows that to face God is to risk perishing before God's judgment (LW 26, 64). To contemplate and confront God as Father without the Mediator thus arouses extreme terror in Luther, a terror "no smaller that was the tremendous and horrible spectacle on Mt. Sinai (Exod 19:16)" (LW 26, 64). As Mediator, Christ causes a person's sin to be "ignored and hidden in the sight of God" (LW 26, 133). As such, Christ, for Luther, is the Dispenser of grace, the Savior, the Pitier (LW 26, 178). Luther's Christ is the Divine Comforter. His Christ does not trouble the heart but gives it peace.

Second, Luther claims that Christ as Divine Comfort comforts the stricken conscience. In Luther's theological lexicon, Christ becomes the Lord, Ruler, and Bridegroom of the conscience. The conscience is not only Christ's chamber. Conscience is also His bride (LW 26, 120).

> [Let] every Christian learn diligently to distinguish between the Law and the Gospel. Let him permit the Law to rule his body and its members but not his conscience. For that queen and bride must not be polluted by the Law but must be kept pure for Christ, her one and only husband; as Paul says elsewhere (2 Cor 11:2): "I betrothed you to one husband." Therefore let the conscience have its bridal chamber.... Here let only Christ lie and reign, Christ, who does not terrify sinners and afflict them, but who comforts them, forgives their sins, and saves them. (LW 26, 120)

According to Luther, Christ and Christ alone must rule the conscience. Here, He and He alone must reign. Writes Luther:

> This Bridegroom, Christ, must be alone with His bride in His private chamber, and all the family and household must be shunted away. But later on, when the Bridegroom opens the door and comes out, then let the servants return.... Then let works and love begin.

Christ, Luther insists, *must* rule the conscience. Why? Because, according to Luther, the "two devils who plague us are sin and conscience, the power of the Law and the sting of sin (1 Cor 15:56)" (LW 26, 26). Christ, Luther argues, mediates a person's sin before God the Father. He also removes the "sting" of sin from within the person, so that the person's conscience no longer makes a person feel guilt as a sinner. The "sting," Luther argues, is guilt. Guilt, Luther continues, is a conscience caught up in fear and turmoil because of personal transgressions. Christ, Luther concludes, "defangs" sin and quiets the unruly conscience. As such, Christ, for Luther, is the conqueror of these two devils: sin and the unruly, guilt-ridden conscience (LW 26, 26). Writes Luther:

> Christ has conquered these two monsters and trodden them underfoot, both in this age and in the age to come. The world does not know this; therefore it cannot teach anything sure

about how to overcome sin, conscience, and death. Only Christians have this kind of teaching and are equipped and armed with it, so that they can overcome sin, despair, and eternal death. It is a teaching that is given only by God; it does not proceed from free will, nor was it invented by human reason or wisdom. These two words, "grace" and "peace," contain a summary of all of Christianity. Grace contains the forgiveness of sins, a joyful peace and a quiet conscience. But peace is impossible unless sin has first been forgiven, for the Law accuses and terrifies the conscience on account of sin. And the sin that the conscience feels cannot be removed by pilgrimages, vigils, labors, efforts, vows, or any other works.... For there is no way to remove sin except by grace. (LW 26, 26–7)

Third, Luther's description of the way in which Christ enters the conscience borders on the mystical. Christ, as the conscience's bridegroom, according to Luther, enters and unites himself with her "in the midst of darkness," in a "cloud" that keeps the act from our sight or knowledge (LW 26, 130). *How* Christ is present Luther does not know. Writes Luther: "[This] is beyond our thought; for there is darkness" (LW 26, 130). Christ is present. Of this Luther has no doubt. Why? Because the presence of Christ in the conscience brings about the personal experience of "confidence of the heart" (LW 26, 130), "a quiet conscience" (LW 26, 27), and the "[conscience] comforted" (LW 26, 52). As such, these *human* feelings become Luther's proof-text that Christ is present within a person. Human assurance, in this way, is born of Christ's presence within the human conscience.[90]

Luther's Incipient Affect Theology

These three strategies cited above lead to Luther's incipient affect theology as the way he explains how emotional distress is transformed into religious feelings of uplift, salvation, and grace. This core strategy of explaining how emotions develop in religious settings and terms is the key to affective theological studies.

Luther's affective theological system tracks how the conscience feels (emotions) the presence of Christ (religious experience) in the conscience. The term *conscience* for Luther is thus a tracking device for his theology of emotions; in short, his affect theology. More precisely, his use of the term *conscience* functions in his theology like an internal combustion engine, which is the spark of the divine that transforms emotional energy into spiritual power. For Luther, the term thus refers to

- Christ's rightful realm within the person,
- Christ's bridal chamber, and
- Christ's bride.

Furthermore, the term *conscience* is used to identify
- one of the two devils that Christ has come to conquer (the other devil, to reiterate, is sin), and
- one of the two devils that plague Christians when they are not united with Christ.

Moreover, the term refers to the place within Christians
- in which their inner confidence, comfort, and peace is born,
- and thus the experience itself of (1) confidence, comfort, and peace is created or that of (2) turmoil, anguish, despair, guilt and the loss or lack of confidence.

This is Luther's affective theological analysis of the spiritual power of the conscience because, to reiterate, he tracks how ravaged emotions are transformed into uplifting religious feelings. This is a bottom up theology, namely, a theology of emotions that starts with feelings rather than with ideas. And he calls his incipient affective theological approach his "theology about Christian righteousness" (LW 26, 127).

According to Luther, his summary of this doctrine of Christian righteousness reveals "the true meaning of Christianity" (LW 26, 126–27). The structure of his summary can be divided into the following nine steps, which track and reveal how Luther's various meanings and uses of the term *conscience* relate to his doctrine of justification.

Step 1. A man first acknowledges that he is in disharmony with God because the man desires to fulfill God's law but is unable to do so. Unable to fulfill God's law, the man is rendered a sinner.

Step 2. Every effort by this man to try to do better, namely, to do good works and thereby fulfill God's law, brings the man to an ever-deepening despair.

Step 3. Each effort to please God by works brings more wrath from God, for God is being offered the man's sin (namely, unfulfilled Law) as if it were good works (namely, fulfilled Law).

Step 4. The man experiences an ever-deepening terror and humiliation in the sight of God because of this.

Step 5. Through such futile efforts to placate God with imperfect works, the man finally "sees the greatness of his sin and finds in himself not one spark of the love of God." In other words, *he now sees himself as God sees him, as an utter sinner.* His view of himself is now that of someone who is an absolute and total negation of the good. He knows that he is all flesh and not spirit.

Step 6. Seeing himself as God sees him, *his view and God's view of him are now aligned and thus one.* As such, *the man and God are now in harmony.* The man "confesses that he deserves death and eternal damnation." Accordingly, his will and view of himself are now in complete accord with that of God's will and view of the man. *The man's will is thus aligned with God's will.* Being in complete accord with God's will is the experience of faith.

Step 7. The experience of faith is the experience of the presence of Christ, who is He who is present in the faith itself.

Step 8. Christ as Divine Mediator hides the man's sins from God by taking the sins upon himself. With this act by Christ, the man is justified.

Step 9. Christ as Divine Mediator also removes the "sting" of sin from the man's conscience so that he no longer feels guilty because he is a sinner.

The role of the Holy Spirit in Luther's doctrine of justification plays a crucial role here. It is the spiritual heat, the spark that triggers his affective theological system.

More precisely, the Holy Spirit for Luther is the means of transition from the externally heard Gospel to the inwardly revealed revelation of the divine Word (LW 26, 73). According to Luther, the Word must be heard if justification is to be attained. Writes Luther, the "external Word must come first" (LW 26, 73).

Initially, the Holy Spirit is the means of transition from the spoken Word to the revealed Word. Writes Luther, "hearing does not come from the flesh, even though it is in the flesh; but it is in and from the Holy Spirit" (LW 26, 171).

As such, the Holy Spirit is the person's *awareness of spiritual energy*. And this spiritual awareness is the *means of transition* from the external to the internal Word. More precisely, this *spiritual transition* is the *means* by which the person moves from step five to step six in the above nine-step schematic. It is a transition point because it sparks the soul. The spark is both a disembodied mental awareness and an embodied emotional experience.

As noted above, step five is the experience of the man as absolute negation before God. The man knows himself to be nothing in God's sight. He is all flesh and not spirit.

Step six recounts the same condition of the man as totally undeserving of justification, but now rather than being in an absolute state of despair over this, the man is in a state of faith because he has been justified. Here's why.

Steps five and six describe the identical state of man as absolute negation. These two steps, however, do not describe two different actions by the man. Rather, what distinguishes the two steps is the change in the person's state of awareness. This change thus indicates a new mindset.

In affective neuroscientific terms, the change in awareness is brought about by a cognitive executive function (frontal cortex) of emotional ruminations and regulations (medial front regions) that creates a sense of freedom to act in a new way.[91] This new way of acting, however, is not the result of an object of contemplation, but rather emerges from an awareness without an object. It is a pure state of nonreflective experience, an ineffable sense of now being an active agent in the world. For Luther, this human state is a mystical awareness and experience that prompts active work in the world.

The neuro-affective awareness, in Luther's terms, is thus a spiritual shift. It is the means of transition between the two steps in which the only thing now present is the Holy Spirit, which is not a thing. It is not an object of thought, namely, something that can be parsed by the human mind. It is not *a word*, but rather it is *the Word* of God.

The Holy Spirit in Luther's schematic is thus the alignment of the man's will with God's will. It is the human awareness that the man is in God's view an absolute sinner. Thus, the condition in step five, which was experienced as absolute despair, is now in step six identified and experienced as grace. This awareness is God's grace. God's grace, in classic Trinitarian terms, is God's Son.

The Holy Spirit is thus the awareness of the identity between God's grace and God's Son. This awareness is the means of transition from the experience of the Holy Spirit's presence to the experience of the presence of Christ because, for Luther, there is no actual (ontic) difference between Christ and the Holy Spirit—both being one and the same God. The Holy Spirit is "simply" the means by which the awareness of Christ's presence in Luther is acknowledged.

The term *awareness* is thus a key term here, for this term denotes, for Luther, the spiritual presence of the Holy Spirit. Spiritual awareness (that one is a sinner) thus becomes, in this affective scheme of things, the felt presence of the Holy Spirit itself.

And thus emerges Luther's inchoate affect theology. A person's experience of the presence of Christ, according to Luther, is the affective experience of a confident and tranquil conscience (an emotional experience) as a state of awareness of the mind (a mental awareness without a determinate object). In other words, a person is *aware of Christ's presence within* when the person is mentally *aware of one's conscience as calmed and comforted*. As such, knowledge of one's justification is born of this affective experience of a comforted conscience. The feeling of comfort is assurance, which is not born of an object of thought but rather is felt as an embodied state of the self.

Conscience, in sum, has become for Luther the access point to Christ. More precisely, it is the way in which a person is immediately aware of one's own spiritual state. Without the affective experience of a peaceful conscience, one has no way of knowing that Christ is present within and that one has thereby been justified.

As such, the nature of the relationship between the human experience of forgiveness and the divine act of forgiveness in Luther's doctrine of justification is that of the relationship between a person's conscience and Christ's presence within it.

The human experience of forgiveness is now in Luther's affective theological system the same as Christ's presence within the conscience. Luther, however, does not equate forgiveness with justification. Rather, the experience of forgiveness, namely, the experience of a tranquil, guilt-free conscience, is the means by which the human being is aware of the fact that the person has been justified.

Conscience, which is related to both Christ (as his bride) and humans, as such, is the experiential basis of awareness of one's justification.

Luther's use of conscience thus functions epistemologically. It is the way in which one knows that one has been justified. This person gains knowledge of one's justification by means of (1) the cessation of torment from a troubled conscience and (2) the experience of peace from a comforted conscience. Such experiences, Luther argues, can only result from the presence and union of Christ, the Divine Bridegroom, with his bride, the conscience.

What has happened to the schoolmen's *synteresis* in Luther's scenario? It's gone.[92] Luther has replaced it with the Bridegroom who comforts and thus guides his bride. Here is a case in point.

In 2 Cor 11 Paul characterizes the Corinthians as Christ's bride and is upset because he fears the bride might be a harlot. Writes Paul:

> I feel a divine jealousy for you, for I betrothed you to Christ to present you as a pure bride to her one husband. But I am afraid … your thought will be led astray from a sincere and pure devotion to Christ. For if someone comes and preaches

another Jesus than the one we preached, or if you receive a
different spirit from the one you receive, or if you accept a
different gospel from the one you accepted, you submit to it
readily enough. (2 Cor 11:2–4)

Paul is upset with the Corinthians, as he is with the Galatians, because they are falling away from his teachings and are embracing
an alien doctrine. In the above-cited passage, Paul does not once
refer to the Corinthians' conscience. But this does not matter to
Luther. Here's why.

Luther now refers to 2 Cor 11:2 in his lecture on the second
chapter of Galatians. Concerning this verse, Luther writes:

[As] Paul says elsewhere (2 Cor 11:2): "I betrothed you to one
husband." Therefore let the conscience have its bridal chamber.... Here let only Christ lie and reign.... (LW 26, 120)

In this citation, Luther equates his understanding of conscience
with Paul's reference to Christ's bride, namely, the betrothed. *For
Luther, that to which Paul refers as the bride can also be referred
to as the conscience.* Thus, in Luther's exegesis of Paul's letters,
Luther can make repeated reference to conscience even though
Paul does not refer to conscience once in the text under review.

It would seem that Luther has engaged in the following implicit reasoning in order to equate Paul's reference to the betrothed
with the conscience:

1. According to Paul, the true Christian is betrothed to Christ.
   Such a Christian is the Bride of Christ. Christ thus unites
   with his bride.
2. This union takes place in the bridal chamber. Such a chamber must be absolutely distinct from the flesh, namely, the
   exterior world where the Law reigns. Such a chamber must
   also be such that a person can experience the presence of
   Christ.
3. Paul has introduced the idea of conscience into the New
   Testament. Conscience, in the New Testament, refers to
   an interior place within a person where self-knowledge of
   one's state of wellbeing is known.

4. For Luther, spiritual awareness and knowledge are received interiorly by means of the Holy Spirit and Christ.
5. Conscience, as such, is the bridal chamber where the Holy Spirit and Christ are received and felt. The bridal chamber is thus, for Luther, the bride to which Paul refers.

Luther, of course, nowhere engages in this kind of explicit logical reasoning. But based on the evidence presented above, the five steps delineated here seem to be the kind of embedded reasoning that led Luther to turn Paul's betrothed into the Christian's conscience.

This is how Paul's message of Christian spiritual freedom[93] *from* the Law has become in Luther's hands a message to Christians that their *conscience* must be free *of* the Law.

For Gabriel Biel and other schoolmen of the *via moderni*, as noted in part two of this chapter, the *synteresis*—the spark of the divine in man—had become the Law internalized. The *synteresis*, so the reasoning went, referred to a gift from God to all so that persons on their own can know how to lead virtuous lives.

Luther, in freeing the conscience from the Law, thus renders the term *synteresis* meaningless in his lexicon. By renouncing Law as the rightful ruler of the conscience, Luther expunged that to which the term *synteresis* refers: God's law.

Christ and not the Law, Luther can now argue, is the rightful ruler of the conscience. Accordingly, conscience, instead of being the storehouse of moral precepts, now has a quasi-ontic status as the bride who *participates* passively and receives the gifts from her beloved Christ. Such a concept of conscience is clearly "transmoral," for it pertains to that which is beyond the rule of Law.

Baylor, as noted in part two of this chapter, disagrees with Tillich's use of the term *participation* in a definition of Luther's transmoral conscience. But Baylor is in error here because he fails to distinguish between (1) Luther's concept of conscience *as* the bride and bridal chamber for Christ and (2) Luther's notion as to what conscience does *after* it is united with Christ: act morally in the world. Writes Luther:

But later on, when the Bridegroom opens the door and comes out, then let the servants return.... **Then let works ... begin.**[94] (LW 26, 137-8)

Baylor, in effect, has failed to make the distinction between the bride's *union* with Christ and the resulting *fruit of this union* with Christ. The result of this failure leads Baylor to the following, only partially correct, conclusion:

Luther's vision of the religious significance that the conscience acquires in faith, as appropriating and reproducing divine judgments about the person, linked the conscience and religious faith in a way totally foreign to scholastic thought.[95]

Baylor has failed to distinguish the *passive* conscience as Christ's bride from the *active* ("appropriating and reproducing") conscience, which is the fruit of the results of the union with the Divine Comforter. Christ's bride—the conscience—does not "appropriate" because appropriation is an action and would seem to refer to a rational act. But rationality, according to Luther, pertains to the Law and is thus a human act of work. Writes Luther:

Human reason has the Law as its object. It says to itself: "This I have done; this I have not done." But faith in its proper function has no other object than Jesus Christ, the Son of God, who was put to death for the sins of the world. It does not look at its love and say: "What have I done? Where have I sinned? What have I deserved?" But it says: "What has Christ done? What has He deserved?" (LW 26, 88)

Baylor, so it seems, has brought notions pertaining to rationality (namely, the Law) into Luther's bridal chamber, while the union between bride and Bridegroom is still underway.

Baylor, so it also seems, has failed to understand a fundamental precept in Luther's concept of the conscience, which states that only Christ must reign in the conscience. The Law for Luther thus does not pertain to the content of the Christian conscience. Christ does.

But Baylor perhaps has not made a textual error. Rather, this distinction that Luther makes so clearly in his *Lectures on Galatians* between the conscience as bride/bridal chamber and the conscience as a work (and therefore subject to the Law) is not fully developed in the thought of the young Luther.[96]

The young Luther, as noted above, is the focus of Baylor's study. The difference between the young and the mature Luther might explain why Baylor's analysis seems in error. But this difference does not justify Baylor's incorrect assessment of Tillich's understanding of the mature Luther because Luther's conscience participates in a reality beyond morality and the Law: the Holy Spirit and Christ.

Luther's confidence thus can be explained, in part, by his experience of a tranquil conscience.

> Where the confidence of the heart is present, therefore, there Christ is present. (LW 26, 130)

> But if there is any [troubled] conscience or fear present, this is a sign that this righteousness has been withdrawn. (LW 26, 9)

Luther thus equates a troubled conscience with the withdrawal of righteousness, namely, the withdrawal of Christ from the conscience. Luther here again equates a confident and peaceful conscience with the presence of Christ within the conscience.

Furthermore, any person who challenges this peaceful presence (namely, the conscience united with Christ) in Luther's schematic is thus actually challenging Christ and as such "was sent by the devil." Luther has but to take a very small step to conclude that anyone who challenges the peacefulness of his conscience is an antichrist. Unfortunately, Luther takes this fateful step. Writes Luther:

> [Any]one who teaches something different or something contrary — we confidently declare that he was sent from the devil. (LW 26, 59)

Luther can now claim that Jews, Papists, Sectarians, Turks, and others are Satan's emissaries. As such, they seek to deny Christ his rightful realm and thus are Christ-tormentors. Luther has equated conscience-troublers with Christ-tormentors. By so doing, Luther has equated the inner subjective feeling of absolute assurance with objective, exterior facts: angry and upset people, persons from different religious traditions, persons who disagree with Luther's doctrinal claims.

By equating inner, personal certainty (namely, a conscience at peace) with objective truth (namely, "Christians are constituted as judges over all kinds of doctrine and become lords over all the laws of the entire world"), Luther has violated a core principle of a sound affective theological approach. He has conflated affective states (the feeling of contentment, for example) with religious truth claims (the claim, for example, that Christ is the source of this feeling).

Schleiermacher, as noted in chapter one, formulated this core principle in affective theological terms when he noted that *all* religious affections are culturally determined. Religious claims are thus not universal truths. Their affective ground, however, is not culturally determined. Culture can determine, for example, if an anger system of the brain is triggered, but biology and culture are not the same in Schleiermacher's scheme. Culture entrains that which precedes the acculturation process: affect. And affect is a neural fact of consciousness. Pious feeling mediates and modifies triggered affect. Pious feelings, Schleiermacher argued, are thus a creation of a religious community and as such are a cultural creation of human experiences in the world.

This core principle is why Schleiermacher claimed that any positive religious pronouncement always entails anthropomorphic claims: they pertain to human self-consciousness linked to experiences in the world.[97] Religious claims are cultural constructions. Christian doctrine, in Schleiermacher's system, thus always pertains to propositions that can be related back to piously determined affections that reflect the interests and patterning principles of a specific, religious community.[98] So, too, in Luther's affective system, but with one major difference: Luther claimed that his feelings were the same as the presence of Christ. He thus turned his cultural experience into a universal truth claim that made him the judge of all laws and all persons.

Luther, in sum, made an affective experience and a rational judgment about that experience the same. The difference between affect and reason, emotions and religious ideas was thus lost in Luther's system.

As a consequence, Luther lost the ability to discern the difference between what he thought and what he felt. And this loss of difference made it impossible for Luther to discern the difference between his ideas, his feelings, and the reality of other people that cannot be reduced to his terms. He stripped others, in effect, of their freedom to exceed his own expectations, beliefs, and judgments. And by so doing, Luther rendered them figments of his terrified feelings and religious imagination. He turned people into devils that must be slain.

The result of Luther's theology is as follows: he justified the experience of extreme personal confidence of the Christian as *the central religious experience of faith*. His affective theological scheme with its emphasis upon the centrality of his own sense of personal assurance in doctrinal terms justified anew the all-too-human tendency to over-confidence as perhaps a psychological defense to protect oneself from a social environment that is crumbling.[99] Luther did indeed live in two domains. But his theory of these two domains conflated civic rule with God's commands and personal feelings with the presence or absence of Christ.

In 1939, the master Swiss theologian Karl Barth watched the rise of the German Third Reich and noted, "every people has its evil dreams." [100] According to Barth, "Hitlerism is the present evil dream of the German pagan who first became Christianized in a Lutheran form."[101]

Is this Christianized Lutheran form to which Barth refers Luther's doctrine on the Christian conscience? Did Luther christen the pagan conscience Paul tried but failed to dismantle in his gentile followers?

Paul urged Gentiles to practice the faithfulness of Christ toward persons through acts of lovingkindness. Luther failed to make the mark. Will we?

Part Four

Contemporary Affect Theology

Chapter Seven

Love Beyond Belief

Introduction

America is a secular nation with a Protestant conscience. This conscience fosters America's public policies and is the shared reference for (the missing) moral values in liberal America and the entrenched religious values in Christian conservative America.[1] The roots of this Christian moral affective evaluation system were created by Paul, schematized by Augustine, conceptualized by Luther, and planted in American soil two centuries ago as self-evident common sense. Liberals rejected the implant.

Does the story of the regnant Protestant moral value system in America reveal liberalism's "shattered moral order," as the former US Secretary of Education under Ronald Reagan, William J. Bennett, puts it?[2] Is the conservative journalist and pundit William Kristol right when he claims that what gets revealed in this story is liberalism's hollow moral core?[3]

Liberalism's moral core, the present chapter argues, is neither shattered nor hollow. Its root system is still the Protestant conscience. Liberals, so the argument goes in this chapter, continue to affirm the Protestant conscience they reject as their moral and spiritual foundation.

There is, however, a different affective foundation for a progressive political and spiritual moral values system in America today. Millions of spiritual but not religious Americans have found its access point: love beyond belief. This discovery marks the dawn of a new era in America's Christian and post-Christian spiritual and political life. The narrative for this new era includes a set of theorems, postulates, and protocols that are laid out and explained in this chapter.

Best to begin with a brief history of how liberals inadvertently affirm the Protestant conscience they reject as the moral judge of human affections. An initial example makes this complex point evident.

Part One
A Brief Historical Narrative

Consider the November 5, 2004, *New York Times* op-ed, "The Day the Enlightenment Went Out," written by Garry Wills, an "ex-conservative"[4] Christian social historian. The essay shows how easy it is for liberals to get blindsided by Christian conservative voters.

Wills' article, a morning-after story, bemoans Senator John Kerry's loss of the presidential election to George W. Bush. To this end, Wills poses a rhetorical question: "Can a people that believes more fervently in the Virgin Birth than in evolution still be called an Enlightened nation?"

His answer, of course, is a resounding "No." And he provides a list of the rational "Enlightenment values" lost because of the outcome of the 2004 presidential election: "critical intelligence, tolerance, respect for evidence, a regard for the secular sciences."

Wills, however, fails to mention one of these enlightenment values: religious affections. This error does not go unnoticed.

Daniel E. Ritchie, director of the humanities program at Bethel University, pointed out this oversight four days later in his letter-to-the-editor response. The actual American Enlightenment, Ritchie argues, "was neither antireligious nor anticlerical." Nor was it "a triumph of conservative religious belief over reason and facts" because, as Ritchie rightly insists, political liberty and religious feelings and practices were inseparable.

After correcting Wills's record of Enlightenment values, Ritchie offers liberals advice from the "heart of an evangelical university with a strongly pro-Bush student body." Liberals and other "elites," Ritchie insists, need to take religion to heart.

In Ritchie's words: "America's elites must ... come to understand American religion, past and present, more deeply. Until they do, they will continue to create the polarization they lament." Simply put, they need a history lesson in America's emotional heartland of moral values and religious feelings.

Conservatives like Ritchie love to recount this affective history and highlight what's missing: common sense, or more precisely, the Christian conscience. Their narratives describe the way Protestant Anglo-Saxons tracked religious affections and shaped the Northern European Enlightenment. The story unfolds in stages.

Strange Bedfellows

First, the Emotional Terrain. Conservative historian Gertrude Himmelfarb in her 2004 book, *The Roads to Modernity: The British, French, and American Enlightenments,*[5] ventures onto the affective terrain liberals tend to avoid.[6] And Himmelfarb invites her reluctant conservative colleagues to join her on the expedition. They have neglected this historical site, she tells them, because it looks like a liberal field.

Himmelfarb thus urges her fellow conservatives not to turn away from values espoused by liberals, but simply to add what the liberals leave out: the "social virtues" and the "social affections." These added factors, Himmelfarb assures her readers, will make conservatives change their minds about liberal cant, namely, "the usual litany of traits associated with the Enlightenment—reason, rights, nature, liberty, equality, tolerance, science progress—[with] reason invariably [heading] the list."[7]

Second, the Moral Philosophers. The real ground of liberal moral values and religious belief, Himmelfarb insists, has always been conservative terrain and always will be because the treasures found there are affective feelings linked to conservative moral values. To find this buried treasure, Himmelfarb tells her readers, they must simply mine the work of the "moral philosophers" who taught moral philosophy at the University of Glasgow in Scotland, namely, men like Frances Hutcheson; Thomas Reid; Dugald Stewart; and Anthony Ashley-Cooper, the third Earl of

Shaftesbury. The work of the Glasgow professors, known collectively as formulators of the Scottish Enlightenment, Himmelfarb rightly argues, became the shared moral values supporting and shaping conservative and liberal politics and Protestant faith in America.

Third, the Common Sense School. This new school of moral philosophy, known at Harvard as the Common Sense School of Philosophy, was linked to the work of Scottish Reformer Thomas Reid (1710–96). Unlike the Protestant Reformers Martin Luther and John Calvin, who both deemed human nature fallen and thus lacking an innate capacity for moral behavior guided solely by God's law,[8] Reid reaffirmed the sanctity of human nature, arguing that it not only had an innate moral faculty, but also an innate capacity to follow moral duty's dictates.

Fourth, the Conscience as Common Sense. The source of this moral capacity, Reid argued, was the conscience, which for him was synonymous with the terms "the moral faculty," "the moral sense," and "intuition."[9] The testimony of the conscience, for Reid, was thus the innate source of moral values, moral law, and moral reasoning in man. It determined, innately, what kinds of human affections are universally right or wrong

Fifth, the Strange Bedfellows. Liberals and conservatives, Unitarians and Calvinists, traditionalists and post-traditionalists, Federalists and anti-Federalists converged in agreement here on this common moral ground of the American Enlightenment. Thomas Jefferson admired the Scottish philosophers even though he dismissed their attempt to preserve organized Christianity, as David Walker Howe notes in *The Unitarian Conscience.*[10] As Howe puts it, John Witherspoon, the president of Princeton, championed a Calvinist "common sense realism." Alexander Madison, James Hamilton, and John Jay, as authors of the Federalist Papers, also understood and affirmed the dignity and values of human faculties from the standpoint of the Scottish philosophers.

These Americans, with their disparate and conflicting political stands and religious interests, were the strange bedfellows here because Common Sense realism was the shared bedding for one and all.

Sixth, Human Nature Upgraded. Human nature was no longer deemed hapless, innately sinful, and thus totally at the mercy of an avenging God. Rather, men and women now were viewed as having moral agency because human nature was considered naturally and potently moral. Discourse on the Protestant conscience was thus universalized and secularized as talk about the innate moral capacity of man to determine and regulate his affections.

This "new"[11] moral standpoint taught Americans how to judge human behavior based on attention to the internal private motivations that prompt it. Accordingly, the heart and soul of this American Enlightenment strategy entailed an internal assessment of human emotions, which is a function of the Protestant conscience and thereby is the prompt for a Christian morality. This is the case because the conscience discerns the "true" motivations for an act that appears moral to others but privately might have been prompted by greed, lust, or other "sinful" feelings, needs, and desires. The conscience tracks down and assesses these hidden, internal emotional operating systems to determine their moral relevancy and value.

Human emotions were no longer viewed by these Enlightenment Protestant minds as fallen from grace and as irreparable because of Adam's (original) sin in the biblical Garden of Eden. And Adam's lustful, disobedient act with Eve was no longer deemed to have been passed down to his progeny as the ongoing corruption of a fallen human nature. There was, however, a catch.

Not all people, so it was now reasoned, had this innate moral capacity to harness their triggered affective impulses and desires. Rather, some people lacked this capacity not because of Adam's bad deed but because some people were simply bad seeds.

Thomas Reid Explains the Bad Seed

Thomas Reid's conclusions about human nature were at first bedrock for both traditional and liberal Christian moral values in America. His system then became the median strip that keeps these two value formation pathways apart. The legacy of Reid's common sense philosophy was, in a word, ironic. [12] A hidden relationship "discovered in the incongruity" between liberal and traditional moral values eventually came to the fore because the traditional way the Protestant conscience evaluates and condemns others was exposed. Here's how it happened.

Reid's arguments, at first glance, seemed to affirm a standpoint that dismissed the Protestant conscience created by Luther and further affirmed and developed by John Calvin, the second-generation Reformer. Luther and Calvin both affirmed an *us versus them* theology about the damned and the elect. Reid, at first glance, seemed to argue against this kind of religiousness. According to Reid, the shared foundation of moral values in man is universal and as such "is the true worth and glory of a man."

Reid could thus claim that the "varieties of education, of fashion, of prejudices, and of habits ... may differ much in opinion with regard to the extent of this [moral] principle, and of what it commands and forbids, but the notion of it, as far as it is carried, is the same in all. It is that which gives a man real worth, and is the object of moral approbation."[13] It is, as such, something not created by man, but rather found in man.

This shared foundation is why man's conscience, Reid argues here, is universal even though there are varied particularities. The cultural differences, Reid insists, are simply variations and riffs on a universal theme, namely, moral values played out in different keys and scales but always as part of one great moral symphony of man's internal value, worth, and dignity.

Reid's explanation and affirmation of the "universality of this principle in men"[14] is linked inextricably to his affirmation of the *Protestant* conscience. More precisely, the reference point is not the external (Catholic) Church and its priests, traditions, and canonical laws. Rather, the reference point for Reid is Protestant, and thus the interior life of man and the direct link of the conscience to Christ, the Holy Spirit, and God.[15]

For Reid, the terms "*Moral Sense*, the *Moral Faculty* [and] *Conscience*"[16] are thus, to reiterate, synonymous. Each term refers to the same thing, namely, the source in man of "both the original conception of right and wrong in conduct, of merit and demerit, and the original judgments that this conduct is right, that is wrong; that this character has worth, that demerit."[17]

Accordingly, the first principles of moral values are the same as the first principles of the Protestant conscience. Writes Reid: the "truths immediately testified by our moral faculty, are the first principles of all moral reasoning, from which all our knowledge of duty must be deduced."[18] Talk about the Protestant conscience is now talk about a universal moral capacity for human value, merit, worth, agency and dignity without at the same time requiring theological talk about God, the Holy Spirit, or Christ. The Protestant conscience has now become a secular, self-evident Protestant principle rather than a religious belief, a denominational creed, or a doctrinal truth claim of the church. Accordingly, knowledge of this conscience is not a religious experience. It is simply a display of man's God-given common sense capacity to know right from wrong and thereby act ethically as a moral duty by regulating his affections.

Reid could thus argue that the knowledge of one's moral responsibilities is a duty and then ask, rhetorically: Of what does this duty consist? Reid replies: If you have to ask, you don't have it because one's moral duty is self-evident. It is common sense for those who have it, which, accordingly is not something that ever demands proof. Either you have this moral faculty that shows you what you ought to do and be—or you don't have it. It's simply a way of knowing truth that does not require empirical proof. For instance, a person might have never argued with a deaf man about sound, Reid argues, and yet the person nevertheless knows that such an attempt is nonsense because it defies common sense.

Writes Reid: "To reason about justice with a man who sees nothing to be just or unjust, or about benevolence with a man who sees nothing in benevolence preferable to malice, is like reasoning with a blind man about colour, or with a deaf man about sound."[19]

Reid offers the following three-part thought experiment to illustrate his point.[20] The threefold strategy is easily summarized as try, try again, stop trying.

Reid's First Strategy: Try. Reid invites his readers to imagine meeting a man who practices polygamy. We now reason with the polygamist showing him the negative consequences for humanity. But we fail to convince the man. The man thus persists in his belief and "does not perceive that he ought to regard the good of society, and the good of his wife and children; the reasoning can have no effect upon him, because he denies the first principle upon which it is grounded," namely, our human moral faculty.

Reid's Second Strategy: Try Again. Redouble your effort, Reid now tells us. This time we "reason for monogamy from the intention of nature, discovered by the proportion of males and of females that are born—a proportion which corresponds perfectly with monogamy, but by no means with polygamy—this argument can have no weight with a man who does not perceive that [he] ought to have regard to the intention of nature." So again, we do not prevail.

Reid's Third Strategy: Stop Trying. Go no farther, Reid now counsels us, because the polygamist lacks a moral capacity. His moral character is innately flawed. The man, Reid concludes, is constrained by his very nature from doing the right thing.

Throughout his work, Reid repeatedly lifts up claims from his own Northern European Protestant values (like the affirmation of monogamy) to a universal status.

As a consequence, Reid still divides humanity into the damned and the elect—as Protestant Reformers and the mainline Protestant traditions they spawned (e.g., Lutheranism, Presbyterianism, Congregationalism) are wont to do based on their own theological understanding of original sin, the damned and the elect, the condemned and the saved. But now the ideas are bundled together to create and affirm the efficacy of the Protestant conscience anew.

The rationale for Reid's Protestant division of the damned and the saved, in sum, is not based on a religious myth about how human nature was brought down by Adam's fall as God's wrathful punishment. Myths offended rational, nineteenth-century enlightenment minds.

Rather, the rationale for this division is now based on Reid's secular philosophic Protestant belief system. Reid's standpoint is secular because it affirms a pervasive cultural bias—polygamy is a sin—using philosophic reasoning rather than relying on theological references, religious doctrines, and canonical texts to explain ostensibly universal laws requisite for monitoring and regulating human affections.

The claim that polygamy is okay would indeed have seemed toxic in a tightly-bound Protestant setting. Such a claim would be the stuff of heresy in the Protestant Church, sedition in the Protestant State, idiocy in the Protestant society, and stupidity in the Protestant academy. Simply put, it would have defied common sense.

Accordingly, the exigencies of a man's own biology, so Reid's culturally-entrained harsh reasoning goes, determines the moral state of his affections and thus his fate. Human beings are now by nature, born innately moral or not. Period.

The Back-Away Move

Liberal Christians began to back away from the Enlightenment moral beliefs and formative values they had previously affirmed. Walter Rauschenbusch (1861–1918), a late nineteenth-century progenitor of the Social Gospel Movement or "New Christianity," explained what was going on: "When I began to apply my previous religious ideas to the [social] conditions I found, I discovered that they didn't fit."[21] The issue here was not the collapse of difference between emotions and ideas. Rather it pertained to issues about exploited communities and people.[22]

The basis for social reform for liberal Christians like Rauschenbusch, as social theorist James Davison Hunter points out in *American Evangelicalism*, was no longer revivals to purge men's hearts—their affections—of sin. Rather, the focal point of liberal Christianity by the end of the nineteenth century became "the social and economic problems associated with industrialization and urbanization (e.g., crowded and inadequate housing, conditions of labor in the factory system, a changing family structure, increasing crime and suicide rates and so on) ... and the religious and cultural pluralism brought by the unprecedented influx of Irish and Italian (Roman Catholic) and Eastern European (Jewish) immigrants."[23] The melting pot of American multiculturalism, racial and ethnic diversity. In short, American pluralism.

And thus emerged the fallout venue. The differences between liberal and traditional moral visions, as Hunter points out, were now "rooted in different systems of moral understanding."[24] People were no longer deemed by liberals to be *born* bad. Rather, they were *made* bad by bad human institutions that plundered and pillaged human souls. So human nature could be improved, the liberal reasoning went, if social institutions were improved. This is a core value of American liberalism: human nature is malleable and thus fixable.

This movement of liberal Protestants into the secular domain to correct the societal sins of modern America, however, had an unintended consequence. The Protestant conscience, which assesses, monitors, and controls human affections, became the moral domain of traditional and conservative Christian stewardship. Talk about America's moral values, virtuous ideas, and principled behavior was now a Christian conservative domain because liberals had abandoned attention to religious affections.

The history of Methodism in America is a case in point, as John Cobb, Jr. points out in the following summary, written explicitly for this present chapter.[25] He writes here in personal inclusive terms as a Protestant theologian who at one point in his life was also a Methodist parish minister. He thus lays out his own history of the emotional demise of Methodist tradition in America in the following way.

> John Wesley was the single most effective evangelist in eighteenth-century England, and unlike others he left a major institution that on his death became the Methodist Church. In the United States his followers became a separate denomination during his lifetime. The Methodist Church here grew to be the largest denomination for some time until recently superseded in numbers by the Southern Baptists.
>
> Wesley constructed his teaching around the centrality of God's love and the actual transformation of believers into loving people by God's activity in the heart. Although doctrinally faithful to the Church of England, Wesley was theologically

tolerant, evaluating people by the purity of their love for one another and for God. His strongest theological position was opposition to predestination. He insisted that God loved everyone and worked in every heart that would open to that work.

Music was an important part of Methodism. John's brother, Charles, wrote hymns some of which are now sung in many Protestant churches. His tunes were "popular" ones in the eighteenth century, but of course sound to people now like traditional church music. Over the centuries his music has had far more influence than Wesley's sermons.

During Wesley's life and for decades afterwards, Methodists were organized into groups who checked each other's progress in love and supported each other. Their use of money was part of their expression of love. Being a Methodist in that period was serious, demanding, and also rewarding business.

Wesley's converts, generally poor, became better workers, saved money, and moved into the middle class. Wesley saw that with this change, the wholeheartedness of his followers diminished and he foresaw a decline in the quality of spiritual lives. Concerns for economic and social advance and security competed with the radical demands of love. As the small groups of intimate self- and mutual-examination disappeared, Methodism became much like other Protestant denominations.

Methodists continued to emphasize the primacy of love and to evaluate their spiritual lives in terms of love. However, a tendency to identify particular practices as expressions of love expected of all developed, i.e., legalism. Wesley had little to say about sex, but in the Victorian period, sexual morality was emphasized. Wesley drank wine, but due to the abuse of alcohol on the frontier where Methodism was growing, Methodists became absolutists in opposition to alcohol. Meanwhile middle class habits weakened the emphasis on motives and emotions. Too often, love took second place to law.

Methodists strongly supported the social gospel and grounded their support in personal piety. Sadly, as the piety declined sometimes the issues of social justice had to stand on their own. Methodism became a form of cultural-Protestantism in which beliefs were largely shaped by education and science, and patriotism became as important as faithfulness to God. Its concern for realistic improvement of the inner life led to a turn to pop psychology. Little of the original conviction and commitment were left. So when the culture ceased favoring the church, it had little to offer.[26]

The result was as follows. When liberals backed away from their own American Enlightenment moral values, they "disestablished" American Protestantism as the foundation of their own liberal faith.[27] They rejected, in effect, the Christian values and claims about human affections and how they should be handled, which they had previously affirmed. As Cobb puts it, "love took second place to law."

Liberal Protestants thus moved beyond the formative moral values, pietism,[28] and theological tradition that "judged human prudence, wisdom and virtue" and could be tracked back, in Reid's words, to the "wise Author of nature [who] has not left us in the dark."[29]

Thanks to the liberals, however, the Protestant conscience was still the common emotional ground of moral value formation in America, but now by default. Liberals, in effect, left the Protestant conscience intact by not replacing it with another internal moral valuation system designed to directly track, shape, and handle human affections. And since the Protestant conscience was the touchstone for talk about Christ and talk about sin and salvation as a change of heart, liberal Christianity lost its Christian emotional and religious moorings and credentials.

Liberal Protestantism became, in effect, talk about social justice issues and concerns rather than talk about man's relationship to and feelings about Christ and God. Mainline liberal Protestant denominations like United Methodism, Presbyterianism, Episcopalianism, and Congregationalism thus gained increasing cultural influence as religious institutions, and decreasing affective recruitment power as religious communities.[30]

Ralph Waldo Emerson, as a nineteenth-century liberal (Unitarian) minister, illustrates the presence of the ongoing role of the Protestant conscience in liberal thought, but now by default. According to Emerson:

> One thing is plain for all men of common sense and common conscience, that here, here in America, is the home of man, here the "new love, new faith, new sight [that] shall restore [creation] to more than its first splendor." What makes this plain is not the men *in* America, but man *as* America, and America not as state of mind but, actually and unequivocally, as "the land," the Bible's *litera-historia* become American *natura-allegoria*.[31]

Sacvan Bercovitch, in his book *The Puritan Origins of the American Self,* cites this text by Emerson and then explains the consequence of such claims.

Emerson, Bercovitch argues, is striving to overcome subjectivity by making nature the vehicle of Emerson's own thoughts. He has done this by aligning nature with Truth and God. Now the "axioms of truth translate into the laws of ethics."[32] And thus the "thing that is plain for all men of common sense and common conscience" is the result of Emerson's conflation of feelings and ideas, emotions and moral values. This kind of conflation became the hallmark of the work of the Protestant conscience in America.

Liberal Christians like Emerson, in effect, did not dismantle the Protestant system when they turned to social reform.[33] They left it intact.

What Happened to Christ?

German theologian and Lutheran minister Dietrich Bonhoeffer (who was part of a failed cabal to assassinate Hitler that cost Bonhoeffer his life) asked this question in 1930–31 when he studied at the liberal bastion of modern Protestant theology in

America, Union Theological Seminary in Manhattan. Bonhoeffer was brutally frank in a letter to a friend about the state of liberal religion in America: "There is no theology here.... The students ... are unfamiliar with even the most basic [theological] questions. They become intoxicated with liberal and humanistic phrases."[34]

Bonhoeffer reached a similar conclusion when attending the liberals' churches. "The sermon," Bonhoeffer bemoaned, "has been reduced to parenthetical church remarks about newspaper events." Bonhoeffer now wondered, "whether one here really can still speak about Christianity.... In New York they preach about virtually everything; only one thing is not addressed or is addressed so rarely that I have as yet been unable to hear it, namely, the gospel of Jesus Christ, the cross, sin and forgiveness, death and life."

Liberal Protestantism, Bonhoeffer concluded, was no longer religious. It had cannibalized its emotions and in the process lost touch with Christ. In paradigmatic Protestant terms, liberal Christians had lost touch with the place where Christ is felt (Luther) or where the laws of God are known (John Calvin): the conscience.

This terrain is the domain of the Protestant conscience as the Bride of Christ (Luther). For John Calvin, it is the "judgment seat of God in man"[35] and part of the original endowment of man.[36] Moreover, it is for Calvin the place where man feels his own sins as if God's summons; a law in nature that cannot be abolished; man's moral tendency and thus more than a cognitive faculty because it pertains to feelings of fear, shame, remorse, and reverence for God.[37]

Reid is heir to this Protestant affirmation of the conscience as the seat of man's moral values without which he lacks moral judgment, dignity, and common sense.

Part Two
The Theological Results of This History

Based on the above historical narrative and illustrations, four theorems regarding the secular Protestant mindset delineated by Reid can now be formulated:

First Theorem: Moral Values = God's Universal Laws
(known through ideas) + Human Affections aligned with
these laws (felt as a person's moral affections).

The conscience in this nineteenth-century scheme of things is equivalent to moral values, so the formula can now be stated as follows:

Second Theorem: Conscience = God's Universal Laws
(known through ideas) + Affections aligned with these laws
(felt as moral affections).

The structural similarities between Luther's religious construction of the Protestant conscience and Reid's secular construction can now be postulated. We simply have to substitute religious terms for Reid's moral philosophy terms as follows.

Third Theorem: Conscience = Affections aligned by Christ
+ the prompt for the moral affections that will conform to
God's Universal Laws (known through moral ideas and expressed as moral behavior).

The term *conscience* with reference to John Calvin's understanding of it as pertaining to the "judgment seat of God in man"[38] and part of the original endowment of man[39] as well as (1) the place where man feels his own sins as if God's summons; (2) a law in nature that cannot be abolished; (3) man's moral tendency and thus more than a cognitive faculty because it pertains to affective experiences, namely, feelings of fear, shame, remorse, and reverence (for God).[40]

Fourth Theorem. Conscience = Feelings of fear, shame, remorse and reverence (for God) + the seat of God's Universal
Laws in man (known through moral ideas and expressed
as moral behavior).

In each of these four theorems, human affections are deemed to be guided by *God's Laws* or the *Divine Presence of Christ* in man. The difference between human affections and religious ideas thus disappears. Several steps make this disappearance evident.

Luther took the first step when he explained his mystical experience.

Luther Describes His Mystical Experience. In the *Lectures on Galatians,* Luther affirms the difference between (1) a felt affective shift of his emotions (a spiritual feeling of uplift he calls "true faith") and (2) the religious beliefs about the cause of this change of heart (Christ). True faith, for Luther, is thus a "sort of knowledge or darkness that nothing can see." Darkness is everywhere, Luther tells us, because the experience takes place in "a cloud in our hearts." Accordingly, Luther describes the experience as "beyond our thought" and thus something that can't be parsed by the rational mind (LW 26, 130).

Luther's Explanation of His Mystical Experience. He now explains this inexplicable affective experience in religious terms. He calls it an encounter with Christ who enters the Christian conscience and becomes one with it (LW 26, 129–30). Luther thus equates the reasoning, arguments, and propositional claims of his religious belief system with the inexplicable experience in the cloud of darkness felt by the human heart.

Luther's Mystical Distinction Vacated. Luther vacated the distinction he himself made between what is affectively felt and what is cognitively believed, thus collapsing the difference between emotions and thoughts. In sum, he conflates religious ideas with spiritual feelings, turning the primordial affective spiritual experience into an anthropomorphic display of Luther's own cultural biases and religious beliefs.

As noted in chapter six, great harm to others resulted from this collapse of difference between Luther's thoughts and affections. This conflation of emotions and ideas allowed Luther to equate his fretful feelings with rebellious peasants whom, Luther concluded, were devils that must be slain in the name of Christ.

More precisely, his theory of the two kingdoms functioned as a tool Luther used to keep his head (civic rules for law and order) and his heart (pious affections) apart. The irony here, of course, is that Luther had already collapsed the difference between them by deeming his subjective feelings and his external world to be directly mediated by God. So he acted as if the laws of civic order were objectively established by God rather than (1) subjectively mediated by vested feelings of fear and loathing, (2) personal judgments, and (3) biased critiques.

Luther's own conflation of emotions and religious ideas, when combined with the four theorems listed above, gives us the conceptual models needed to lay out two corollaries to the four postulates listed above.

Both corollaries are needed to understand the distinction between religious and spiritual experiences.

The First Corollary: Religious experience is constructed by vacating the difference between what is affectively felt and what is conceptually believed. More precisely, a religious experience in this Protestant scheme of things collapses the difference between feelings and thoughts by conflating (1) religious ideas, legends, myths, and other culturally-created traditions with (2) a primordial spiritual experience of affective resonance with life itself, namely, with the experience of cosmic consciousness.

The Second Corollary: Spiritual experience is constructed by maintaining the difference between (1) an affective shift in emotions felt as an exalted state and (2) all religious ideas, concepts and claims about the source of the shift and transformative state. More precisely, a spiritual experience expands the difference between emotions and thoughts by (1) setting aside all religious ideas, legends, myths, and other culturally-created faith traditions and (2) remaining steadfastly present in an inexplicable affective feeling of enormous uplifting life.[41]

This second corollary helps us understand why Schleiermacher called spiritual experiences the "natal hour" of everything living in religion, rather than calling it an "actual religious experience." Nothing can be said about the spiritual experience, Schleiermacher argued, without reducing the affective state to a culturally-determined, anthropomorphic religious claim.[42] Luther, as noted above, by violating this distinction reduced his resonant, affective spiritual experience to the biases of his culturally-constructed, religious beliefs.

This second corollary also helps us understanding the term "the Ungiven God," which, Schleiermacher insisted, was different from the churchgoer's God of religious conviction because when one had a truly spiritual experience, all thinking ceased.[43] There was only "nothing" left to consider about God, as one commentator has put it, when in this spiritual state. But this "nothing" was empty only of *ideas*. It was filled with feelings of awe, love, gratitude, caring, joy, and more. The mind, as an opened space, was simply filled up with what the body felt: life. All of it, at once. This state of being is the affective experience of cosmic consciousness. It's access point is affect.

For Schleiermacher, the feeling of being part of an infinite creation, namely, the affective sense of wonder, the ensuing awe, care, and love beyond belief are simply the spiritual experiences available to all persons because of human nature's capacity to feel the infinite universe as a finite moment of personal experience. It is the cosmic interior of human life affectively felt.

Luther's conscience, as noted in chapter six, became archetypal for the Protestant world. His rendition of the Gentile conscience accidentally created by Paul, then filled out by Augustine and formulated by Luther as the affective foundation for gentile faithfulness to Christ, makes evident a major patterning principle of the Protestant conscience today, namely, the elimination of the difference between what is felt and thought. The elimination of this difference, as repeatedly noted throughout this book, eliminates cosmic consciousness, which is found between thoughts in the resonant affective expanse of infinite life.

The Protestant conscience, from this paradigmatic perspective, has the markings of what John B. Cobb Jr., in his book *Spiritual Bankruptcy*, calls "religiousness,"[44] namely human mentalities that handle religious traditions, legends, and myths as if they are empirically verifiable secular facts rather than as what they really are: fictions born of religious mindsets.[45] As Cobb notes: "Believing that some one set of ancient legends is literally true is crazy, especially when it leads to discrimination against believers in the literal truth of other legends. When religiousness is co-opted for purposes that run diametrically against the needs of the world, the insanity becomes vicious."[46]

Is America's Protestant conscience by this standard vicious?

It is best to begin with Reinhold Niebuhr's answer to this question because he tracked how both liberal and traditional conservative Protestant minds incapacitate their ability to understand and "experience ... the claims and counter-claims of man's social existence, either domestically or internationally."[47]

Niebuhr turned to talk of God for the religious resolution to this problem. I suggest a spiritual solution.

Reinhold Niebuhr's Irony of American History

Reinhold Niebuhr, in his classic twentieth-century work *The Irony of American History*, describes what happens when the difference between thoughts and feelings, critical reasoning and vested affective interests is eliminated. Our faculty for emotional intelligence is gravely compromised.

According to Niebuhr:

> We [Americans] can understand the neat logic of either economic reciprocity or the show of pure power. But we are mystified by the endless complexities of human motives and the varied compounds of ethnic loyalties, cultural traditions, social hopes, envies and fears which enter into the policies of nations, and which lie at the foundation of their political cohesion.[48]

Three claims are spotlighted here. First, Americans cannot grasp these complex emotional factors and signature interests in others, Niebuhr concludes, because they are unable to discern it in themselves.

Second, the highest and most esteemed realms of reason, Niebuhr insists, are also linked to emotional dispositions, personal needs, and motivations, and thus express vested interests.

Third, Americans do not know how to deal with this "complex 'self' whether in its individual or in its collective forms."[49]

The result, for Niebuhr, is the necessary affirmation of original sin. Original sin, for Niebuhr, is the failure to see the links between emotions, reason, and behavior in moral value systems.

Emotional dispositions, personal needs, and motivations, after all, are linked to rational ideals and thus bias them. Accordingly, these overlooked emotional factors turn reason's rule into personal agendas that limit a person's ability to act reasonably, morally, and forthrightly.[50]

And thus the consequence is "the rejection of the reality of original sin in the mind of the controllers of social process ... has bred either cruelty or confusion. It has bred cruelty if the elite managed to achieve power proportioned to their pretentions, and confusion if they only wistfully longed for it."[51] It has bred, in a word, viciousness.

Human affections are at the base of Niebuhr's theological system. Niebuhr, however, does not lay hold of them. Rather, he exposes them. For Niebuhr, evil, is not an independent force that fights against God. Rather, it is a human limitation that can't be seen by the light of human judgment but only by using the standard of God's grace.

The transformation of human feelings, says Niebuhr, is God's terrain. In Niebuhr's words, it's the place where "moral resoluteness about ... immediate issues [combine] with a religious awareness of another dimension of meaning and judgment." For Niebuhr, the combination of these two dimensions—spirit and nature—is "almost a perfect model of the difficult but not impossible task of remaining loyal and responsible toward the moral treasures of a free civilization on the one hand while yet having some religious vantage point over the struggle."[52]

Niebuhr's discourse on the Protestant conscience begins here because he describes God's terrain in classic Protestant terms. More precisely, his focus is on the individual's reference to God without reliance on the mediating power of the Catholic Church. And this Protestant terrain is found in the place where human affections and ideas meet and are handled in the presence of God or Christ or the Holy Spirit by the Protestant's conscience.

The role of the Protestant conscience is discussed in Niebuhr's systematic theology, *The Nature and Destiny of Man*. Here we find the framework for Niebuhr's claim in *The Irony of American*

History that Americans cannot grasp the complex affective factors and signature interests in others or themselves. The source of this problem, we now learn, is the "easy conscience." Or more precisely, again in Niebuhrian terms: our inability to live in the self-contradiction resulting from the tensions in spiritual freedom and embodied reality as an embedded part of organic life. In short, our inability to live with the "uneasy conscience."

Niebuhr sets up the argument for these two states of the Protestant conscience as follows. He first describes the "uneasy conscience" as the result of a self-contradiction in human nature caused by man's essence—his freedom—and the sin created within this freedom because man in his freedom stands at the juncture of nature and spirit. This juncture, Niebuhr argues, lets man break with the natural world without also seeking a harmonious way of living in it.[53]

In contrast, Niebuhr calls man's "easy conscience" the belief that "human virtue is guaranteed by the rational preference for the benevolent as against the egoistic impulses."[54] Here, spirit is identified with reason too completely, which prevents reason from understanding its organic relationship to nature,[55] namely, its embodied feelings, impulses, and desires (and those of others) triggered by life in the world.

And thus I return full-circle to the major argument of this chapter, which can now be stated in Niebuhrian terms: Liberals and conservatives, traditionalists and New Christians are guided by an "easy" Protestant conscience that collapses the tension between thoughts and affections, reasons and feelings, spiritual exaltation and religious experiences into something called common sense.

Niebuhr tracked this kind of Protestant conscience as the reigning form of American consciousness in modern American life. The tension produced in the "uneasy conscience" by maintaining the difference between thought and feeling was gone.

I update Niebuhr's claim about the easy American conscience.

First, by way of an argument of absence (Argumentum ex Silentio). Here I point out the *absence* of affective expressions when liberals talk about moral values.

Second, by way of an argument of presence. I focus here on the enormous affective interests and emotional protocols displayed by traditionalists, social and political conservatives, and Christian evangelicals when discussing America's moral values.

Part Three
Examples of America's "Easy" Conscience

The First Example: Drew Westen's Study on the Liberal Democrats' Emotion-Deficiency Disorder

Drew Westen, a political psychologist, was hired by liberal Democrats to teach them how to overcome their inability to act with emotional forthrightness. Westen's 2007 book, *The Political Brain: The Role of Emotion Deciding the Fate of the Nation*, documents his findings, using firsthand case studies of the liberal brain disorder of hamstrung emotions. This condition is a brain disorder, Westen argues, because the political brain is "not a dispassionate calculating machine, objectively searching for the right facts, figures, and policies to make a reasoned decision."[56] Rather, it's thinking with your guts, which Westen calls the emotional brain.[57]

This brain state of emotional deficiency is the disorder Westen documents using his clinical work with liberal Democrats. Liberal Democrats during the George W. Bush era, as Westen repeatedly observed, seemed to "place their stock in the market place of ideas."[58] By so doing, Westen concluded, "they have been trading in the wrong futures."

The Democratic Party, as noted above, thus established itself as "the party of the profane" by "staking its claims on policies, bread-and-butter issues, rationality, expertise, and expected utility." By contrast, the Republican Party, by consistently casting its appeals "in the language of the sacred," became the party promoting America's religious and moral values. As Westen trenchantly notes:

> I have it on good authority (i.e., off the record) that leading
> conservatives have chortled with joy (usually accompanied
> by astonishment) as they watched their Democratic counter-
> parts campaign by reciting the best facts and figures, as if they

were trying to prevail in a high school debate tournament.... One can only imagine the relief of the Bush campaign in 2004 when no one thought to pull out the classic television footage of a smiling Secretary of Defense Dick Cheney shaking hands in the 1980s with an equally charming Saddam Hussein, with the narration "Why was Vice President Cheney sure Saddam had weapons of mass destruction? Because he sold them to him." And they must certainly have appreciated the Kerry Campaign's failure to juxtapose footage of President Bush running for his first term as president with his arm around his biggest campaign contributor, Ken Delay, promising to "run this country like a CEO runs a company."

These kinds of failures by liberal Democrats to seize the political fodder of conservatives, using emotion-protocols, Westen concludes, "are systematic, not incidental."[59]

Westin chronicles but does not explain a formative source of these endemic liberal political affective failures. In contrast, I can do so by using my third postulate about the American liberal moral mindset. For liberals:

Moral Values = Universal Laws (known through reason and empirically verifiable ideas about the natural world) + institutional procedures, policies, and practices that treat human beings (and the wider world) with dignity and respect so that human life on earth not only survives but also flourishes.

This postulate explains the consequences of the back-away move by nineteenth-century liberal Christians who did not replace the affective-organizing value system left behind: the "easy" Protestant conscience. The heirs to these nineteenth-century forebears are American liberals today.

And thus the result is that liberal moral value reasoning does not parse the American heart. More precisely, liberal reasoning can't peer into the emotional heart of a political issue. Why? The liberals Westen dealt with and observed, for example, had collapsed the difference between emotions and ideas—and in the process left the emotions behind. The easy Protestant conscience was thus still operative here because the liberal strategy Westen repeatedly witnessed is what the American "easy conscience" does. It cannot understand and "experience ... the claims and counter-claims of man's social existence, either domestically or internationally"[60] in affective terms. The next examples illustrate this point in more specific detail.

The Second Example: The Lament of Andrei Cherny

Andrei Cherny, a writer and advisor for the presidential campaigns of both John Kerry and Al Gore, wrote a post-election op-ed essay, "Why We Lost," published by *The New York Times* on November 5, 2004. In it, Cherny declared that Democrats lacked "a clear sense of what the party stands for."

According to Cherny: "What we don't have, what we sorely need, is what President George H. W. Bush so famously called '*the vision thing*'—a worldview that makes a thematic argument about where America is headed and where we want to take it."

And like most liberals, Cherny seemed clueless about how to find this so-called vision thing. And so his confession continued:

> I don't pretend to know exactly what the party should do now. But I do know we better start answering some important questions. What is our economic vision in a globalized world? How do we respond to the desire of many Americans to have choices and decision-making power of their own? How can we speak to Americans' moral and spiritual yearnings? ... Long after midnight in November 2000, I stood in the rain in Nashville and listened to the Gore campaign chairman, William Daley, tell us there would be no victory speech. On Wednesday, long after midnight, I stood in the rain in Boston listening to John Edwards tell us the same thing. I'm sick of standing in the rain."

Cherny was "standing in the rain" because he was looking for the wrong thing to give him shelter: reasoning, namely, (1) arguments, (2) the presentation of choices to stoke decision-making power, and (3) thematic arguments for the purpose of speaking to moral and spiritual yearnings.

The "yearnings" referred to by Cherny in the above passage, however, weren't about ideas. They were about human affections, triggered feelings, namely, emotions, desires, feelings, and affective needs, rather than ideas, logical arguments, and rational choices. But Cherny did not mention these feelings.

Thus the result was Cherny standing in the rain because he mistakenly thought that the Democratic problem was "the vision thing." It was actually "the affection thing." He could not find shelter because he was standing in the wrong place.

More precisely, what's missing in Cherny's essay are references to emotional strategies the brain can use to create an affective moral evaluation system. Liberals backed away from the system devised to handle and adjudicate such emotional states, namely, the common sense values of the nineteenth-century Protestant conscience. They turned instead to social reform agendas, to reiterate this crucially important point, without also establishing a new system designed to judge, mediate, and explain the affective content of American moral values.[61]

In Thomas Reid's terms, Cherny's behavior (and those of his liberal Democratic colleagues) defied common sense.[62] Standing in the rain and complaining about it is, in a word, nonsense.

The Third Example: Barack Obama's Low Emotional Thermostat

Four years before he became America's forty-fourth president, Barack Obama sounded like someone who could solve the emotion problem in liberal Democratic politics by returning the party to its affective religious moral values roots.

The December 19, 2004, *Newsweek* cover story on the new US Senator from Illinois seemed to make this point when it highlighted the case he made for a new liberal vision. The Democratic Party, Obama said, must "reconnect to ... roots in a moral imperative."

The *Newsweek* story claimed that although Obama stopped short of "calling for a 'religious left' [that would] counter the political power of the religious right," his manifest destiny for the Democratic Party was clear. Dig deep into liberalism's religious roots, Obama preached, and you will reach its moral vision. This work won't be hard to do, Obama insisted, because it's been done before—by Martin Luther King, Jr.; the abolitionists; and Catholic Worker Dorothy Day. "Most of the reform movements that have changed this country," Obama said, "have been grounded in religious models. We don't have to start from scratch." Obama, however, was not cited as also talking about the role of emotions embodied in such a moral vision, namely, an emotional capacity liberal Christians must now develop and hone.

Three years later, Senator Obama talked about his liberal vision and its Christian moral roots with *New York Times* columnist David Brooks. Brooks discovered this ongoing interest of Obama's when looking around for something to jump-start a lifeless interview—as Brooks put it—with a fatigued, political stump-wearied presidential candidate. Here's what happened next.

> Out of the blue I asked, "Have you ever read Reinhold Niebuhr?" Obama's tone changed. "I love him. He's one of my favorite philosophers." "So I asked, What do you take away from him?"
>
> "I take away," Obama answered in a rush of words, "the compelling idea that there's serious evil in the world, and hardship and pain. And we should be humble and modest in our belief we can eliminate those things. But we shouldn't use that as an excuse for cynicism and inaction. I take away … the sense we have to make these efforts knowing they are hard, and not swinging from naïve idealism to bitter realism."
>
> My first impression was that for a guy who's spent the last few months fund-raising, and who was walking off the Senate floor as he spoke, that's a pretty good off-the-cuff summary of Niebuhr's "The Irony of American History." My second impression is that his campaign is an attempt to thread the Niebuhrian needle, and it's really interesting to watch.[63]

But something significant went unmentioned in Brooks's April 26, 2007 account of their exchange. Neither Brooks nor Obama talked about Niebuhr's intense focus on the neglect of human emotions in American politics. Niebuhr, as earlier noted, called the use of reason unmoored from emotional intelligence the "easy conscience." This is the Protestant conscience that collapses the difference between thoughts and feelings. Obama, in effect, failed to understand that "evil, for Niebuhr, pertained to the inattention to the emotional protocols embedded in rational decisions. Obama thus flunked Niebuhr's own emotional intelligence test.

Journalists Carol E. Lee and John F. Harris pointed out Obama's affective deficiency in laymen's terms in their January 22, 2010 online *Politico* essay "Obama's First Year: What Went Wrong."

Obama mistakenly believed, Lee and Harris argued, that his election flagged a shift in American affections away from "George W. Bush's brash conservatism [and] Bill Clinton's tepid and defensive-minded progressivism." It didn't. Most Americans remained distrustful of government activism on things like bailouts, health care, and global warming.

Moreover, the internecine wars he set off within his own party while unemployment went up "meant that Obama spent the year bleeding momentum rather than steadily increasing public confidence in his larger governing vision."

But something more systemic was amiss, the journalists argued. Obama's belief in his ability to inspire folks through well-reasoned ideas and well-crafted words prevented him from seeing the emotional shift in America from 2008 to 2010. He was their hope in 2008. He was part of their problem two years later, Lee and Harris rightly concluded.

In classic Niebuhrian terms, Obama failed to recognize how his own emotions, vested interests, and loyalties had biased his political reasoning.

And thus the problem was this: Obama's "emotional thermostat," as Frank Rich put it in his June 5, 2010, *New York Times* column, was way too low. The source of this problem, Rich argued, is Obama's "unshakable confidence in the collective management brilliance of the best and the brightest he selected for his White House team" and also his default assumption that his peers are as well-intentioned as he.

Obama's former Defense Secretary, Leon Panetta, made a similar claim about Obama in *Worthy Warrior* as someone who too
often "relies on the logic of a law professor rather than the passion of a leader." A President needs the heart of a warrior, Panetta
insists, but this hasn't happened with Obama because he lacks the
ability to engage.

Obama, like most liberal Democrats, undervalued the role of
human affections in making policy decisions, in expressing moral
values, and thus in making common sense in the heartland of
American politics. He collapsed the difference between thoughts
and feelings in moral value formation. Affects were lost as unmoored ideas soared.

The result was that the "easy" Protestant conscience that conflates reason and emotions was in full force in Obama's presidency.
This is why Obama's own ability to understand and "experience
... the claims and counter-claims of man's social existence"[64] was
incapacitated. His political brain was not also an emotional brain.
This incapacity is the legacy of a liberal agenda that did not replace what was left behind: an emotional operating monitoring
system that creates affective values as the emotional content of
America's moral vision. The common sense conscience thus remained operative in liberal policies and protocols by default.

The next round of examples focuses on American political
leaders who actively affirm and use the affective content of the
moral value system created by the easy Protestant conscience.
Ideas and emotions are also conflated here. This time, however,
the dominant trait affirmed is not reason but the common sense
importance of moral feelings.

The Fourth Example: George W. Bush, America's First Common Sense King

When President George W. Bush proclaimed in his West Point
Address on June 3, 2002, that he knows—as does everyone else—
the absolute difference between right and wrong, he was applauded. Here's part of his speech with the applause interruptions
included:

Some worry that it is somehow undiplomatic or impo-
lite to speak the language of right and wrong. I disagree.
(Applause). Different circumstances require different meth-
ods, but not different moralities. (Applause.) *Moral truth is the
same in every culture, in every time, and in every place.* Targeting
innocent civilians for murder is always and everywhere
wrong. (Applause.) Brutality against women is always and
everywhere wrong. (Applause.) There can be no neutrality
between justice and cruelty, between the innocent and the
guilty. *We are in a conflict between good and evil, and America will
call evil by its name.* (Applause). By confronting evil and law-
less regimes, we do not create a problem, we reveal a problem. And we will lead the world in opposing it. (Applause)
(Emphasis added.)

Bush's judgment calls were not based on logic. Rather, their stay-
ing power was his religiousness as a born-again Christian. Bush
was using American Common Sense reasoning to affirm in secular terms the invincibility of his own Protestant moral judgments
and religious intuitions.

Bush's claim that "Moral truth is the same in every culture, in
every time, and in every place," for example, entailed the classic
common sense schematic:

Moral Values = God's Universal Laws (known as ideas)

So, too, did Bush's claim that "We are in a conflict between good
and evil, and America will call evil by its name" follow this schematic. His emotions are aligned with God's Laws, which are felt as
moral affections that occur because Christ has been with his bride,
the Christian conscience (Luther) or because this conscience is the
access point to direct knowledge of God's Laws (Calvin).

Bush has, in effect, equated human affections with a set of
God's divine attributes (God's Laws) and the Divine Presence of
Christ (in the conscience felt as the feeling of assurance). Or in the
tradition of Calvinist theology of the Puritans, Bush knows that
man's moral tendency is more than a cognitive faculty because

it pertains to feelings of fear, shame, remorse, and reverence for God.[65]

What liberals kept missing was that Bush was being religious in the core common sense secular way of the nineteenth-century secular Protestant conscience. While liberals spoke policy-talk, much of Protestant America resonated to the affective force of Bush's words, namely, his God-talk in the secular terms of nineteenth-century American common sense. Bush affirmed the moral values of the easy Protestant conscience that stoke and control human affections by removing the tension between what's felt and thought.

The Fifth Example: General Richard B. Myers, a Common Sense Warrior

General Richard B. Myers, the chairman of the Joint Chief of Staff from October 1984 to September 1985, used common sense moral valuation logic to dismiss accusations by the International Committee of the Red Cross that the tactics used in the American military's treatment of detainees at Guantánamo Bay, Cuba, was "tantamount to torture" (*New York Times*, December 1, 2004). Myers said he didn't think it was torture. He continued: "Let's not forget the kind of people we have down there." And he concluded: "These are people that don't know any moral values."

Think Thomas Reid here.[66] Persons have moral values or they don't have them. Period. Myers' logic was constructed by the common sense Protestant conscience. Reasoning with persons lacking a moral capacity, by Reid's common sense definition, is nonsense and thus a waste of time. So the only thing that can alter their behavior, so the reasoning seems to go for Myers, is pain and the only way to control the behavior is confinement. In short, Gitmo.[67]

The Sixth Example: The Reformicons, Tea Party Politicians, and Donald Trump

1. The Ethics and Public Policy Center (EPPC)—a preeminent conservative think tank in Washington—is a fine example of the emotions and logic of the common sense easy conscience at work in America today for three basic reasons.

First, Yuval Levin—the Hertog Fellow at EPPC and editor of its journal *The New Atlantis*—is regaled as "a one-man Republican brain-trust" (David Frum), and called "the pre-eminent conservative intellectual of the Obama era" (Jonathan Chait), as Sam Tanenhaus notes in his July 6, 2014, *New York Times Magazine* "Can the G.O.P. Be a Party of Ideas?" cover story on Levin. His Center's mission statement: EPPC is "dedicated to applying the Judeo-Christian moral tradition to critical issues of public policy."

Second, Levin, a former policy advisor to George W. Bush as well as founder and editor of *National Affairs* quarterly, believes that conservatives must back away from a "blinding nostalgia" for times long gone. "What's needed now is work on forming a thriving and appealing subculture, or network of subcultures." Christianity has a great deal of experience in this work, Levin says. But it's just not being practiced right now. Levin thus wants to clean up this act by putting traditional religious values back into practice using three basic principles of the Edmund Burke (the father of modern British-American conservatism)[68] tradition:

- A reliance upon God (traditional religious values)
- Strict allegiance to the US Constitution
- A resolute commitment to a moral vision of human nature that explains human emotions and keeps them in check through universal rules and values. (These rules, Levin argues, are first established by God and then articulated— incrementally—by the traditions of America's religious, cultural, and political founders and their moral heirs.)

Third, Levin's list (cited above) affirms, in the following ways, the Common Sense school of philosophy that made the Protestant conscience the secular religious referent for America's moral values. Like Reid, Levin affirms God as the universal Lawgiver. And like Reid, Levin also assesses human emotions using the measuring rod of universal God-given values without attending to their cultural biases.

The origins of such universal visions in America are the purview of the Protestant conscience in secular moral values terms. More generally, they are the purview, in Levin's words, of the Judeo-Christian God. Levin thus affirms the traditions of America's religious, cultural, and political moral enlightenment founders and their common sense moral heirs. In classic, Protestant terms, this tradition is moored in the secularized values of the Protestant conscience.

2. The Tea Party is a political party that, at heart, is a nineteenth-century Common Sense Christian movement writ large in twenty-first-century terms. Eighty-five per cent of its members—as the chief political correspondent for CBN (Christian Broadcasting Network) news David Brody notes in *The Teavangelicals: The Inside Story of How the Evangelicals and the Tea Party Are Taking Back America*—are "Bible-believing Christians [who want] a strict interpretation of the Constitution [and] focus on a crucial additional layer: all of these founding documents are rooted in a belief in Almighty God."[69]

Consider some of the rallying cries of these nineteenth-century troops in their twenty-first-century garb, as chronicled by Jonathan Weisman in his September 29, 2014, front page *New York Times* article headlined "House Hopefuls in G.O.P. Seek Rightward Shift."

- Ryan Zinke, a former Navy SEAL team member who seeks the House seat being vacated by its incumbent, called Hillary Rodham Clinton the Antichrist.
- Jody Hice, the radio host and Southern Baptist preacher who went after the House seat of Georgia's Paul Broun, believes that evolution is a lie from "the pit of hell" and he believes it is OK for a woman to enter politics today "if the woman's within the authority of her husband."

Reporter Weisman kicks off this story by chronicling more of these beliefs: "One nominee proposed reclassifying single parenthood as child abuse. Another ... said Islam was not a religion but a 'complete geopolitical structure' unworthy of tax exemption." This candidate also suggested that four "blood moons" would herald "world changing, shaking-type events."

These are the kinds of claims wrought by the Protestant conscience that equates religious ideas, religious feelings, and moral values and renders the religious other the antichrist. Or in the philosophic terms of Thomas Reid, they are persons without moral capacities.

3. Finally, the rise of Donald J. Trump in the 2016 US presidential race. Trump represents a disheartened white American populace. Trump did not create the toxic system of white voter anger, fear, rage, desperation and frustration that brought him to the forefront of American electoral politics in 2016. Rather, the toxic mix of aggrieved emotional passions in white Americans created him.

Trump simply cornered the political market on white men without a college education and white college-educated men who knew their prospects for advancement were tanking. Their suffering, as Trump affirmed, wasn't imagined but real.[70] Trump played on white fears of non-white outsiders and coyly cuddled his relationship with the unapologetically racist Ku Klux Klan.[71]

Trump, in effect, grabbed hold of white anger and fear, then drum rolled it to a swelling pitch that swept enraged whites into the streets as part of a right-wing, authoritarian political movement.

As *New York Times* reporters Patrick Healy and Maggie Haberman noted in their December 5, 2015, analysis of ninety-five thousand words spoken by Trump ("95,00 Words, Many of Them Ominous, From Donald Trump's Tongue"), the "specter of violence looms over much of his speech, which is infused with words like kill, destroy and fight."[72] Trump became America's new Common Sense King because he equated emotions with ideas and deemed those who opposed him demonic forces who must be battled in the streets, in politics, and by Christian and Judaic religious communities.

The Seventh Example: Stephen Bannon's 2014 Vatican Address

Consider the fourfold moral values affirmed by Stephen K. Bannon to get what's going on now. Bannon, as President Donald Trump's former chief strategist with, for a time, a full seat on the principals committee of the National Security Council,[73] laid out these four values in his 2014 speech at the Vatican:[74]

First, work.

Second, "Judeo-Christian capitalist values" that create wealth. Third, Christian worship.

Fourth, a Christian affirmation of the US Constitution as a document sanctioned by God.

Three of his four core values are expressed in Christian terms. Bannon, in effect, envisions and champions, as he puts, it a "global Tea Party movement" and he dismisses a term like "racism" as a label that won't "stick."

According to Bannon, the racist elements attracted to this movement "will all burn away over time and you'll see more of a mainstream center-right populist movement" that draws on an "'enlightened capitalism' of the Judeo-Christian West."

The Evangelical churches that support Tea Party candidates, as Brody so carefully documents, now constitute a network of co-ordinated religious communities that are a political force field in an otherwise vacant religious lot. They politically harness human affections in the name of Christ.

All of the liberal and conservative political examples presented here display a pervasive common sense American Protestant moral value system. This system uses the nineteenth-century, common sense hegemonic values of the Protestant conscience to explain twenty-first-century issues and concerns.

The result is that America's Protestant conscience has made human emotions difficult for most Americans to fathom, explain, or explore in terms that do not conflate feelings with Protestant lore. This "easy" conscience incapacitates the ability of Americans to understand and experience the claims and counter-claims of the social existence of persons and nations, either domestically or internationally.[75]

The easy, common sense Protestant conscience is the irony in America's moral values history then and now. This conscience not only fosters America's moral values and shapes its public policies, but it is also a major source of talk about "American exceptionalism," which describes the "terrible consequences" of what happens when America abandons "a strong military, strong alliances, strong international institutions, strong support for global development and democracy promotion," namely, its homegrown tools of internationalism.[76] A power vacuum appears on the world stage, so the argument goes, because America has retreated from its global role as *the* freedom fighter for democratic rights.[77]

This pervasive view of America heralded by mainstream liberals and conservatives is the vision of the unreconstructed Protestant conscience in America that can't discern the difference between its pious affections and its militarism at home and abroad.[78]

This conscience fosters America's moral values and shapes its public policies as America's reigning moral evaluation system.[79] More often than not, this mindset operates by eliminating the difference between what is felt and thought. As a consequence, it monitors, assesses, and judges human behavior without a sustained ability for empathy, compassion, or love.

The Rev. Dr. Martin Luther King, Jr. tried to make a similar point in 1967 at the Riverside Church in Upper Manhattan by leveling, as David J. Garrow notes in his astute April 4, 2017 *New York Times* op-ed essay, "When Martin Luther King Came Out Against Vietnam," a blistering attack on the American war in Vietnam, comparing American military actions to those of the Nazis during World War II. King was vilified across the political spectrum. Chronic domestic poverty and military adventurism overseas, King insisted, are as deeply endemic in America as its racism.[80] Liberals and conservatives, as Garrow pointed out, skewered King. Both sides could do so because the same common sense "easy" conscience was operative.

Part Four
Contemporary Affect Theology

A New Constructive Theology for Spiritual but Not Religious Souls

America's twenty-three million spiritual but not religious people are setting aside the Protestant conscience from their secular minds.

When atheists and humanists, for example, talk about their personal spiritual experiences of "the uplifting of the human spirit," they do so without referring to "a god." [81] Or when they affirm their prayer life as "the equivalent of a highly versatile, always reliable, perfectly legal, free, nonphysical addictive or intoxicating drug,"[82] they are talking about their personal experiences by redefining the religious term "prayer" in a nonreligious way. They thus maintain the difference between what they feel (spiritual uplift) and what they think by not making religious claims.

The common ground of these spiritual but not religious examples is the attempt to maintain the difference between affective states and conceptual truth claims.

Consider the Not-Church people who gather together in Northern Baja California for services in their "Not Church" sanctuary. They create their own ways of avoiding religious terms. According to Erin Dunigan, an ordained Presbyterian evangelist who serves as the spiritual leader and chaplain for these "Not Church"[84] folk, the work is experimental.

> [W]e ... realize that there are many, like ourselves, who are seeking something more—whether we call that God, love, or that in which we live and breathe and have our being. We realize that language and dogma have often gotten in the way of being able to encounter that "something more." So, we are an experiment, in a sense, to see what happens when a very diverse group of people is able to enter into this journey together.

These "Not Church" folk talk about a "something more" to describe an encounter that exceeds religious beliefs. They have cleared their minds of all religious ideas. And their minds, thanks to their communal service, become a gateway to something beyond the reach of religious ideas, something that exalts their feelings and transforms the emotional fiber of their lives. They become spiritual pioneers in an unchartered terrain.

Can the spiritual insights of Americans like the "Not-Church" folk serve as the common ground for a new set of moral values in secular America? Will these values be deeper and more original to Christian faith than the easy Protestant conscience? And if so, will America's spiritual but not religious leaders be the new priests in secular congregations millions upon millions strong? Will these congregations, networked together, launch a new spiritual era in American moral consciousness and behavior because they have found the lost emotional foundation of Christian faith, a foundation that is not Christian, but strictly speaking is and remains spiritual?

The various formulae laid out in this chapter seem to make one answer to these questions evident. Spiritual but not religious Americans need contemporary affective theological analysis to explain their spiritual experiences in nonreligious spiritual terms. Such a strategy can help them remember not to collapse the difference between thoughts and feelings, but rather to expand that difference until they feel the infinite universe incarnating itself affectively in the moments of their lives. They cannot build such a vocabulary by drawing on the experiences of the Protestant conscience and the liberal and conservative moral values systems linked to it.

Two things must be kept in mind here. First, if spiritual but not religious Americans want more access to spiritual feelings of wellbeing, they will have to create secular congregations that celebrate these feelings without reducing or explaining the experiences in religious terms.

Second, the need for such communities is evident. Millennials are five times more likely than other Americans to self-identify as suffering from a "great deal of stress."[85] And they want "emotional rescue."[86] (They are often referred to as *Generation Rx* because so many of them eat "prescription drugs like candy".)[87] In five years, they will make up almost half (46 percent) of America's workforce. Following current trends, this workforce could become disaffected and dangerous.

Moreover, a third of Americans under thirty do not go to church or to other religious institutions. As a 2010/2011 Gallup poll discovered, "Americans who are the most religious have the highest levels of wellbeing." Religion in principle "provides mechanisms for coping with setbacks and life's problems, which in turn may reduce stress, worry, and anger." If churches do not provide attention and support to these emotional needs, they tank and the religion "consumers" go elsewhere.

Millennials thus need secular sanctuaries but they lack access to places that can spiritually rescue them. Mainline churches, on the other hand, have the sanctuaries for this kind of work. What they do not have are the programs or the leaders to inspire and empower.

Millennials and mainline churchgoers, however, tend to share a similar progressive political bent of mind. Mainline Christian churchgoers tend to affirm the big government principles of American liberalism. So, too, do a great many Millennials. They "tilt left."[88]

Can spiritual leaders create new "secular" congregations in mainline sanctuaries if they develop a vocabulary to talk about what they have found: ultimate care, namely, a love beyond belief that exceeds religion's reach? Can they help create a moral valuation system based on these experiences?

Three things must be kept in mind for this kind of work.

1. *The Individual's Personal Experience of a Change of Heart*: Congregants should feel better by the end of the service than they felt before the service began so that they have new energy to handle the struggles, difficulties, trials, and triumphs in their lives with wholehearted spiritual and moral integrity.

2. *The Congregation's Liturgical Template*: An ethos of care and compassion should be created liturgically within the sanctuary through music, song, and other practices that support and encourage uplifting experiences of a change of heart within the gathered community. Music should compose at least half of each service.

3. *The Spoken Word*: Narratives, poetry, and more that support and affirm personal and congregational experiences of transformed hearts. The wisdom traditions of humanity can be used here to affirm experiences of love beyond belief as a spiritual experience and a moral value system.

Spiritual but not religious Americans constitute the fastest growing demographic in the country in religion surveys. If these Americans create secular congregations for themselves and network them together, can they launch a new progressive era in American moral values? And can they do so by replacing what the Protestant conscience blocked from sight: affective states that resonate with infinite life as the access point to cosmic consciousness?

Can spiritual leaders be trained for this movement of Love Beyond Belief secular congregations? Can mainline congregations become Love Beyond Belief religious churches in which authentic spiritual experience of the God of love is found?[89] Yes!

The first step has been taken by presenting the historical and emotional contexts for such work in *Love Beyond Belief* secular and religious congregations.

Bibliography

Ascough, Richard S. "Social and Political Characteristics of Greco-Roman Association Meals." In *Meals in the Early Christian World: Social Formation, Experimentation, and Conflict at the Table*. Ed. Dennis E. Smith and Hal Taussig. New York: Palgrave MacMillan, 2012.

Andrejč, Gorazd. "Bridging the gap between social and existential-mystical interpretations of Schleiermacher's 'feeling.'" *Religious Studies* (September 3, 2012): 377–401.

Apuzzo, Matt, Sheri Fink, and James Risen. "U.S. Torture Leaves a Legacy of Detainees With Damaged Minds" (October 9, 2016), *The New York Times*.

Augustine. *Retractationes (Retractions)*. Ed. A. Mutzenbecher. CCSL, 1984. Reprinted 2003.

——. *Confessions*. Trans. William Watts. Cambridge: Harvard University Press, Vols. 26 and 27, reprinted 1999.

——. *"The Confessions": Saint Augustine*, trans. Maria Boulding, O.S.B. New York: A Vintage Spiritual Classics, 1997.

——. "Sermon 90A." In *The Complete Works of St. Augustine: A Translation for the Twenty-First Century. Sermons III/I: Newly Discovered Sermons.*, Trans. Edmund Hill. Hyde Park, New York: New City Press, 1990.

Balibar, Étienne. "Is There a 'Neo-Racism.'" In *Race, Nation, Class: Ambiguous Identities*, trans. Chris Turner. London: Verso, 1991.

Bannon, Stephen K. 2014 Vatican speech and commentary: https://www.buzzfeed.com/lesterfeder/this-is-how-steve-bannon-sees-the-entire-world?utm_term=.px23276Ee#.glyKBjyN3. Accessed January 30, 2017.

Barclay, J. M. G. "Introduction: Diaspora Negotiations," in Barclay, ed., *Negotiating Diaspora*. London and New York: T. & T. Clark International, 2004.

——. "Using and Refusing. Jewish Identity Strategies under the Hegemony of Hellenism." In *Ethos und Identität, Einheit und Vielfalt des Judentums in hellenistisch-römischewr Zeit*. Edited by M. Konradt and U. Steinert. Paderborn: Schöningh, 2002.

Barth, Karl. "The Christian Faith." In *The Theology of Schleiermacher: Lectures at Göttingen, Winter Semester of 1923–24*. Ed. Dietrich Ritschl. Trans. Geogrey W. Bromiley. Grand Rapids, MI.: Eerdmans, 1982.

——. *Evangelical Theology: An Introduction*. New York: Holt, Rinehart and Winston, 1963.

——. *Protestant Thought: From Rousseau to Ritschl*. New York: Harper, 1959.

——. *This Christian Cause (A Letter to Great Britain from Switzerland)*. New York: MacMillan, 1941.

——. "Das Wort Gottes als Aufgabe der Theologie." In *Vorträge und kleinere Arbeiten, 1922–25*. Hoger Finze, ed. Zurich: TVZ 1990.

Barth, Ulrich. *Christentum und Selbstbewußtsein*. Göttingen: Vandenhöck & Ruprecht, 1983.

Baylor, Michael G. *Action and Person: Conscience in Late Scholasticism and the Young Luther.* Leiden: E. J. Brill, 1977.

Beck, James R. *The Psychology of Paul: A Fresh Look at His Life and Teachings.* Grand Rapids, MI: Kregel Publications, 2002.

Beckworth, David. "Praying for Recession: The Business Cycle and Protestant Religiosity in the United States." *https://papers.ssrn.com/sol3/papers. cfm?abstract_id=1103142.* Accessed February 21, 2018.

Bennett, William. "The Moral Origins of the Urban Crisis." In *Backward and Upward: The New Conservative Writing.* Edited by David Brooks. New York: Vintage Books, 1996.

Bercovitch, Sacvan. *The Puritan Origins of the American Self.* New Haven: Yale University Press, 1975.

Bernecker, Karl. *Kritische Darstellung der Geschichte des Affektbegriffes (Von Descartes bis zur Gegenwart), Inaugural-Dissertation zur Erlangung der philosophischen Fakultät der Königlichen Universität Greifswald.* Berlin: Druck von Otto Godemann, 1915.

Billing, Einar. *Our Calling.* Philadelphia: Fortress Press, 1947.

Blackwell, Albert L. "The Role of Music in Schleiermacher's Writings." In *Internationaler Schleiermacher Kongreß Berlin 1984,* vol 1.1. Ed. Kurt-Victor Selge. Berlin: Walter de Gruyter, 1985.

Boersch, Ekkehard. "Zur Entstehung der 'Weihnachtsfeier' von Friedrich Schleiermacher." In *Theologische Zeitschrift* 13 (1957): 355–56.

Bosman, Philip. *Conscience in Philo and Paul: A Conceptual History of the Synoida Word Group.* Tübingen: Mohr Siebeck, 2003.

Bosman, Philip. "Why Conscience Makes Cowards of Us All: A Classical Perspective." *Acta Classica* 40 (1997): 270–1.

Boyarin, Daniel. *Border Lines: The Partition of Judaeo-Christianity.* Philadelphia: University of Pennsylvania Press, 2004.

——. *A Radical Jew: Paul and the Politics of Identity.* Berkeley: University of California Press, 1994.

Brandt, James M. *All Things New: Reform of Church and Society in Schleiermacher's Christian Ethics.* Louisville: Westminster John Knox Press, 2001.

Brodkin, Karen. *How Jews Became White Folks: And What that Says about Race in America.* New Brunswick, NJ: Rutgers University Press, 2000.

Brody, David. *The Teavangelicals: The Inside Story of How the Evangelicals and the Tea Party Are Taking Back America.* Grand Rapids, MI: Zondervan, 2012.

Brown, Peter. *Augustine of Hippo: A Biography.* Berkeley: University of California, 2000.

Bucke, Richard Maurice. *Cosmic Consciousness: A Study in the Evolution of the Human Mind.* Mineola, NY: Dover Publications, Inc, 2009.

Buelow, George J. "Johann Mattheson and the Invention of the Affektenlehre." Pp. 393–407 in *New Mattheson Studies.* Ed. George J. Buelow and Hans Joachim Marx. Cambridge: Cambridge University Press, 1983.

Bultmann, Rudolf. *Theology of the New Testament. Vol. II.* New York: Charles Scribner's Sons, 1955.

Cage, John. *Silence.* Cambridge: The M.I.T. Press, 1961.

Callan, Terrance. *Psychological Perspectives on the Life of Paul: An Application of the Methodology of Gerd Theissen.* Lewiston: The Edwin Mellen Press, 1990.

Capps, Donald. "Augustine as Narcissist: Of Grandiosity and Shame." In *The Hunger of the Heart: Reflections on the Confessions of Augustine.* Ed. Donald Capps and James E. Dittes. West Lafayette, IN: Society for the Scientific Study of Religion, 1990.

Cobb, John Jr. *Spiritual Bankruptcy: A Prophetic Call to Action*. Nashville: Abingdon Press, 2010.

Collins, Raymond F. *First Corinthians*. Sacra Pagina Series Volume 7. Ed. Daniel J. Harrington, S.J. Collegeville, MN: A. Michael Glazier, 1999.

Collins, John J. *Jewish Cult and Hellenistic Culture: Essays on the Jewish Encounter with Hellenism and Roman Rule*. Leiden: Brill, 2005.

Crouter, Richard, ed. *On Religion: Speeches to Its Cultured Despisers*. English translation of the 1799 first edition of *Über die Religion*. Cambridge: Cambridge University Press, 1998.

Damasio, Antonio. *Descartes' Error: Emotion, Reason and the Human Brain*. London: Vintage, 2000.

——. *The Feeling of What Happens: Body and Emotion in the Making of Consciousness*. San Diego: Harcourt Inc, 1999.

Davies, W. D. "Conscience." In *The Interpreter's Dictionary of the Bible*. Vol. 1. Nashville: Abingdon Press, 1962.

——. *Paul and Rabbinic Judaism: Some Rabbinic Elements in Pauline Theology*. London: SPCK, 1955.

Demos, E. Virginia. "Affect and the Development of the Self: A New Frontier." In *Frontiers in Self Psychology: Progress in Self Psychology*, Vol. 3. Ed. Arnold Goldberg. Hillsdate, NJ: The Analytic Press, 1988.

——. "Empathy and Affect: Reflections on Infant Experience." In *Empathy II*. Ed. Joseph Lichtenberg, Melvin Bornstein, Donald Silver. Hillsdale, NJ: The Analytic Press, 1984.

Dilthey, Wilhelm. *Aus Schleiermacher's Leben*. Berlin: Georg Reimer, 1860.

Dixon, Sandra Lee. *Augustine: The Scattered and Gathered Self*. St. Louis: Chalice Press, 1999.

Dorrien, Gary. "Introduction." In *The Making of American Liberal Theology: Crisis, Irony, and Postmodernity, 1950–2005*. Louisville: Westminster John Knox Press, 2006.

Dowey, Edwards A., Jr. *The Knowledge of God in Calvin's Theology*. Grand Rapids, Michigan: William B. Eerdmans Publishing Co, 1994.

Duke, James O., ed. *Christian Caring: Selections from Practical Theology*. Trans. James O. Duke and Howard Stone. Philadelphia: Fortress Press, 1988.

Dülon, Friedrich Ludwig. *Dülons des blinden Floetenspielers Leben und Meynungen von ihm selbst bearbeitet*. Ed. C. M. Wieland. Zurich, 1807–8.

Ebeling, Gerhard. *Luther: An Introduction to his Thought*. Philadelphia: Fortress Press, 1972.

Eckstein, Hans-Joachim. *Der Begriff Syneidesis bei Paulus: Eine heustestamentlich-exegetische Untersuchung zum, Gewissensbegriff*. Tübingen: J. C. B. Mohr (Paul Siebeck), 1983.

Epstein, Greg M. *Good Without God: What a Billion Nonreligious People Do Believe*. New York: Harper, 2009.

Firchow, Peter. *Friedrich Schlegel's "Lucinde" and the Fragments*. Minneapolis: University of Minnesota Press, 1971.

Fisher, Max. "Measuring Action Against a Government Already Under Siege." *New York Times* (April 8, 2017).

Fisher, Max, and Amanda Taub. "Syrian War Magnifies Tension in America's Global Mission." *The New York Times* (April 7, 2017).

Fitzgerald, Frances. *The Evangelicals: The Struggle to Shape America*. New York: Simon & Schuster, 2017.

Flusser, David. "A New Sensitivity in Judaism and The Christian Message." *Harvard Theological Review* 61,2 (April 1968): 107–27.

Fredriksen, Paula. *Jesus of Nazareth, King of the Jews: A Jewish Life and the Emergence of Christianity*. New York: First Vintage Books, 2000.

———. "Paul and Augustine: Conversion Narratives, Orthodox Traditions, and the Retrospective Self." In *Journal of Theological Studies* (1986): 3–34.

———. "Augustine and his Analysts: The Possibility of a Psychohistory." *Soundings* 57 (1978): 207–27.

Fox, Robin Lane. *Augustine: Conversions to Confessions*. New York: Basic Books, 2015.

Gager, John, G. *Reinventing Paul*. Oxford: Oxford University Press, 2002.

———. *The Origins of Anti-Semitism: Attitudes Toward Judaism in Pagan and Christian Antiquity*. Oxford: Oxford University Press, 1985.

Garrow, David J. "When Martin Luther King Came Out Against Vietnam." *New York Times* (April 4, 2017).

Gaston, Lloyd. *Paul and the Torah*. Eugene, OR: Wipf & Stock Publishers, 2006.

Gay, Volney. "Augustine: The Reader as Selfobject." In *The Hunger of the Heart: Reflections on the Confessions of Augustine*. Ed. Donald Capps and James E. Dittes. West Lafayette, IN: Society for the Scientific Study of Religion, 1990.

———. "Augustine: The Reader as Selfobject." *Journal for the Scientific Study of Religion* 21,1 (March 1986): 64–76.

Gerrish, B. A. *Grace and Reason: A Study in the Theology of Luther*. Oxford: Clarendon Press, 1962.

Gilson, Étienne. *The Christian Philosophy of Saint Augustine*. Trans. L. E. M. Lynch. New York: Random House, 1960.

Goldberg, Arnold. *Being of Two Minds: The Vertical Split in Psychoanalysis and Psychotherapy*. Hillsdale, NJ: The Analytic Press, 1999.

Goldstein, Saiving. "The Human Situation: A Feminine View." *Journal of Religion* 40,2 (April 1960): 100–12.

Gorday, Peter. *Principles of Patristic Exegesis: Romans 9–11 in Origin, John Chrysostom, and Augustine*. New York: The Edwin Mellen Press, 1983.

Guenther-Gleason, Patricia. "Schleiermacher's Feminist Impulses in the Context of His Later Work." In *Schleiermacher and Feminism: Sources, Evaluations, and Responses*. Ed. Iain G. Nicol. Lewiston, NY: The Edwin Mellen Press, 1992.

Harland, Philip A. *Associations, Synagogues, and Congregations: Claiming a Place in Ancient Mediterranean Society*. Minneapolis: Fortress Press, 2003.

Han, Shihui, and Georg Northoff. "Understanding the Self: A Cultural Neuroscience Approach." In *Progress in Brain Research* 178 (2009): 203–12.

Harrison, Carol. *Augustine: Christian Truth and Fractured Humanity*. Oxford: Oxford University Press, 2000.

Hempton, David. *Methodism: Empire of the Spirit*. New Haven: Yale University Press, 2005.

Herdt, Gilbert. *Sambia Sexual Culture: Essays from the Field*. Chicago: University of Chicago Press, 1999.

Hermann, Rudolf. *Luthers Theologie, Gesammelte und nachgelassene Werke*. Göttingen: Vandenhoeck & Ruprecht, 1967.

Herzog, Frederick. *European Pietism Reviewed*. San Jose, California: Pickwick Publications, 2003.

Heyward, Carter. "We're Here, We're Queer: Teaching Sex in Seminary." Pp. 78–96 in *Body and Soul: Rethinking Sexuality as Justice-Love*. Ed. Marvin M. Ellison and Sylvia Thorson-Smith. Cleveland: Pilgrim Press, 2003.

Hillesum, Etty. *An Interrupted Life the Dairies, 1941–1943, and Letters from Westerbork*. New York: Henry Holt and Company, Inc, 1996.

Himmelfarb, Gertrude. *The Road to Modernity: The British, French, and American Enlightenments*. New York: First Vintage Books Edition, 2005.

Hirsch, Emmanuel. *Lutherstudien*. Vol. 1. Gütersloh: C. Berterlsmann, 1954.

Hodge, Caroline Johnson. *If Sons, Then Heirs: A Study of Kinship and Ethnicity in the Letters of Paul*. Oxford: Oxford University Press, 2007.

Holl, Karl. *What Did Luther Understand by Religion?* Eds. James Luther Adams and Walter F. Bense. Trans. Fred W. Meuser and Walter R. Wietzke. Philadelphia: Fortress Press, 1977.

Howard, Thomas Albert. *Protestant Theology and the Making of the Modern German University*. Oxford: Oxford University Press, 2006.

Howe, David. *The Unitarian Conscience: Harvard Moral Philosophy, 1805–1861*. Middletown, CT: Wesleyan University Press, 1988.

Hunter, James Davison. *Culture Wars: The Struggle to Define America*. New York: BasicBooks, 1991.

——. *American Evangelicalism: Conservative Religion and the Quandary of Modernity*. New Brunswick, NJ: Rutgers University Press, 1983.

James, William. *The Varieties of Religious Experience*. Cambridge: Harvard University Press, 1985.

Jewett, R. *Paul's Anthropological Terms: A Study of their Use in Conflicting Settings*. Leiden: Brill, 1971.

Joest, Wilfried. *Ontologie der Person bei Luther*. Göttingen: Vandenhoeck & Ruprecht, 1967.

Jones, Robert P. "White Christian America ... has died." *The End of White Christian America*. Simon and Schuster, 2016.

Josephus. *Jewish Antiquities, The Complete Works of Josephus*, trans. William Whiston. Grand Rapids, MI: Dregel Publications, 1999.

——. "The Jewish War." In *The New Complete Works of Josephus*. Trans. William Whiston. Commentary by Paul L. Maier. Grand Rapids, MI: Kregel Publications, 1999.

Kavanagh, Aidan. *On Liturgical Theology*. Collegeville, Minnesota: A Pueblo Book, 1984.

Kirk, Russell. *The Conservative Mind: From Burke to Eliot*. Abridged by Aaron McLeod. Birmingham, Alabama: The Alabama Policy Institute, 2005.

Klinghardt, Matthias. "A Typology of Communal Meals." In *Meals in the Early Christian World: Social Formation, Experimentation, and Conflict at the Table*. Ed. Dennis E. Smith and Hal Taussig. New York: Palgrave MacMillan, 2012.

Kristol, William. "A Conservative Looks at Liberalism." In *Backward and Upward: The New Conservative Writing*. Ed. David Brooks. New York: Vintage Books, 1996.

Lee, Carol E. and John F. Harris. "Obama's First Year: What Went Wrong." *Politico* (Pavia, Italy) (January 2010): 22.

Leith, John H., ed. *Creeds of the Churches: A Reader in Western Christian Doctrine from the Bible to the Present*. 3rd ed. Atlanta: John Knox Press, 1982.

Levine, Amy-Jill. *The Misunderstood Jew: The Church and the Scandal of the Jewish Jesus*. New York: HarperCollins, 2006.

Levy, Sanford S. "Thomas Reid's Defense." In *History of Philosophy Quarterly* 16 (October 1999): 413–35.

Lohse, Bernhard. *A Short History of Christian Doctrine: From the First Century to the Present*. Philadelphia: Fortress Press, 1978.

——. "Conscience and Authority in Luther." In *Luther and the Dawn of the Modern Era*. Ed. Heiko A. Oberman. Leiden: E.J. Brill, 1974.

Luther, Martin. "An Open Letter on the Harsh Book Against the Peasants: 1525." In *Luther's Works*, Vol. 46. Eds. Helmut T. Lehmann and Robert T. Schultz. Philadelphia: Fortress Press, 1967.

———. "Admonition to Peace: A Reply to the Twelve Articles of the Peasants in Swabia: 1525." In *Luther's Works*, Vol. 46. Eds. Helmut T. Lehmann and Robert T. Schultz. Philadelphia: Fortress Press, 1967.

———. "Against the Robbing and Murdering Hordes of Peasants: 1525." Trans. Charles M. Jacobs. Revised by Robert C. Schultz. In *Luther's Works*, Vol. 46. Ed. Robert C. Schultz. Philadelphia: Fortress Press, 1967.

———. "On the Jews and Their Lies," 1543, *Luther's Works*, Vol. 47. Excerpts from this text can be found at the following website address: http://www.jewishvirtuallibrary.org/jsource/anti-semitism/Luther_on_Jews.html. Accessed August 21, 2016.

———. *Lectures on Galatians (1535)*, Chapters 1–4 in *Luther's Works*. Volume 26. Ed. Jaraslov Pelikan. Saint Louis: Concordia Publishing House, 1963.

———. "Ninety-five Theses or Disputation on the Power and Efficacy of Indulgences" http://www.stpaulserie.org/95%20Theses.pdf Accessed August 20, 2016.

———. "Secular Authority: To What Extend It Should Be Obeyed." In *Martin Luther: Selections From His Writings*. Ed. John Dillenberger. New York: Anchor Books, 1961.

Marietta, Don E., Jr. "Conscience in Greek Stoicism." In *Numen* 17,3 (Dec. 1970): 176–87.

Massey, Marilyn Chapin. *Feminine Soul: The Fate of an Ideal*. Boston: Beacon Press, 1985.

Meckenstock, Günter, ed. 1831 edition of *Über die Religion: Reden an die Gebildeten unter ihren Verächtern*. In *Schleiermacher*. Ed. Kritische Gesamtausgabe. Berlin: Walter de Gruyter, 1995.

Merton, Thomas. *Mystics and Zen Masters*. New York: Noonday Press, 1967.

Metaxas, Eric. *Bonhoeffer: Pastor, Martyr, Prophet, Spy*. Nashville: Thomas Nelson, 2010.

Mikulincer, Mario, Phillip R Shaver, Omri Gillath, and Rachel A Nitzberg. "Attachment, caregiving, and altruism: Boosting attachment security increases compassion and helping." *Journal of Personality and Social Psychology* 89,5 (Nov 2005): 817–39.

Miles, Margaret. *Desire and Delight: A New Reading of Augustine's Confessions*. New York: Crossroads, 1992.

Miller, Leta E. "C. P. E. Bach and Friedrich Ludwig Dülon: Composition and Improvisation in Late 18th-century Germany." *Early Music* 23,1 (Feb 1995): 65–81.

Moore, George Foote. *Judaism in the First Centuries of the Christian Era*. Vol. 1. New York: Schocken Books, 1971.

Murphy, Lawrence S. J. "Martin Luther, the Erfurt Cloister, and Gabriel Biel: the Relation of Philosophy to Theology" (Archiv für Reformationsgeschichte - Archive for Reformation History Volume, 70, Issue jg, Dec 1979: http://www.degruyter.com/view/j/arg.1979.70.issue-jg/arg-1979-jg01/arg-1979-jg01.xml).

Nanos, Mark D. *Reading Paul Within Judaism*. Eugene, OR: Cascade Books, 2017.

Narvaez, Darcia. "The Individual, Relational and Social Neurobiological Development of Morality." In *After You. The Ethics of The Pastoral Counseling Process*. Ed. M. Rieslagh, R. Burggraeve, J. Corveleyn, and A. Liégeois. Leuven, Belgium: Bibliotheca Ephemeridum Theologicarum Lovaniensium, 2013.

Narvaez, Darcia and Tracy R. Gleason. "Developmental Optimization." In *Evolution, Early Experience and Human Development: From Research to Practice and Policy*. Eds. Darcia Narvaez, Jaak Panksepp, Allan N. Schore, and Tracy R. Gleason. New York: Oxford University Press, 2013.

Neusner, Jacob. *The Program of the Fathers According to Rabbi Nathan A.* Lanham: University of America, Inc, 2009.

———. *Building Blocks of Rabbinic Tradition: The Documentary Approach to the Study of Formative Judaism.* Lanham: University Press of America, Inc., 2008.

———. *The Systemic Analysis of Judaism.* Atlanta: Scholars Press, 1988.

———. *Vanquished Nation, Broken Spirit: The Virtues of the Heart in Formative Judaism.* Cambridge: Cambridge University Press, 1987.

———. *Early Rabbinic Judaism: Historical Studies in Religion, Literature, and Art.* Leiden: E. J. Brill, 1975.

———. "Two Pictures of the Pharisees: Philosophical Circle or Eating Club." *Anglican Theological Review* 64 (1982): 525–38.

———. *Judaic Law From Jesus to the Mishnah: A Systematic Reply to Professor E. P. Sanders.* New York: Rowman & Littlefield, 1993.

Neusner, Jacob, and Bruce Chilton. *The Intellectual Foundations of Christian and Jewish Discourse: The Philosophy of Religious Argument.* London: Routledge, 1997.

Niebuhr, Reinhold. *The Nature and Destiny of Man: Volume One—Human Nature.* New York: Charles Scribner's Sons, 1964.

———. *The Irony of American History.* New York: Charles Scribner's Sons, 1952.

O'Connell, Robert J. "The *Confessions* at Cassiciacum." Pp. 259–309 in *Images of Conversion in St. Augustine's Confessions.* New York: Fordham University Press, 1996.

O'Daly, Gerard. *Augustine's Philosophy of Mind.* Berkeley: University of California Press, 1987.

Oberman, Heiko A. *The Two Reformations: The Journey from the Last Days to the New World.* Ed. Donald Weinstein. New Haven: Yale University Press, 2003.

———. *The Harvest of Medieval Theology.* Cambridge: Harvard University Press, 1963.

Oman, John. *On Religion: Speeches to Its Cultured Despisers.* English translation of the 1821 edition of *Über die Religion.* New York: Harper Torchbooks, 1958.

Pagels, Elaine. *Adam, Eve, and the Serpent.* New York: Random House, 1988.

Panksepp, Jaak. "'A Synopsis of Affective Neurosis,' The Philosophical Implications of Affective Neuroscience." *Journal of Consciousness Studies* 19,3–4 (2012): 6–48.

———. "A Synopsis of Affective Neuroscience—Naturalizing the Mammalian Mind." *The Philosophical Implications of Affective Neuroscience Cognitive Science Society.* Jaak Panksepp, Stephen Asma, Glennon Curran, Rami Gabriel & Thomas Greif. Cognitive Science Society (CogSci10), Portland, Oregon, 12 August *2010.*

———. *Affective Neuroscience: The Foundations of Human and Animal Emotions.* New York: Oxford University Press, 1998.

Panksepp, Jaak, and Georg Northoff. "The trans-species core SELF: The emergence of active cultural and neuro-ecological agents through self-related processing within subcortical-cortical midline networks." Journal homepage: www.elsevier.com/licate/concog. *Consciousness and Cognition* 18,1 (Mar 2009): 193–215.

Pierce, C. A. *Conscience in the New Testament.* Chicago: Alec R. Allenson, Inc., 1955.

Pies, Ronald W. *The Ethics of the Sages: An Interfaith Commentary on Pirkei Avot.* Northvale, NJ: Jason Aronson Inc., 2000.

Porter, Frank Chamberlin. *The Yeçer Hara: A Study in the Jewish Doctrine of Sin.* New York: Charles Scribner's Sons, 1902.

Porter, Stanley E., ed. *The Pauline Canon.* Leiden: Brill, 2004.

Proudfoot, Wayne. *Religious Experience.* Berkeley: University of California Press, 1985.

Redeker, Martin. *Schleiermacher: Life and Thought*. Trans. John Wallhausser. Philadelphia: Fortress Press, 1973.

Reid, Thomas. "On the Active Powers." In *Thomas Reid: Inquiry and Essays*. Ed. Ronald E. Beanblossom and Keith Lehner. Indianapolis: Hackett Publishing Company, Inc., 1983.

Rice, John A. "The Blind Dülon and His Magic Flute." *Music & Letters* 71,1 (Feb 1990): 25–51.

Richardson, Ruth Drucilla. *The Role of Women in the Life and Thought of the Early Schleiermacher (1768–1806): An Historical Overview*. Lewiston, NY: The Edwin Mellen Press, 1991.

Rosen-Zvi, Ishay. "Two Rabbinic Inclinations? Rethinking a Scholarly Dogma." *Journal for the Study of Judaism* 39 (2008) 1–27. www.brill.nl.jsj.

Rothert, Hans-Joachim, ed. *Über die Religion: Reden an die Gebildeten unter ihren Verächtern*. Hamburg: Felix Meiner, 1970.

Rousselle, Aline. *Porneia: On Desire and the Body in Antiquity*. Trans. Felicia Pheasant. Cambridge, MA: Blackwell, 1988.

Sadie, Julie Anne. "Johnann Mattheson." In *Companion to Baroque music*. Berkeley: University of California Press, 1990.

Samuelsson, Gunnar. *Crucifixion in Antiquity: An Inquiry into the Background of the New Testament Terminology of Crucifixion*. Götenborg, Sweden: University of Gothenburg, Department of Literature, History of Ideas and Religion, 2010.

Schechter, Solomon. *Some Aspects of Rabbinic Theology*. Kessinger Publishing@ Legacy Reprints, originally published in 1923.

Schleiermacher, Friedrich. *On Freedom*. Trans. Albert L. Blackwell. Lewiston, NY: The Edwin Mellen Press, 1992.

——. *On Religion: Speeches to its Cultured Despisers*. Ed. and Trans. Richard Crouter. Cambridge: Cambridge University Press, 1988.

——. *Über den Begriff der Kunst* (1831/32). Ed. Thomas Lehnerer. Hamburg: Felix Meiner Verlag, 1984.

——. *Sämmtliche Werke*. Berlin: G. Reimer, 1850. *Photomechanischer Nachdruck*. Berlin: Walter de Gruyter, 1983.

——. *On the Glaubenslehre: Two Letters to Dr. Lücke*. Trans. James Duke and Francis Fiorenza. Chicago: Scholars Press, 1981.

——. *Brouillon zur Ethik (1805/6)*. Ed. Hans-Joachim Birkner. Based on the edition of Otto Braun. Hamburg: Felix Meiner Verlag, 1981.

——. *Weihnaschtsfeier*. Ed. Hermann Mulert. Leipzig: Dürr'schen Buchhandlung, 1908.

——. *Über den Umfang des Begriffs der Kunst in Bezug auf die Theorie Derselben*, Anhang. Akademie-Abhandlungen, 1831/32.

——. *The life of Schleiermacher: As Unfolded in his Autobiography and Letters*. Vol. II. Trans. Frederica Rowan. London: Smith, Elder and Co., 1860.

——. *Die Praktische Theologie nach den Grundsaezen der evangelishchen Kirche im Zusammenhange dargestellt, Aus Schleiermachers handschriftlichen Nachlasse und nachgeschriebenen Vorlesungen*. Berlin, 1850.

——. *Ästhetik: Im Auftrage der Preußischen Akademie der Wissenschaften und der Literatur-Archiv-Gesellschaft zu Berlin nach den bisher unveöffentlichten Urschriften zum ersten Male herausgegeben*. Ed. Rudolf Odebrecht. Berlin, Leipzig, 1931.

Schofer, Jonathan Wyn. *Confronting Vulnerabilities: The Body and the Divine in Rabbinic Ethics*. Chicago: University of Chicago Press, 2010.

——. *The Making of a Sage: A Study in Rabbinic Ethics*. Madison: University of Wisconsin Press, 2005.

Scholtz, Gunter. *Ethik und Hermeneutik: Schleiermachers Grundlegung der Geisteswissenschaften*. Frankfurt: Suhrkamp, 1995.

———. *Schleiermachers Musikphilosophie*. Goettingen: Vandenhoeck & Ruprecht, 1981.

Schore, Allan N. *Affect Regulation and the Origin of the Self: The Neurobiology of Emotional Development*. Hillsdale, NJ: Lawrence Erlbaum Associates, 1994.

Schrage, W. *Der erste Brief an die Korinther*. 2 Teilb. (1 Kor. 1,1–6, 11; 2 Kor. 6, 12–11, 16). Düsseldorf: Benziger, 1991.

Schwartz, Seth. *Imperialism and Jewish Society from 2000 BCE to 640 CE*. Princeton, NJ: Princeton University Press, 2001.

Scrutton, Anastasia. "Emotion in Augustine of Hippo and Thomas Aquinas: A Way Forward for the Im/passibility Debate." *International Journal of Systematic Theology* 7,2 (April 2005): 169–77.

Siegfried, Theodor. *Luther und Kant ein Geistesgeschichtlicher Vergleich im Anschluss an den Gewissensbegriff*. Berlin: Walter de Gruyter, 1930.

Smith, Dennis. *Social and Political Characteristics of Greco-Roman Association Meals*. New York: Palgrave Macmillan, 2012.

Smith, Dennis E., and Hal Taussig, eds. *Meals in the Early Christian World: Social Formation, Experimentation, and Conflict at the Table*. New York, Palgrave MacMillan, 2012.

Smith, Preserved. *Luther's Table Talk: A Critical Study*. Thesis submitted in partial fulfillment of the requirements for the degree of Doctor of Divinity in the Faculty of Political Science, Columbia University, 1907.

Soskice, Janet Martin and Diana Lipton. "General Introduction." In *Feminism and Theology*. Oxford: Oxford University Press, 2003.

Stauffer, John. *The Black Hearts of Men: Radical Abolitionists and the Transformation of Race*. Cambridge: Harvard University Press, 2001.

Steinert, U., ed. *Ethos und Identität, Einheit und Vielfalt des Judentums in hellenistisch-römischewr Zeit*. Paderborn: Schöningh, 2002.

Stendahl, Krister. *Paul Among Jews and Gentiles and Other Essays*. Philadelphia: Fortress Press, 1976.

Stout, Hilary. "Oh, to Be Young, Millennial, and So Wanted by Marketers." New York Times (June 20, 2015) [http://www.nytimes.com/2015/06/21/business/media/marketers-fixation-on-the-millennial-generation.html?_r=0.] Accessed April 26, 2016.

Striker, Giesela. *Essays on Hellenistic Epistemology and Ethics*. Cambridge: Cambridge University Press, 1996.

Stuart, G. H. Cohen. *The Struggle in Man between Good and Evil: An Inquiry into the Origin of the Rabbinic Concept of Yeṣer Hara'*. Uitgeversmaatschappij J. H. Kok—Kampen, 1984.

Sumney, J. L. "Identifying Paul's Opponents: The Question of Method in 2 Corinthians" In Sheffield: *Journal for the Study of the Old Testament*, 1990: 69–73.

Taterta, Kelly. "Generation RX Eats Prescription Drugs Like Candy." *Millennial Magazine*, (January 27, 2016) [http://millennialmagazine.com/generation-rx-eats-prescription-drugs-like-candy/millennialmagazine.com]. [Accessed April 26, 2016.]

Taylor, Jill Bolte. *My Stroke of Insight: A Brain Scientist's Personal Journey*. New York: Viking, 2006.

Thandeka. "Future Designs for American Liberal Theology." *The American Journal of Theology and Philosophy* 30,1 (January 2009): 72–100.

———. "Schleiermacher's *Affekt* Theology," *The International Journal of Practical Theology* 9,2 (December 2005): 199.

———. "Ministering to Anxiety: Take Abortion, for Example." *Tikkun Magazine* 20,3 (2005): 19–21.

———. *Learning to Be White: Money, Race, and God in America.* (New York: Continuum, 1998), 28–37, *passim.*

———. *The Embodied Self: Friedrich Schleiermacher's Solution to Kant's Problem of the Empirical Self.* New York: New York State University Press, 1985.

Thandeka and Darcia Narvaez, "Neurobiology, Emotions and Faith: From White Self-Destruction to Healing through Contemporary Affect Theology," *Ethics: Contemporary Perspectives* 1:1 (in press).

Theissen, Gerd. *Psychological Aspects of Pauline Theology.* Trans. John P. Galvin. Philadelphia: Fortress Press, 1983.

Thompson, Derek. "Who are Donald Trump's supporters, really?" *The Atlantic* (March 1, 2016) http://www.theatlantic.com/politics/archive/2016/03/who-are-donald-trumps-supporters-really/471714/. Accessed April 17, 2016.

Tice, T. Terrence N. *Christmas Eve: Dialogue on the Incarnation.* Lewiston, NY: The Edwin Mellen Press, 1990.

Tillich, Paul. *Morality and Beyond.* New York: Harper & Row, 1963.

Tomson, Peter J. *Paul and the Jewish Law: Halakha in the Letters of the Apostle to the Gentiles.* Assen/Maastrich: Van Gorcum and Minneapolis: Fortress Press, 1990.

Van Voorst, Robert E. *Jesus Outside the New Testament: An Introduction to the Ancient Evidence.* Grand Rapids, MI: Eerdmans Publishing Company, 2000.

von Ranke, Leopold. *History of the Reformation in Germany.* Trans. Sarah Austin. Philadelphia: Lea and Blanchard, 1844. https://books.google.com/books?id=TMA8AAAAYAAJ&pg=PA93&lpg=PA93&dq=but+if+he+would+live+joyously+all+the+days+of+his+life,+then+let+him+turn+priest.&source=bl&ots=rrFka2jvpF&sig=9_5lJeBPJTFjCy-QRaJCdXLkesc&hl=en&sa=X&ved=0ahUKEwictfWLwtHOAhVBgx4KHSl6BMsQ6AEIHDAA#v=snippet&q=1525%20&f=false. Accessed August 20, 2016.

Wan, Sze-kar. "Does Diaspora Identity Imply Some Sort of Universality? An Asian American Reader on Galatians." In *Interpreting Beyond Borders.* Ed. Fernando F. Segovia. Sheffield: Sheffield Academic Press, 2000.

Watson, Gerard, trans. *Saint Augustine: Soliloquies and Immortality of the Soul.* Warminster, England: Aris & Phillips Ltd., Teddington House, 1990.

Weisman, Jonathan. "House Hopefuls in G.O.P. Seek Rightward Shift." *New York Times* (September 29, 2014).

Westen, Drew. *The Political Brain: The Role of Emotion Deciding the Fate of the Nation.* New York: Public Affairs Books, 2007.

Westin, Drew. *The Role of Emotion in Deciding the Fate of the Nation.* New York: Public Affairs, 2007.

Wittgenstein, Ludwig. *Philosophical Investigations: The English Text of the Third Edition.* Trans. G. E. M. Anscombe. New York: MacMillan Publishing Company, 1968.

Zachman, Randall C. *The Assurance of Faith: Conscience in the Theology of Martin Luther and John Calvin.* Minneapolis: Fortress Press, 1993.

Notes

Acknowledgements

1. Schleiermacher, *On Freedom*, 131.
2. Panksepp, *Affective Neuroscience*, 9.

Introduction

1. Panksepp and Northoff, "The trans-species core SELF," 198.
2. Cage, *Silence*, 8.
3. James, *Varieties*, 316. See Bucke, *Cosmic Consciousness*, 3. As James notes, "It was Dr. Bucke's own experience of a typical onset of cosmic consciousness in his own person which led him to investigate it in others." Bucke's work, first published in 1901, is filled with the Eurocentric and androcentric biases of his era of someone born of "good English middle class stock" (15–16), who has an experience of cosmic consciousness (16) that he then explains in enormously prejudicial terms.
4. ["*das Innere des Ich selbst*"] Schleiermacher, Über die Religion (*KGA*, 1.12), 170; *On Religion*, Oman, 137.
5. Collins, *Jewish Cult*, 15.
6. Reiner Maria Rilke, The Duino Elegies: http://www.poetryintranslation.com/PITBR/German/Rilke.php. Accessed February 20, 2018.
7. Etty Hillesum, *An Interrupted Life*, 207.
8. James, *Varieties*, 308.
9. Merton, *Mystics*, 17–18.
10. Cage, *Silence*, xi.
11. Schleiermacher, *On Religion*, 31.
12. Schleiermacher, *Speeches*, 32.
13. Schleiermacher, *Speeches*, 21–26, and *passim*.
14. Schleiermacher, *Speeches*, 21.
15. A commentary by Richard Crouter, the translator and editor of Schleiermacher's *Speeches*, 27n.
16. Schleiermacher, *Speeches*, 13–14.
17. Schleiermacher, *Speeches*, 46.
18. Schleiermacher, *Speeches*, 31
19. Schleiermacher, *Speeches*, 12.

Chapter One

1. Schleiermacher's analysis of affect will be studied in detail—and also translated into twenty-first-century neuroscientific terms—later in this chapter.
2. Schleiermacher, *On the Glaubenslehre*, 57. See also Thandeka, *The Embodied Self*, 8–9.

3. The origin of the foundation problem in liberal religion is described as Schleiermacher's misbegotten attempt to define "the real essence of religion." Wayne Proudfoot highlights this standard view of Schleiermacher's project in *Religious Experience*. Schleiermacher failed in his attempt because, as Proudfoot puts it, "There is no such essence to capture" (179). Schleiermacher, Proudfoot insists, confused experience with description:

> Schleiermacher's insistence on the immediacy of religious experience is descriptively accurate, but it is theoretically inadequate…. The experience seems to the subject to be immediate and noninferential, but it is not independent of concepts, beliefs, and practices. This confusion between the phenomenological and theoretical senses of *immediate* is central to Schleiermacher's program and is important for understanding contemporary religious thought and the study of religion. (3)

4. Schleiermacher, *On the Glaubenslehre*, 34–35.

5. Schleiermacher, *On the Glaubenslehre*, 36.

6. Barth, *Christentum und Selbstbewußtsein*, 7–27.

7. This paragraph is taken from Thandeka, *The Embodied Self*, 9.

8. Dorrien, "Introduction," 1–8.

9. Dorrien, "Introduction," 1–8.

10. Dorrien, "Introduction," 529. See Heyward, "We're Here, We're Queer," 78–96, quote, 93.

11. Thandeka, "Future Designs."

12. See Fitzgerald, *The Evangelicals* for a fine study of the rise and fall in power of evangelical churches and their survivalist link to the Tea Party. And Cobb, *Spiritual Bankruptcy* presents a lucid analysis of the decline of liberal mainline churches in America.

13. Schleiermacher, *The Life of Schleiermacher*, 38.

14. Schleiermacher, *The Life of Schleiermacher*, 45; *Aus Schleiermacher's Leben*, 45–46.

15. Rice, "The Blind Dülon and His Magic Flute," 25.

16. Dilthey, Br. IV, *Schleiermacher an Reimer* (10 Feb 06), 122.

17. Schleiermacher, *Weihnaschtsfeier*. References in this essay are to the translation of the 1826 second edition (Berlin, 1826) by Tice, *Christmas Eve: Dialogue on the Incarnation*, 46. References to this translation are given in the text of this essay as CE.

18. Chapter Two lays out these various standpoints in illustrated detail.

19. Cited by Terrence Tice, 'Introduction,' to *Speeches*, 9. *Aus Schleiermacher's Leben*, 47.

20. See Sadie, "Johann Mattheson," 171–72, and Buelow, "Johann Mattheson and the invention of the Affektenlehre," 393–407.

21. Dülon, *Dülons des blinden Floetenspielers Leben und Meynungen von ihm selbst bearbeitet*, 151–52. Cited by Miller, 66.

22. Miller, 72–75. Cited by Miller, C. P. E. Bach's text *Versuch über die wahre Art das Clavier zu spielen* (Berlin, 1753, 1762), ii. 325–26.

23. Miller, 72–75.

24. Boersch, "Zur Entstehung der 'Weihnachtsfeier,'" 355–56.

25. See Scholtz, *Schleiermachers Musikphilosophie* for a fine overview of the entire topic of the development of Schleiermacher's interest in music and its function in his life and work. See also Blackwell, "The Role of Music in Schleiermacher's Writings," 446.

26. Schleiermacher, *Ästhetik*, 52. (Hereafter AO.)

27. Scholtz, *Ethik und Hermeneutik*, 217.

28. Schleiermacher, *Die Praktische Theologie*; Schleiermacher, *Sämmtliche Werke*. Two selections from this work have been published in English in Duke, *Christian Caring*, 81.

29. Bernecker, *Kritische Darstellung der Geschichte des Affektbegriffes*, 1–3.

30. Schleiermacher, *Über den Umfang*. Schleiermacher, *Sämmtliche Werke* (n. 5), III/3, 181–224. Schleiermacher read the first two parts of this essay on 11 August 1831 in the plenary session of the Royal Academy of the Sciences.

31. This is a hotly debated claim in Schleiermacher scholarship. James M. Brandt, for example, wonders whether "you can separate Affect from God/Christ/Spirit" in Schleiermacher's work. "He sees Christ/Spirit as the stimulus of *Affekt* bringing about communion with God." Personal correspondence, February 14, 2017. See Brandt, *All Things New*.

32. See Schleiermacher, *Christian Faith*, §6.2 for details of this perspective. My analysis here focuses on Schleiermacher's Introduction to his *Christian Faith* and his *Speeches on Religion*. In these two works, Schleiermacher makes a distinction between religious claims and affective experiences. As will be seen in the work that follows, this distinction made by Schleiermacher was two centuries ahead of his times. Indeed, this distinction made between affect and religious ideas is difficult for a great many theists to affirm today because Schleiermacher raised the feeling of cosmic consciousness and the experience of love beyond belief above what can be said about the experience in religious terms. Cosmic consciousness is an innate state of human nature; religious beliefs and notions like "God" are human cultural creations that draw on the specific historical liturgical traditions, creeds, canons, doctrines and beliefs of a specific faith tradition to explain the cosmic state.

Personal correspondence between the author and Terrence N. Tice, one of the translators (with Catherine L. Kelsey and Edwina Lawler) adds further clarity to the ongoing debate among Schleiermacher scholars about Schleiermacher's interest in Affekt and its link to pious versus religious feelings. Terry's email was written on November 17, 2016. The author's response was sent on November 18, 2016.

> Yes, Thandeka … I did struggle over the regular translation of "*fromm*" as "pious," because I could not get around the fact that he places the very nature of "religion," at all its levels and permutations as lying in what Christians would call an "inner faith," grounded in a level of feeling and perception above sensory perception (*Wahrnehmung*) and logically prior to its expression in thought, action or belief (also *Gnade*) but different from elemental "faith," just as "*fromm*" can refer to "piety" at both the prior, essential level of perception and feeling (which did not have to be experienced simultaneously, but both ingredients are necessary to each other in any case). So, it seemed to me clearer to English readers to use "religious" at its basic meaning rather than meaning the entire extent of piety (*Froemmigkeit*), a perfectly good German term to stand for religious expressions in thinking and acting. Naturally, I had to indicate why we chose in each case options closer to Schleiermacher's meaning where that meaning is clearly indicated and in the very few instances where it could mean either level of functioning in the context. For example, in *Reden II* it is crucial to recognize that what grounds either "religion" or "piety" in their full extent is "religious" (*fromm*) experience within, e.g., in a relationship with the divine, theistically speaking with God, or primary, "inner faith."

By the way, I think *Affekt*, in its infrequent use, refers especially to the grounding of all feeling (or "being affected," "affective events in the self," within a larger "affective domain") in sensory functioning, whereas *Gefuehl* always sits somewhere above that level, though unescapably affected by it, depending on the actual and then grammatical context. Is that what you are doing?

Thandeka's response:

We are indeed on the same page when it comes to *Gefuehl* as different from *Affekt*.... I use affective neuroscience to explain in contemporary terms this difference found in what I call Schleiermacher's neuro-conceptual understanding of human consciousness....

I am so very, very pleased that you and I seem to be on the same page about the differences among *Anschauung*, *Gefuehl*, *Wahrnehmung*, and *Affekt*, since these terms are foundational building blocks for Schleiermacher's theological system. I still might take issue with your translation of "*fromm*" as "religious" where as you put it "it could mean either level of functioning in the context." I think the ambiguity here is of critical importance in order to highlight in English the ambiguity requisite for discourse on the null point of human consciousness, as Schleiermacher describes this state in his *Dialektik*.

But now I understand the logic of your decision much more clearly and can appreciate it without me having to fully agree with you. I thus think that your further reflections on the way you "did struggle" over the translation are of enormous importance for English-only readers of your work. Of course, you speak of your decision in your editor notes in CF, but I believe readers of your work would find these further thoughts about your decision truly helpful and enlivening. May I have your permission to include your commentary in your email to me in my book with the citation for your text as "personal correspondence"? [Terry gave his permission.]

I believe it of crucial importance that readers of Schleiermacher wrestle with his work now because of all the trials and tribulations in the world today over the use of religion and religious language as prompts for deadly actions against others. Schleiermacher took his insights to the churches and beyond to help heal and transform a broken world through love. So, too, must we.

33. Schleiermacher, *Christian Faith*, §6.2. This use of the English term *contagion* here to refer to Schleiermacher's notion of the way in which consciousness of kind makes a transition into living imitation or reproduction (*in lebendige Nachbildung*) is based on Douglas F. Watt's important essay, "Toward a Neuroscience of Empathy." In this essay, Watt discusses emotional contagion as a neurological process entailed in empathy. Direct references of the German second edition of *Christian Faith*, *Der christliche Glaube nach den Grundsätzen der evangelischen Kirche im Zusammenhang dargestellt* is subsequently referred to as KGA 1.13 in this book.

34. Schleiermacher, *Christian Faith*, §6.2.

35. Schleiermacher, *Christian Faith*, §4.1–4.

36. Schleiermacher, *Christian Faith*, §4.4.

37. Schleiermacher, *Christian Faith*, §4.4.

38. Schleiermacher, *Christian Faith*, §4.4.

39. Barth, *Protestant Thought*, 341–54.

40. Barth, "The Christian Faith," 278.

41. Thandeka, "Schleiermacher's *Affekt* Theology," 199. Howard, *Protestant Theology*, 197–216. As a fine introduction to Schleiermacher's ethics, see Brandt, *All Things New*.

42. Thandeka, "Schleiermacher's *Affekt* Theology." As James Brandt notes in personal correspondence with the author, Schleiermacher "does talk of propositions 'borrowed' from ethics that he employs to place piety within human experience and theology within the academy." (Email correspondence, February 14, 2017.) This distinction Schleiermacher makes between human experience and theology is of critical importance to the arguments laid out in the present work.

43. Karl Barth made this point forcefully when questioning the appropriateness of a theology as an academic science in a secular university, in his 1922 address, "The Word of God and the Task of Religion," stating: "It is the paradoxical but undeniable truth that as a science like other sciences theology has *no* right to its place: for it becomes then a wholly unnecessary duplication of the disciplines of knowledge belonging to the other faculties. Only when a *theological* faculty undertakes to say, or at least points out the need for saying, what the others ... dare not say, or dare not say aloud, only when it keeps reminding them that a chaos, though wonderful, is not a cosmos, only when it is a question mark and an exclamation point at the outmost edge of scientific possibility—or rather, in contrast to the philosophical faculty, beyond the outermost edge—only then is there a *reason* for it." "Das Wort Gottes als Aufgabe der Theologie," in Karl Barth, *Vorträge und kleinere Arbeiten*, 1922–25, 155–57. This passage is cited and translated by Howard in *Protestant Theology*, 412–13.

44. See chapters six and seven for details.

45. As Schleiermacher scholar James M. Brandt notes in personal correspondence to the author on February 14, 2017, "Traditional theological claims were certainly not prooftexts for FS, but he did go to great pains to demonstrate how his theological system had a certain kind of continuity with previous tradition. So that continuity was important to him."

46. The following abbreviations are used in citations to Über die Religion: Reden an die Gebildeten unter ihren Verächtern: KGA 1.12 refers to the 1831 edition of Über die Religion; OR, Oman refers to Oman, *On Religion*; OR, Crouter refers to Crouter, *On Religion*; R, Rothert refers to the 1799 first edition of Rothert, Über die Religion.

47. Panksepp, *Affective Neuroscience*.

48. Panksepp and Northoff, "The trans-species core SELF," 198. For a bibliography of the almost 200 citations used by the two neuroscientists in their essay, I direct readers to the authors' essay. Special thanks here to Jaak Panksepp for sending a copy of this essay to me in 2009.

49. Terrence Tice and Catherine Kelsey, in a footnote commentary on their translation of Schleiermacher's *Christian Faith*, provide a fine summary of Schleiermacher's new affective theological enterprise: "The term *Affekt*, in Schleiermacher's usage, refers to a stirring in the body, literally an 'emotive' stirring component by which feeling consciously rises and is registered somewhere in the body (in what we call the brain and nervous system today). In his psychology lectures, the human psyche is always body-mind never separately body and mind. Thus, an 'affective' state, such as an experience of joy or a mood of depression, is an expression of body-mind/mind-body" (16n).

50. Schleiermacher, Über die Religion, R. Rothert, 37–38; *On Religion*, Crouter, 109–10

51. Panksepp and Northoff, "The trans-species core SELF," 193–215 (journal homepage: www.elsevier.com/licate/concog), 194. For a bibliography of the almost 200 citations used by the two neuroscientists in their essay, I direct readers to the authors' essay.

52. Schleiermacher, Über die Religion (*KGA*, 1.12), 58–59; *On Religion*, Oman, 41.

53. Panksepp and Northoff, 198

54. Schleiermacher, Über die Religion (*KGA*, 1.12), 132 note 4, 64; *On Religion*, Oman, 105, note 4; 46

55. Schleiermacher, Über die Religion (*KGA*, 1.12), 143, note 15; *On Religion* Oman, 113, note 15.

56. Schleiermacher, Über die Religion (*KGA*, 1.12), 143, note 15; *On Religion* Oman, 113, note 15.

57. Schleiermacher KGA 1.13, §13.1.

58. Schleiermacher, Über die Religion (*KGA*, 1.12), 141 note 13; *On Religion*, Oman, 112, note 13.

59. [*daß für uns, an unserem Ort und auf unserer Bildungsstufe das Gemüth die eigentliche Welt der Religion sei*]. Schleiermacher, Über die Religion (*KGA*, 1.12), 140–41. *On Religion*, Oman, 122.

60. [*so sind es doch immer Gemüthzustände, auf welche die religiösen Erregungen sich beziehen*] Schleiermacher, Über die Religion (*KGA*, 1.12), note 13; *On Religion*, Oman, 112, note 13.

61. Schleiermacher, Über die Religion (*KGA*, 1.12), 141 note 13; *On Religion*, Oman, 112, note 13. There is disagreement among Schleiermacher scholars on this point, as James M. Brandt notes in personal correspondence with the author on February 14, 2016: "In my read, FS's view of consciousness is that there is simultaneously an objective self-consciousness of the world and a subjective self-consciousness of God or the whole, that these two are inseparable although distinct for purposes of analysis. And that the latter is tied to certain manifestations of the former, at least in the Glaubenslehre [*Christian Faith*]." I agree with Brandt that this link is inseparable in the *Christian Faith*, but not in the Introduction to this work. My analysis focuses on this Introduction and other work by Schleiermacher that further elucidates the distinction he makes between affect and culturally created religious ideas. This distinction is of critical importance if one wants to understand cosmic consciousness as a species wide human trait that is then explained in different and often contradictory terms by disparate faith traditions. Schleiermacher strove to affirm the common affective ground of these disparate claims. So do I.

62. Schleiermacher, *Christian Faith*, §3.2.

63. Schleiermacher, *Christian Faith*, §3.2. Andrejč, in his essay "Bridging the gap," masterfully summarizes Matthew Radcliffe's delineation of "existential feeling" as an attempt to expand Merleau-Ponty's phenomenology with its emphasis on embodied existence (385–56). I am suggesting here an alternative approach to Andrejč's reliance on Radcliffe to help bring unity to the diverse ways in which contemporary theologians have parsed Schleiermacher's analysis of feeling. Andrejč's explanation of my "existential-mystical understanding" of nature, for example, can be expanded to include the social world if he takes into account my own use of contemporary affective neuroscientific insights. My empirically-based approach, I am arguing, enables philosophers of religion and theologians to enter into conversation with neuroscientists on a common ground: the human brain as an experience-generating organ. And it enables them to translate Schleiermacher's complex understanding of religious feeling without

adding to it that which Schleiermacher tried to exclude: positive constructions of God-consciousness accompanied by anthropomorphic projections and culturally-defined claims. Finally, this approach affirms the affective revolution in Protestant theology Schleiermacher began, but few understood because it starts with *Affekt* as a study of the human nervous system.

64. Schleiermacher, *Christian Faith*, §3.4

65. As neurologist Antonio Damasio notes in *The Feeling of What Happens*, the pervasive affective states give our lives and thoughts definition and color. They are our body's native tongue and are observable as "body postures, the shape and design of our movements, and even the tone of our voices and the prosody in our speech as we communicate thoughts that may have little to do with the background emotions" (286). Schleiermacher made a similar distinction between the background *feeling* and the foreground immediate *affective* shifts in subjective self-awareness.

66. Schleiermacher, Über die Religion (*KGA*, 1.12), 132 note 4, 64; *On Religion*, Oman, 105, note 4, 46.

67. Schleiermacher, Über die Religion (*KGA*, 1.12), 143, note 15; *On Religion*, Oman, 113, note 15.

68. Schleiermacher, *Christian Faith*, §3.4.

69. Schleiermacher, Über die Religion (*KGA*, 1.12), 132 note 4, 64; *On Religion*, Oman, 105, note 4, 46.

70. More details of the way in which such pious dispositions of the mind are created by religion as an affective trigger of feeling are presented in the final section of the present chapter.

71. [*(d)rei verschiedene Gebiete des Sinnes*] Schleiermacher, Über die Religion (*KGA*, 1.12), 170; *On Religion*, Oman, 137.

72. He writes, for example, "daß Handlungen nicht unmittelbar *aus den Erregungen des Gefühls einzelne aus einzelnen hervorgehen sollen*," Schleiermacher, Über die Religion (*KGA*, 1.12), 142, note 15; *On Religion* Oman, 113, note 15.

73. [*"das Innere des Ich selbst"*] Schleiermacher, Über die Religion (*KGA*, 1.12), 170; *On Religion*, Oman, 137.

74. Schleiermacher, Über die Religion (*KGA*, 1.12), 58–59; *On Religion*, Oman, 41.

75. Schleiermacher, Über die Religion (*KGA*, 1.12), 170; *On Religion*, Oman, 137.

76. Schleiermacher, Über die Religion (*R*, Rothert), 31; *On Religion*, Crouter, 104.

77. This example is taken from my essay, *Schleiermacher's Affekt Theology.*

78. Schleiermacher, Über die Religion (*KGA*, 1.12), 170; *On Religion*, Oman, 137–38.

79. Schleiermacher, Über die Religion (*KGA*, 1.12), 58–59; *On Religion*, Oman, 41.

80. Schore, *Affect Regulation and the Origin of the Self*, 6.

81. As Panksepp notes, "This nomenclature RAGE, FEAR, GRIEF/PANIC AND PLAYFULNESS is capitalized to highlight that the focus is on primary-process emotions and their associated affects" (Personal email correspondence, March 12, 2010).

82. Panksepp, *Affective Neuroscience*, 9.

83. Panksepp, "On the Embodied Neural Nature of Core Emotional Affects," 169.

84. Ibid., 101.

85. Ibid., 169-170, passim.

86. Panksepp, *Affective Neuroscience*, 135.

87. The term SELF is Panksepp's acronym for "A Simple Ego-type Life Form." It refers to the primordial structure of agency found "deep within the brain." Panksepp explains the SELF as our "primordial self-schema" or "self-representation," and characterizes its content as the ineffable feeling of being alive and an active agent in the perceived world of events. *Affective Neuroscience*, 309.

88. Panksepp and Northoff, "The trans-species core SELF," 198.

89. Panksepp and Northoff, "The trans-species core SELF," 198.

90. This filtering system is "based upon [the stimuli's] relationships to the emotions and other affective states of the organism." Further integration of the stimuli by the organism is thus determined at this level not by what the self thinks, but by what the self feels. Panksepp and Northoff, "The trans-species core SELF," 198.

91. Taylor, *My Stroke of Insight*, 19.

92. Panksepp and Northoff, "The trans-species core SELF," 206.

93. Panksepp and Northoff, "The trans-species core SELF," 206.

94. Panksepp and Northoff, "The trans-species core SELF," 199.

95. Panksepp and Northoff, "The trans-species core SELF," 207.

96. Panksepp and Northoff, "The trans-species core SELF," 198.

97. Panksepp and Northoff, "The trans-species core SELF," 205.

98. The following five paragraphs are taken from my essay, "Future Designs."

99. Panksepp and Northoff, "The trans-species core SELF," 197. Some of the higher moods and feelings, the authors argue, "arise potentially through cognitive conceptualizations [of generalized negative and positive affects]."

100. Panksepp and Biven, *The Archaeology of Mind*, 417.

101. Northoff refers to the content of this domain of human consciousness as "exteroceptive stimuli within an organism," "incoming stimuli from the environment," "externally derived sensory stimuli," and "sensory stimuli." Moreover, when such sensory stimuli within perceptual consciousness get linked up with the first domain ("intrinsic affective values") the process turns, as both authors note affirming other research, from "something informational or neurophysical into something phenomenological." The stimuli, in short, becomes "mine." This sense of "mineness"—an awareness that the personal experience is self-referential—is not created by the sensory data. Rather, it is created through a "self-perspectival organization" within the brain through affective neural substrates that Panksepp, Northoff and Schleiermacher attempt to delineate.

102. Schleiermacher, *Christian Caring: Selections from Practical Theology*, 81.

103. Panksepp, *Affective Neuroscience*, 316, 77.

104. Panksepp and Northoff, "The trans-species core SELF," 204.

105. "The trans-species core SELF," 200. Northoff's approach to brain imaging of the higher systems and Panksepp's investigations of the lower regions enable the two neuroscientists to integrate their perspectives and produce their co-authored study.

106. Schleiermacher, *Über die Religion* (KGA, 1.12), 170; *On Religion*, Oman, 137–38.

107. Schleiermacher, *Über die Religion* (KGA, 1.12), 58–59; *On Religion*, Oman, 41.

108. Panksepp and Northoff , "The trans-species core SELF," 205.

109. Schleiermacher, *Über die Religion* (KGA, 1.12), 142, note 14; *On Religion*, Oman, 114, note 14.

110. Schleiermacher, *Über die Religion* (KGA, 1.12), 132, note 4; *On Religion*, Oman 105, note 4.

111. Schleiermacher, Über die Religion (*KGA*, 1.12), 182; *On Religion*, Oman, 148.

112. Schleiermacher, *KGA, 1.13*, §6.2.

113. Narvaez, "The individual, relational and social neurobiological development of morality," 109. Narvaez refers here to the work of D.J. Siegel, *The Developing Mind: How Relationships and the Brain Interact to Shape Who We Are*, New York, NY, Guilford Press, 1999.

114. Panksepp, Affective Neuroscience, 30.

115. Panksepp, *Affective Neuroscience*, 262.

116. Panksepp, *Affective Neuroscience*, 77.

117. See Narvaez and Gleason, *Developmental Optimization*.

118. Narvaez and Gleason, *Developmental Optimization*, 120.

119. Redeker, *Schleiermacher: Life and Thought*, 187; 188–99.

120. More evidence for the merits of this argument will be laid out in the chapters that follow. Schleiermacher is used here to jump starts the discourse. The goal of this present chapter is "simply" to introduce the notion of cosmic consciousness using (1) insights from Schleiermacher's work elucidated by (2) insights from affective neuroscience. From beginning to end this entire project will be a tough sell for theists who link what they feel to what they believe without a space of difference between the two. They are like the dancing priest and need not be persuaded otherwise. Persons who call themselves spiritual but not religious and who want to know how to make sense of what they have experienced in nonreligious terms, on the other hand, will perhaps have an easier time with the arguments and evidence. Schleiermacher, after all, gives them a way to affirm their spiritual experiences without having to describe them in religious terms or define them as religious beliefs about God, Christ, or the Holy Spirit.

Chapter Two

1. Schleiermacher, *On the Glaubenslehre*, 57. See also Thandeka, *The Embodied Self*, 8–9.

2. Soskice and Lipton, "General Introduction," in *Feminism and Theology*, 5.

3. Soskice and Lipton, "General Introduction," in *Feminism and Theology*, 5. As the authors note, this conclusion was reached by Goldstein in her article, "The Human Situation: A Feminine View."

4. Guenther-Gleason, 113–27.

5. Soskice and Lipton, 6.

6. Schleiermacher, *Weihnaschtsfeier*. References in this chapter are to the translation of the 1826 second edition by Terrence N. Tice, *Christmas Eve: Dialogue on the Incarnation*.

7. Schleiermacher, *Christmas Eve*, 46.

8. Schleiermacher, *Christmas Eve*, 58.

9. Schleiermacher, *Christmas Eve*, 61.

10. Schleiermacher, *Christmas Eve*, 71–75.

11. Schleiermacher, *Christmas Eve*, 77.

12. Schleiermacher, *Christmas Eve*, 79.

13. The work of Ruth Drucilla Richardson is outstanding in this area. See her book, *The Role of Women in the Life and Thought of the Early Schleiermacher (1768–1806)*. Schleiermacher's "Idee zu einem Katechismus der Vernunft für edle Frauen" is found in Schleiermacher's *Schriften aus der Berliner Zeit 1796–99*. An English translation is given by Richardson (60–61) and can also be found in Peter Firchow's translation, *Friedrich Schlegel's "Lucinde" and the fragments*, 220–21.

Schleiermacher's "Catechism" originally was published as one of the fragments of the first volume of the magazine *Athenaeum*, published by Friedrich von Schlegel and his brother August Wilhelm von Schlegel.

14. See Massey, *Feminine Soul* for a vivid presentation of this perspective.

15. See Patricia Guenther-Gleason's essay, "Schleiermacher's Feminist Impulses," 127 and 95–127, for a strong summary of the textual incongruities for contemporary scholars posed by Schleiermacher and his work.

16. Massey, *Feminine Soul*, 146,

17. Massey, *Feminine Soul*, 5–9.

18. Herdt, *Sambia Sexual Culture*, 245.

19. Schleiermacher, *Brouillon zur Ethik*.

20. Richardson, *The Role of Women*, 150–51.

21. Richardson, *The Role of Women*, 151.

22. Jaak Panksepp and Günther Bernatzky, Panksepp and Bernatzky, "Emotional Sounds and the Brain," 146. This and the following paragraphs are taken from the author's essay, co-authored with Darcia Narvaez, "Neurobiology, Emotions and Faith."

23. Panksepp and Bernatzky, "Emotional Sounds and the Brain," 146.

24. Panksepp and Bernatzky, "Emotional Sounds and the Brain," 144.

25. Kavanagh, *On Liturgical Theology*, 79, *passim*.

26. Letter of A. Müllers 25. 2. 1805. Cited by Borsch, 356.

27. Schleiermacher, *On religion*, 32.

28. Schleiermacher, *On religion*, 32.

29. The term *Vorstellung ("representation")*, for Schleiermacher, refers to images and concepts rather than to sounds and movements. Schleiermacher, *Ästhetik*, 95

30. Schleiermacher, *Christian Faith*, §100.3.

31. Schleiermacher, *Die Praktische Theologie; Schleiermachers* Sämmliche Werke. Two selections from this work have been published in English in Duke, *Christian Caring*, 81.

32. Schleiermacher, *Christian Faith*, §100.2.

33. Schleiermacher, *Christian Faith*, §100.2.

34. Schleiermacher, *Christian Faith*, §101.

35. Schleiermacher, *Über den Umfang*, 208–9.

36. Schleiermacher, *Über den Umfang*, 192. Schleiermacher read the first two parts of this essay on 11 August 1831 in the plenary session of Royal Academy of the Sciences. This work has also been published as part of the book Ästhetik (1819/25), Über den Begriff der Kunst (1831/32), 151–88.

37. Schleiermacher, *Über den Umfang*, 192.

38. Schleiermacher, *Über den Umfang*, 182.

39. Schleiermacher, *Über den Umfang*, 181.

40. Schleiermacher, *Über den Umfang*, 223.

41. Collins, *First Corinthians*, 355.

Chapter Three

1. I paraphrase here a claim by Seth Schwartz, but substitute the term "conscience" for his terms "Christianization" and "religion" so as to make a similar claim, namely, to identify the creation of a new discrete category (in this case "conscience") used to think about human experience. Writes Schwartz: "Christianization, and what is in socio-terms its sibling, the emergence of religion as a discreet category of human experience—religion's disembedding."

Imperialism and Jewish Society, 179. Cited by Boyarin, *Border Lines*, 11. Boyarin elaborates upon Schwartz's point: "the production of Christianity is, itself, the invention of religion as such—a discrete category of human experience. The production of this category does not imply that many elements of what would form religions did not exist before this time, but rather than the particular aggregation of verbal and other practices that would now be named as constituting a religion only came into being as a discrete category as Christianization itself."

2. This strategy is akin to Daniel Boyarin's work in his path-breaking book *Border Lines: The Partition of Judaeo-Christianity*. He put "together the different bits and pieces that other scholars have constructed into a new mosaic." His goal was not to discard them but rather to honor and suspect them. *Border Lines*, 141, 227.

3. Bosman, in *Conscience in Philo and Paul*, 191, lists these texts as: 1 Cor 4:4; 8:7–12; 10:25–29; 2 Cor 1:12; 4:2; 5:11; Rom 2:15; 9:1, and 13:5; and once in its negative verb form in 1 Cor 4:4. For an overview of the ongoing scholarly discourse about which of Paul's New Testament letters (and what parts of them) were written by Paul, see *The Pauline Canon*, ed. Stanley E. Porter.

4. As W.D. Davies notes in his essay, "Conscience," the term does not even appear once in the four gospels. Davies argues that this fact points to the Hellenistic origin of the term. Writes Davies: "in the four gospels, which are concerned with a tradition which however much under Hellenistic influences, was primarily Hebraic or Palestinian, the term does not occur."

5. Pierce, *Conscience*, 60.

6. Davies, "Conscience," 671. As Davies also notes, the Hebrew word עַדָּע also occurs in 2 Chr 1:10–12 and Dan 1:17, is translated into Greek as σύνεσις and in English is rendered "knowledge." The Hebrew context, writes Davies, shows that the reference is to "mind" or "the inner, secret place of thoughts." Most significant for Davies, is the Wisdom of Solomon text 17:10, because here "conscience emerges with a moral connotation, as a witness within man, which condemns his sin. This approximates to what we find in the [New Testament]." But as Davies goes on to note, "the Wisdom of Solomon shows marked Hellenistic influences, and the emergence of the term 'conscience,' with a moral significance points to the Hellenistic world as its source." Special thanks to Bronson BrowndeVost for the extended observations on the Hebrew word *madda*.

7. Paul, after all, believed he had received grace and apostleship from Christ to work with the Gentiles (Rom 1:4–5). To this end, he aligned with them to work with them (Gal 4:12).

8. Pierce, *Conscience*, 63.

9. Stendahl, *Paul Among Jews*, 76.

10. Paul's use of the term *syneidesis* as a *response* to the Corinthians' own use of the term, as Philip Bosman notes in *Conscience in Philo and Paul*, is "a vexing problem confronting the exegete of 1 Cor 8–11" (205). Without the actual letter from Corinth, the exegete must reconstruct the historical context. But it seems evident, Bosman concludes, that Paul followed a strategy integral to his ministry: borrowing and then modifying the Corinthians' own terms. Citing Sumney, "Identifying Paul's Opponents," and also Schrage, *Der erste Brief an die Korinther*, 39–47.

11. Boyarin, *A Radical Jew*, 220.

12. Gaston, *Paul and the Torah*, 15. Cited by Gager in *The Origins of Anti-Semitism*, 15.

13. Gager, *Reinventing Paul*, 151.

14. Gager, *Reinventing Paul*, 151.

15. Gager, *Reinventing Paul*, 54, passim.

16. Boyarin, *A Radical Jew,* 15, 215, passim.

17. Boyarin, *A Radical Jew,* 242. Citing Etienne Balibar's concept of "ethnocide." See Balibar, "Is There a 'Neo-Racism'?," 21–22. Also worth noting here is that in Rom 2:28, when Paul writes that someone "is a Jew who is one inwardly," the Greek term Paul uses—"Ioudaios/ Ἰουδαῖος"—usually translated today as "Jew," would have been understood by the ancient hearer as having geographic and cultural connotations, and thus referring to a Judean, namely, an immigrant from Judea. The plural form (Ἰουδαῖοι/Ioudaioi) would have meant "an immigrant association of Judeans." See Harland's discussion in *Associations, Synagogues, and Congregations,* 202. Boyarin's claim of "ethnocide" refers to the killing of this socio-cultural, geographic identity.

18. Harland, *Associations, Synagogues, and Congregations,* 220.

19. Levine, *The Misunderstood Jew,* 84.

20. Levine, *The Misunderstood Jew,* 84.

21. Levine, *The Misunderstood Jew,* 95–99.

22. Neusner and Chilton, *Intellectual Foundations,* 38.

23. Neusner *and* Chilton, *Intellectual Foundations,* 32.

24. Neusner *and* Chilton, *Intellectual Foundations,* 38–39.

25. Neusner, *The Systemic Analysis of Judaism,* 104.

26. Neusner, *The Systemic Analysis of Judaism,* 102.

27. Boyarin, *Border Lines,* 21.

28. Boyarin, *Border Lines,* 85–86.

29. John Gager defines himself as "Christian only in the broad cultural sense of that word: I am affiliated with no religious institution of any kind" (Gager, Reinventing Paul, 17).

30. As Mark D. Nanos wisely notes in *Reading Paul Within Judaism,* Paul used the "widely held stereotype that Jews by definition served as the model for practicing what one preaches [in order to create] a rhetorical gambit to illustrate a principle he wants his readers as non-Jews to grasp for themselves by employing a fictive Jew," 143. Paul's strategy failed, I argue, because this rhetorical gambit included strategies that undermined his intended goal.

31. Collins, *First Corinthians,* 355.

32. Gaston, *Paul and the Torah,* 78.

33. Gaston, *Paul and the Torah,* 78.

34. An easy way to understand the function of this principle is to recall what your kindergarten teacher often said to you and the other members of your class: "Well children, what are *we* going to do today"? She spoke to you as if she were a member of your class in order to win your allegiance and marshal your class as her troops.

35. Gaston suggests that the function of the law in Rom 7:13ff, for example, "seems closest to the Jewish concept of the 'evil impulse,'" but he does not interrogate possible links between the Apostle Paul's invention of the Christian conscience and Paul the Pharisee's commerce with the narratives of the evil impulse in his first-century Jewish era (*Paul and the Torah,* 31). A major section in this chapter investigates these links.

36. Gaston, *Paul and the Torah,* 136.

37. Panksepp and Northoff, "The trans-species core SELF," and Han and Northoff, "Understanding the Self," for a full discussion of this process as well as for references to more work in the field.

38. Striker's *Essays on Hellenistic Epistemology and Ethics* is an excellent reference for considering the diversity of interests and approaches within Greek philosophy. I have drawn especially on insights from chapter 9 of this book,

"*Ataraxia*: Happiness as tranquility" (183–99), in my discussion.

39. Boyarin, *A Radical Jew*, 240–41. So, too, for Protestants and Catholics, for example, who are raised within these respective religious traditions. Their way of being in the world tends to have a different dispositional signature. Religion, simply put, is not just a set of religious ideas. It's a learned way of making sense of and acting in the world because of an embedded dispositional, nature/nurture mindset.

40. Boyarin, *A Radical Jew*, 240-1.

41. And he was probably proficient in Aramaic or Hebrew, even though the only writings we have of Paul are his New Testament missionary letters as Apostle, which were written in Greek. Peter J. Tomson, for example, makes a strong case for Paul's Jewish Hellenism, concluding that Paul's mother tongue was quite probably the Hebrew and Aramaic of Jerusalem rather than Greek of his native Tarsa, and that there was, as Tomson puts it, a close relationship between elements of Paul's teachings and Pharisaic-Rabbinic tradition. I refer readers to Tomson's book and its references for support of his conclusions, which are wisely stated as probable rather than absolute fact since his arguments and evident are based, in part, on historical reconstruction. Tomson, *Paul and the Jewish Law*, 52–53, *passim*.

42. Neusner, *Early Rabbinic Judaism*, 43.

43. Neusner, *Building*, 4. Moreover, as Neusner and Chilton note in *Intellectual Foundations*, "what both formally and intellectually sets the Mishnah apart from all Israelite law codes [is] the provision of disputes on points of law, on the one hand, and the names of authorities that are party to those disputes, on the other hand…" (9). Boyarin's book *Border Lines* updates these insights, interrogates and expands upon them by theorizing that "Judaism was evolving within the context of the world that Christianity, Christendom, and the Christian empire had made for it," and he dissents "in some measure [from Neusner's] specific time frame," 219.

44. Boyarin, *Border Lines*, 170, 164, *passim*.

45. Neusner, *Building Blocks*, 4–5.

46. The only assumption I make here is that human beings have some predictable and shared neurological patterns that *do* make it possible—however cautiously—to explore Paul's brain.

47. Neusner, *Building Blocks*, 4–5.

48. Boyarin, *Border Lines*, 92.

49. Boyarin, *Border Lines*, 235, n. 73. Boyarin also refers here to the claim made by Saldarini in *Scholastic Rabbinism*: "The emergence of definable sects, Pharisees, Sadducees, etc., and more importantly, the attention given to them fits most comfortably into the Greco-Roman world with its recognized philosophical schools, religious societies, and craft associations."

50 Boyarin, *Border Lines*, 7. Collins sites insights from Barclay, "Using and Refusing," and Barclay's introductory comments, "Introduction: Diaspora Negotiations," to help substantiate Collins' claims.

51 My emphasis upon the differences among these texts is directly influenced by Ishay Rosen-Zvi's groundbreaking essay, "Two Rabbinic Inclinations?" in which he convincingly argues—after having read and systematically analyzed all rabbinic reference to the *yetzer*—that the notion of a good as well as a bad *yetzer* in this work is marginal rather than dominant. He thus successfully challenges the scholarly "dogma" that posits a good and bad *yetzer* as the standard, and replaces it with a "single-*yetzer* model." My special thanks to Professor Jonathan Wyn Schofer for alerting me to this groundbreaking essay.

52. Rosen-Zvi, "Two Rabbinic Inclinations?," 6.

53. Neusner, *The Fathers According to Rabbi Nathan*, ch. 18.

54. Rosen-Zvi, "Two Rabbinic Inclinations?," 6.

55. Rosen-Zvi, "Two Rabbinic Inclinations?," 6.

56. Rosen-Zvi, "Two Rabbinic Inclinations?," 7.

57. Rosen-Zvi, "Two Rabbinic Inclinations?," 7.

58. Rosen-Zvi, "Two Rabbinic Inclinations?," 8.

59. Rosen-Zvi, "Two Rabbinic Inclinations?," 8.

60. Rosen-Zvi, "Two Rabbinic Inclinations?," 8–9.

61. Rosen-Zvi, "Two Rabbinic Inclinations?," 10.

62. Schofer, "Redaction." For references, refer to Schofer's text.

63. Schofer notes here his own preference for the term "bad" rather than "evil" for the negative *yeser* because the rabbinic sources do not denote man as taking pleasure (thus an *evil* act) in doing what is wrong (thus a *bad* act). Schofer, "Redaction," 26, note 22.

64. Stuart, *The Struggle in Man*, 81.

65. Jacob Neusner presents a reference list for uses of this term with passages cited in his book, *Theology of Normative Judaism*, 113–17.

66. Schechter, *Some Aspects of Rabbinic Theology*, 267.

67. Schechter, *Some Aspects of Rabbinic Theology*, 269.

68. As Daniel Boyarin notes in his commentary on this translation, which is his translation of the text: "it's actually a reference to the penis." Personal email correspondence to author (June 27, 2018).

69. *Bavli-Tractate Sukkah* 5:1D II. 13/52B. Listed and cited by Neusner in *Theology of Normative Judaism*, 144.

70. See Neusner's arguments and evidence in his book, *Judaic Law*, for reading the rabbinic redactions as essentially accurate representations of the rules of the sect of the Second Temple Pharisaic Houses (260ff).

71. See the Introduction to Goldin's פִּרְקֵי אָבוֹת *Ethics of the Fathers* for more details, xiiff. [Complete reference needed for Bibliography]

72. Neusner's book, *The Fathers According to Rabbi Nathan*, in which he translates the text and provides extensive commentary on it, is a fine introduction to this text with commentary on *Tractate Abot* as further elaborations and additions.

73. Schofer, *Making of the Sage*, 28.

74. Boyarin, *Border Lines*, 85.

75. Boyarin, *Border Lines*, 57.

76. Schofer, *Confronting Vulnerabilities*, 11.

77. Neusner, *Vanquished*, 58.

78. I will use the non-inclusive gender language of the text in this discussion so as to avoid distorting the male gender bias of the text and the conversations linked to this male perspective.

79. Goldin, *Ethics of the Fathers*, 31 note 121a.

80. Pies: *The Ethics of the Sages*, 102–3.

81. Cohen Stuart, 19. Citing a tract noted by Schechter, 267. *A. R. N.*, 9a, text and note 9.

82. Schofer, *The Making of a Sage*, 11.

83. Schofer, *The Making of a Sage*, 31.

84. Rosen-Zvi, "Two Rabbinic Inclinations?," 12.

85. Rosen-Zvi, "Two Rabbinic Inclinations?," 13.

86. Schofer, *The Making of a Sage*, 59.

87. Schechter, *Some Aspects of Rabbinic Theology*, 278.

88. Schechter, *Some Aspects of Rabbinic Theology*, 280.

89. Schofer, "Redaction," 29.

90. Schofer, "Redaction," 29. Schofer quotes from *The Fathers According to Rabbi Nathan*, to make these points: "They said, the bad *yeser*, is thirteen years older than the good *yeser*. From the belly of a person's mother it grows and comes with him. He begins to desecrate the Sabbath, and nothing in him protests. He kills people and nothing in him protests. He goes to do an act of transgression, and nothing in him protests. After thirteen years, the good *yetzer* is born. When he desecrates Sabbaths, it says to him 'You idiot! Look, it says, "The one who desecrates it will surely die!"' (Exod 31:14). He kills people, and it says to him, 'You idiot! Look, it says, "If a man spills blood of another man, his blood will be spilled"' (Gen 9:6). He goes to do an act of sexual transgression, and it says to him, 'You idiot! Look, it says, "the adulterer and the adulteress will surely die"' (Lev 20:10)...." See Schofer for bibliographic detail and further commentary.

91. Because the rabbis portray the good yetzer as an internal voice that monitors and regulates evil impulses, Jacob Neusner characterizes it anachronistically as "what we should now call the private counsel and conscience." But just as the bad *yetzer* differs dramatically from Christian theological notions of sin, so, too, the good *yetzer* bears little resemblance to "the Christian conscience"—a point I've made above and I will explore more extensively in chapter 4 and succeeding chapters.

92. Schechter, *Some Aspects of Rabbinic Theology*, 269.

93. Schofer, "Redaction," 30.

94. Schofer, "Redaction," 30.

95. Flusser, "A New Sensitivity in Judaism," 113.

96. Flusser, "A New Sensitivity in Judaism," 119.

97. Flusser, "A New Sensitivity in Judaism," 113.

98. Davies, *Paul and Rabbinic Judaism*, 20.

99. Porter, *The Yeçer Hara*, 134.

100. A fuller discussion of the rabbinic literature on the *yetzer* is developed later in this present chapter.

101. Porter, *The Yeçer Hara*, 134–35.

102. Davies notes in *Paul and Rabbinic Judaism*, 21. See Davies for the numerous, detailed references he gives to Rabbinic literature to support this claim.

103. Stendahl, *Paul Among Jews*, 51.

104. Pierce, *Conscience in the New Testament*, 40–53.

105. Stuart, *The Struggle in Man*, 81. Citing J. Hadot, *Penchant mauvais et volunté libre donc la Segesse de Ben Sira (l'Ecclésiastique). Bruxelies, 1970, 16f.*

106. Flusser, "A New Sensitivity in Judaism," 113.

107. Flusser, "A New Sensitivity in Judaism," 116.

108. Flusser, "A New Sensitivity in Judaism," 119.

109. Flusser, "A New Sensitivity in Judaism," 118–21.

110. Flusser leads off this discussion with an analysis of the logion of Antigonos of Sokho (*Aboth* I.3): second century BCE, prior to the Maccabean uprising. Flusser cites the text in which persons are urged to serve their masters "not on condition of receiving a reward." Flusser, "A New Sensitivity in Judaism," 109.

111. Flusser, "A New Sensitivity in Judaism," 109–11.

112. Flusser, "A New Sensitivity in Judaism," 115.

113. Flusser, "A New Sensitivity in Judaism," 115. Citing Ben Sira (27:30–28:7).

114. Flusser, "A New Sensitivity in Judaism," 116. See Sir. 18:13a.

115. Schofer, *The Making of a Sage*, 87.

116. Schofer, *Confronting Vulnerabilities*, 175.

117. Rosen-Zvi, "Two Rabbinic Inclinations?," 25.

118. Rosen-Zvi, "Two Rabbinic Inclinations?," 2.

119. Rosen-Zvi, "Two Rabbinic Inclinations?," 10.

120. Rosen-Zvi, "Two Rabbinic Inclinations?," 26.

121. Rosen-Zvi, "Two Rabbinic Inclinations?," 14.

122. Rosen-Zvi, "Two Rabbinic Inclinations?," 14.

123. Neusner, *Vanquished Nation*, 18–20.

124. Neusner, *Early Rabbinic Judaism*, 51.

125. Neusner, *Early Rabbinic Judaism*, 61–63.

126. Neusner's arguments and evidence in his book, *Judaic Law*, 291.

127. Neusner, *Early Rabbinic Judaism*, 47.

128. Neusner, "Two Pictures of the Pharisees," 530, 535–37, and *passim*.

129. Harland, *Associations*, 191–92.

130. Harland, *Associations*, 237–43, passim.

131. Harland, *Associations*, 14. Philip Harland has successfully challenged the dominant approach of scholars who "do not pay adequate attention to the concrete and complex ways in which local associations, synagogues, and assemblies found a place in polis and empire."

132. Neusner, *Early Rabbinic Judaism*, 47.

133. Theissen, *Psychological Aspects of Pauline Theology*, 33. Callan, *Psychological Perspectives* for a Freudian psychoanalytic analysis of Paul and his "conversion," as Callan puts it. The approach of the present author does not attempt to analyze the subjective life of Paul and the Jewish era in which he lived psychoanalytically, but rather to track inculcated affective behavior patterns of the era. To this end, I draw on neuropsychological, affective neuroscience, and related contemporary fields of inquiry about emotions and how they become triggered, informed, and habituated by nature/nurture systems. Unlike Beck in his book *The Psychology of Paul*, who wants to examine "Paul and his thought from a psychological perspective," I do not assume that "We are not that distant from him and his way of thinking" (22). Rather, I argue that this "we" of Western Christian consciousness reconstructed Paul in its own image and lay out how this process was inadvertently begun by Paul and subsequently formulated by Augustine and Luther.

134. As Daniel Boyarin notes, in the Hebrew text the word Neusner is translating is yetzer not enemy. Thus, the correct translation should be: "strength consists of winning over one's yetzer." Personal email correspondence to author (June 27, 2018).

135. Neusner, *Vanquished Nation*, 19–20. Emphasis added.

136. Van Voorst, *Jesus Outside the New Testament*.

137. Josephus, cited by Fredriksen, 170. Josephus, "The Jewish War,", 675. Josephus, it should be pointed out here, was despised. As Van Voorst notes in *Jesus Outside the New Testament*, Josephus was a commander of Jewish troops in the Galilee during the Jewish Revolt in 66 CE, but then surrendered his troops on the battlefield, became a Roman citizen, took on a Roman name and worked for subsequent Roman emperors, living in an apartment in their palaces. Writing his histories as a defender of Rome, he became, as Van Voorst notes, an admonisher to the Jewish people to live peaceably with Romans. As a result, Josephus is never mentioned in rabbinic literature, but is a standard reference for Christian scholarship on this era because of his references to Jesus, John the Baptizer, and James as leader of the early Jerusalem church. Van Voorst, *Jesus Outside the New Testament*, 81–83.

138. Fredriksen, *Jesus of Nazareth*, 149–50, citing Josephus. See Josephus, *Complete Works*, "Jewish Antiquities," 578, 648, 650, and "The Jewish War," 745, 861.

139. Samuelsson, *Crucifixion in Antiquity*, 327–71. Special thanks to my gradu-

ate student assistant Bronson Brown-deVost for making me aware of this path-breaking work.

140. Scarry, *The Body in Pain*, 5.

141. Josephus, *Jewish Antiquities*, xvii 2, 4 § 41; xviii. 1, 3 §12–5, §22.

142. Indeed, the Greek term for Pharisee—Φαρισαῖος—seems to make this point. It comes from the vernacular Aramaic form *Parisha* (פְּרִישָׁא), which is in turn derived from the verb *parash* (פְּרַשׁ) (Hebrew *parash* [פְּרַשׁ]), which as used in various rabbinical texts (in its Hebrew form parush [פָּרוּשׁ]), means "one who is separated, or is separate." *A Lexicon of the Talmud* by Nathan ben Jehiel of Rome (died 1106), cited by Moore, in *Judaism in the First*, 60. I wish to thank my graduate assistant Mr. Brown-deVost for helping me sort out the Aramaic and Hebrew terms used here.

Chapter Four

1. Bosman, "Why Conscience Makes Cowards," 270–71.

2. Gager in *The Origins of Anti-Semitism*, 3.

3. Gager, *Reinventing Paul*, 3.

4. See Smith and Taussig, *Meals in the Early Christian World*. Special thanks to Kathleen Corley for introducing me to this field in general and Smith's work in particular.

5. Smith and Taussig, *Meals in the Early Christian World*.

6. Ascough, "Social and Political Characteristics of Greco-Roman Association Meals," Kindle eBook, 59.

7. Ascough, "Social and Political Characteristics of Greco-Roman Association Meals," Kindle eBook, 60–62, 67, and *passim*.

8. Klinghardt, "A Typology of Communal Meals," Kindle eBook, 16.

9. Ascough, "Social and Political Characteristics of Greco-Roman Association Meals" (Kindle EBook, 27–28).

10. Collins, *First Corinthians*, 22.

11. Collins, *First Corinthians*, 22.

12. Collins, *First Corinthians*, 24.

13. Collins, *First Corinthians*, 24.

14. Collins, *First Corinthians*, 24.

15. Jewett, *Paul's Anthropological Terms*, 421.

16. Bosman, *Conscience in Philo and Paul*, 205.

17. Collins, *First Corinthians*, 384.

18. Collins, *First Corinthians*, 371.

19. Collins, *First Corinthians*, 355.

20. Ascough, "Social and Political Characteristics of Greco-Roman Association Meals," 29–30.

21. Collins, *First Corinthians*, 324. See Collins for examples of such claims by Plutarch and Cicero.

22. And more precisely, as Collins notes, the sin of idolatry. 377–78, 389–90.

23. Collins, *First Corinthians*, 371.

24. Marietta, "Conscience in Greek Stoicism," 178.

25. Marietta, "Conscience in Greek Stoicism," 178.

26. Bosman, "Why Conscience Makes," 66–67. I have cited Bosman's translation of Democritus fragment 297, Diels *Vorsokr*.

27. Marietta Jr., "Conscience in Greek Stoicism," 178.

28. Marietta Jr., "Conscience in Greek Stoicism," 178. Nevertheless, as Marietta notes, even as the terms gradually developed literarily into a kind of moral consciousness, the "original meaning of consciousness or awareness was basic to the

meaning of the term" in the widely varied work of such writers as Sophocles, Xenophon, and Plutarch, Euripides, Aristophanes, Xenophon, and Plato. Although scholarship, observes Marietta, is divided regarding the Stoic use of the term, scholars are nevertheless in substantial agreement that *syneidesis* did not originate as a technical philosophic term. Rather, Marietta notes, the term "seems to have been part of the syncretistic religious and ethical thought which permeated the Graeco-Roman world [and] as a term for moral consciousness developed in the common speech of the people." The new uses of the term, in short, "originated in the common speech, growing out of the experience of the people."

29. Marietta Jr., "Conscience in Greek Stoicism," 182, 184.

30. Marietta Jr., "Conscience in Greek Stoicism," 178–80.

31. Bosman, "Why Conscience Makes Cowards," 69.

32. Marietta, "Conscience in Greek Stoicism," 178.

33. Marietta, "Conscience in Greek Stoicism," 178.

34. Bosman, *Conscience*, 274.

35. Bosman, *Conscience*, 41. As Bosman notes, "an entity (in an objectifying sense in a person)." As Bosman also observes, the use of this term [*Instanz*, in the German text] by Eckstein, *Der Begriff Syneidesis bei Paulus* "does not explain how the inner entity gives its evidence or rather how the individual experiences the inner entity. For this, one has to trace the evolution of the [*synoida*] word group back to the particular awareness of inner turmoil, pain, and fear" (229).

36. Bosman's summary of Eckstein's analysis of moral consciousness/conscience, *Conscience*, 41. Eckstein, 6.

37. Bosman, *Conscience*, 280.

38. Bosman, *Conscience*, 263.

39. Bosman, "Why the Conscience Makes Cowards," 70.

40. Rosen-Zvi, "Two Rabbinic Inclinations?," 8–9.

41. Gaston, *Paul and Torah*, 31.

42. Schechter. *Some Aspects of Rabbinic Theology* , 267.

43. This conclusion provides a gateway to a form of Jewish consciousness distinct from gentile consciousness. This gateway is closed, however, when the Jews and Gentiles in Paul's era are treated today as if their internal life and access point to untoward feelings were the same. There is, to reiterate, no equivalent notion in Hebrew Scriptures for this Greek term (Davies, "Conscience," 671).

44. Davies, "Conscience," 74–75.

45. See Goldberg, *Being of Two Minds* for a remarkably fine and pioneering delineation of the difference between a split self and the repressed self. One is aware of the former but unaware of the latter condition within oneself.

46. Goldberg, *Being of Two Minds*.

47. Goldberg, *Being of Two Minds*, 73

48. Bosman, *Conscience*, 262.

49. Bosman, *Conscience*, 212.

50. Bosman, *Conscience*, 215.

51. Bosman, *Conscience*, 227.

52. Bosman, *Conscience*, 278.

53. Pierce, *Conscience in the New Testament*, 40–53.

54. Schechter, *Some Aspects of Rabbinic Theology*, 148.

55. Hodge, *If Sons, Then Heirs*, 66–67.

56. Hodge, *If Sons, Then Heirs*, 149.

57. Hodge, *If Sons, Then Heirs*, 149–50; citing Wan, "Does Diaspora Identity Imply Some Sort of Universality?," 126.

58. Hodge, *If Sons, Then Heirs*, 141.

Chapter Five

1. The appropriateness of using such terms as "emotional" and "emotion" in Augustine's work is an issue of contemporary scholarly debate, which Scrutton summarizes and examines in her important essay, "Emotion in Augustine of Hippo and Thomas Aquinas." Scrutton questions the viability of using the term *emotion* when analyzing Augustine's work. As she notes, contemporary scholars and psychologists have been unable to provide a single definition of the term *emotion* and explain exactly what emotions are (170). Accordingly, Scrutton presents a more informed and nuanced approach to this current debate by analyzing the distinctions Augustine himself makes between passion and affection in his book, *City of God* (172). Affections, for Augustine, Scrutton argues, tend to refer to emotions that are in agreement with reason and truth and have God as their object. Passions, on the other hand, refer to acts of the "arational," "appetitive soul" that must be subjected to reason (172). Writes Scrutton: "passions [are] disordered movements of the lower, animal soul [while] other 'emotions'—affections that are movements of the rational soul—are at once aspects of the rational mind and what modernity would distinguish as subjectively-experienced 'emotional' states" (171). In the present chapter, I augment Scrutton's approach to the emotion debate by using insights from affective neuroscience and related fields to define the term emotions based on reproducible clinical research studies. And I use these insights to delineate the differences—which Scrutton notes—between the arational, animal, appetitive soul and the rational soul in Augustine's work. I focus on Augustine's *Confessions*. Scrutton refers to the neurological work of Antonio Damasio in *The Feeling of What Happens: Body, Emotion and the Making of Consciousness* and *Descartes Error: Emotion, Reason and the Human Brain* (London: Vintage, 2000) to support her claim that Augustine repudiates the idea that "the head" and "the heart" are separate and often in conflict (174 and 174n). I first use Augustine's own terms about this conflict that rages within him and I show how he constructed a rational theology and an affect theology to explain how these two distinct aspects of the soul function and are reconciled. I then translate his insights into contemporary affective neuroscientific terms using the work of affective neuroscientist Jaak Panksepp and neuropsychologist Darcia Narvaez, among others, to show how Augustine in his *Confessions* struggles to resolve the raging conflicts between his head and his heart, his rational soul and his appetitive animal soul. See Scrutton's work for bibliographic references to the current debate, which I have set out to update using my contemporary affect theological approach.

2. Augustine wrote his *Confessions* as if his narratives weren't personal stories about a particular "self" or a "life-writing" autobiography, as classicist Fox notes in his book, *Augustine: Conversions to Confessions*, 2 and also 289. Rather, as Fox rightly observes, "From start to finish [Augustine's confessions] are a prayer addressed to God, but intended to be overheard by readers." Accordingly, readers must simply listen attentively to Augustine's prayers and learn lessons about how they, too, should understand themselves as the broken souls saved by Christ. This same narrative also turns Paul into someone who "became a Christian" (498), which is an anachronistic claim, since Paul and others who followed Christ considered themselves part of a Jewish sect. Moreover, Christianity did not yet exist. See Fredriksen's masterful work, *Jesus of Nazareth, King of the Jews*.

3. Leith, *Creeds of the Churches*, 37. The Catholic Church councils of 418, 431, and 529 accepted Augustine's new definition of sin, which insisted on "man's

lack of freedom insofar as he is related to God, a belief in the necessity of the divine work of grace, and an understanding of the primacy of grace rather than of human merit." See also Lohse, *A Short History of Christian Doctrine*, 114.

4. Lohse, *A Short History of Christian Doctrine*, 114. As Lohse notes, "Augustine imparted to the traditional doctrine of sin a profundity which it had not had before. For him sin is not merely this or that wrongful deed. Hence sin is not something which can be removed by a mere appeal to the good in man, or through instruction. Sin is, rather, the wrong orientation of all human existence since Adam's fall, an orientation from which no man can free himself." More pointedly, as Peter Gorday notes in his study of every commentary Augustine made about Romans 9–11, "As a patristic exegete Augustine … is the first exegete to hammer out the intensely individualistic, introverted interpretation of the epistle that will allow chapters 9–11 to be consigned to the status of a more or less interesting locus" (*Principles of Patristic*, 233). I show in the present chapter how Augustine turned his "introverted interpretation" of himself into his interpretation of Paul, the Gentile, as someone who suffered just like Augustine.

5. Pagels, *Adam, Eve, and the Serpent*, 106. Pagels refers to the work of Peter Gorday—cited in the above footnote—to help explain her insight.

6. Pagels, *Adam, Eve, and the Serpent*, 129.

7. Pagels, *Adam, Eve, and the Serpent*, 147.

8. All translations of Augustine's *Confessions* are taken from either *The Confessions: Saint Augustine*, trans. Maria Boulding, O.S.B. or *Augustine: Confessions*, trans. William Watts. I use the Loeb texts because they provide a parallel translation of English with the Latin text. Readers will thus have an easier time identifying Augustine's different usages of the two Latin references to the soul (*animus* and *anima*), which cannot be tracked in the English texts because both terms are usually referred to as the "soul." When recounting Augustine's conversion narrative in the garden in Milan, I make note that I have made certain implicit dramatic elements within the text explicit for the purpose of spotlighting peak experiences in his story.

9. *The Confessions*, book VIII, chapter 7, paragraph 9. Thus the citation [VIII. 7.18]. Subsequent references to Augustine's work will be placed in the body of this chapter. Boulding's text lists the paragraph number of the chapter but the Watts' translation cites only the book and chapter.

10. Brown, *Augustine of Hippo*, 492.

11. The references to findings from the newly discovered sermons and letters in this paragraph are taken from the new epilogue to Brown's *Augustine of Hippo*, 441–520.

12. Brown, *Augustine of Hippo*, 500.

13. Miles, *Desire and Delight*, 7, 78.

14. The question of "two Augustines" is usually posed as a debate between (1) Augustine the Neoplatonist interested in the human soul as a philosophic query and (2) Augustine the Catholic bishop who was interested in saving the souls of his flock. A succinct summary of this debate can be found in O'Connell's chapter on this problem, "The *Confessions* at Cassiciacum," 259–309. Of particular interest are Paula Fredriksen's contributions to this debate in her essay "Paul and Augustine: Conversion Narratives, Orthodox Traditions, and the Retrospective Self," n.s.37: 3–34. Fredriksen analyzes the difference between Augustine as Neoplatonist and Augustine as North African Catholic bishop when he endeavors to explain his conversion experience with the use of references to Paul. As part of this analysis, she notes a basic problem of all conversion accounts: dis-

guise. A conversion account, Fredriksen argues, is a "condensed, or disguised description of the convert's *present*, which he legitimates through his retrospective creation of a past and a self." This type of narrative leaves the historian with a problem, Fredriksen concludes: "What *actually* happened, what the convert actually thought or experienced at the time of the conversion, is ... not accessible to the historian.... The historian works with the available evidence, the conversion narrative; and that narrative can reveal to him only the retrospective moment, and the retrospective self." This is not a complete answer. Fredriksen, in an earlier essay, "Augustine and his Analysts: The Possibility of a Psychohistory," turns to Heinz Kohut's self psychology and other psychological studies of the "conflicts of the narcissistic personality" as a way of investigating Augustine that transcends the limits of his own retrospective self. During this discussion, she notes that "alienation from the body" marked the age in which Augustine lived. Fredriksen investigates the possibilities of the historian's use of personality theory ("psychohistory"), and she affirms the importance of historians paying attention to the bodies of the persons they study. Other major analyses using a self-psychological approach to Augustine and his *Confessions* include Dixon's *Augustine: The Scattered and Gathered Self*, and Harrison's *Augustine: Christian Truth and Fractured Humanity*. Essays on Augustine's fragmented self from a self-psychological perspective include Gay's "Augustine: The Reader as Selfobject," and Capps's "Augustine as Narcissist: Of Grandiosity and Shame." Both essays are found in *The Hunger of the Heart: Reflections on the Confessions of Augustine*. The present chapter pays particular attention to affective neuroscientific theory (and related fields) when analyzing Augustine as a split self. And it also uses insights from self-psychology.

15. I agree with O'Daly's claim, in *Augustine's Philosophy of Mind* that although the terms *anima* and *animus* are used by Augustine to refer to the soul, they "do not represent a systematic usage in any sense, [but, nevertheless, they] are sufficiently consistent to be classifiable. *Anima* can refer to the soul of both animals and men.... *Animus* can, however, also mean `mind' ... and is not used with reference to the souls of non-rational beings" (7). I make this distinction between *anima* and *animus* in the following discussion. *Animus* is classifiable as the rational part of man's soul. Furthermore, O'Daly rightly argues that man's mind (*mens, ratio*) in Augustine's scheme is part of the soul. As O'Daly notes, it is the best part of the soul for Augustine. Furthermore, as O'Daly notes later in his book, Augustine waivers, but usually argues that the soul is not purely rational. It has both rational and nonrational or irrational powers (60). Augustine's analysis of the human soul entails a person's emotional and mental powers and activities. Thus, O'Daly concludes, we do not find in Augustine a pure mind or "ego" distinct and totally independent of a body. In Augustine's *Confessions*, we find a description of personality but, O'Daly argues, "that is not the same as an articulated concept of 'personality'" (58). I agree with O'Daly that Augustine is being misread when we attempt to read into Augustine a concept of an isolated "mind" or "self" or "ego" for which his work is a forerunner for this kind of speculative work rather than an actual primary example of it. My own discussion of Augustine's two terms focuses on his analysis of the human soul as having both a purely rational aspect as well as a nonrational principle of vitality (*anima*) that links it to the body. Augustine's anthropology thus entails man as having exterior (*corpus*), inner (*anima*), and inmost (*animus*) aspects of the self. (O'Daly here refers to the insight of Vincentius Victor's trichotomic view of man as *spiritus-anima-corpus* (59)).

16. My reading of Augustine in this regard is in agreement with Étienne Gilson's comment in his work *The Christian Philosophy of Saint Augustine*, that the "faculties" which Augustine described are not "a power of the soul … distinct from mind and reason. These real distinctions are foreign to Augustine's thought, since for him intelligence is rather the result attained by the mind in virtue of its activity as reason" (259, note 10).

17. Watson makes this observation in the Preface to *Saint Augustine: Soliloquies and Immortality of the Soul*, iv.

18. This passage is cited by Watson in the Preface to his translation of *Saint Augustine: Soliloquies and Immortality of the Soul*, iv. Augustine, *Retractationes* (Retractions), xiii.

19. Lohse, *A Short History of Christian Doctrine*, 110.

20. In 372, Augustine became a Manichaean "hearer," which was a "pseudo-Christian" sect created in the third century by its founder, Mani. Hampl, "Chronology of the Life of Saint Augustine, Bishop of Hippo A.D. 345–430," *The Confessions*.

21. I have taken dramatic liberty with the English translations by Maria Boulding and the Latin text and English translation by William Watts in the Loeb Classical Library edition of Augustine's *Confessions*. More precisely, I have combined elements of their translations with a more direct and informal narrative line to spotlight what Augustine did not explicitly say but nevertheless seemed to feel—as subsequent references to his experiences in the later books of his *Confessions* would seem to indicate.

22. For a philosophical analysis of Augustine's error in his theory of language see Wittgenstein, *Philosophical Investigations*, propositions 1–3. Wittgenstein, however, acknowledges that Augustine "does describe a system of communication." Wittgenstein develops vivid examples of this system later in this work (propositions 206–12). I explore Augustine's "system of communication" rather than his "theory of language" in the following discussion.

23. Demos, "Affect and the Development of the Self," 27.

24. Demos, "Empathy and Affect: Reflections on Infant Experience," 11.

25. Demos, "Empathy and Affect: Reflections on Infant Experience," 32.

26. Panksepp, "A Synopsis of Affective," 9.

27. Panksepp, "A Synopsis of Affective," 9.

28. Panksepp and Northoff, "The trans-species core SELF," 198.

29. Panksepp and Northoff, "The trans-species core SELF," 198.

30. Narvaez, "The individual, relational and social neurobiological development of morality," 109–35.

31. Narvaez, "The individual, relational and social neurobiological development of morality," 109–35.

32. Narvaez, "The Individual, relational and social neurobiological development of morality," 109-35.

33. Rousselle, *Porneia: On Desire and the Body in Antiquity*, 55. Mnesitheus, another physician, believed the mother's milk was harmful for forty days.

34. Rousselle, *Porneia: On Desire and the Body in Antiquity*, 57.

35. Rousselle, *Porneia: On Desire and the Body in Antiquity*, 44, 36.

36. Rousselle, *Porneia: On Desire and the Body in Antiquity*, 46.

37. Rousselle, *Porneia: On Desire and the Body in Antiquity*, 54.

38. Rousselle, *Porneia: On Desire and the Body in Antiquity*, 62.

39. Thus Augustine cannot recall any outbursts by Patricius toward her. Instead, Augustine remembers Monica waiting for a favorable moment, when

she saw that his mood had changed and he was calm again, so that she could explain her action, in case he had given way to wrath without due consideration.

40. Augustine, "Sermon 90A," 81–82.

41. Neurobiologist Darcia Narvaez and co-writer Tracey R. Gleason (Psychological Director of the Wellesley College Child Study Center) offer a vivid and succinct statement of this problem: "If we accept Western culture as normal, than humans are on a fast train to self-demise." "Developmental Optimization," 319.

42. Goldberg, *Being of Two Minds*.

43. Goldberg, *Being of Two Minds*, 43–58.

44. Goldberg, *Being of Two Minds*, 9.

45. Goldberg, *Being of Two Minds*, 10.

46. Goldberg, *Being of Two Minds*, 73.

47. Goldberg, *Being of Two Minds*, 9.

48. Goldberg, *Being of Two Minds*, 27.

49. Goldberg, *Being of Two Minds*, 27.

50. Gay, "Augustine: The Reader as Selfobject," 64–76.

51. Gay, "Augustine: The Reader as Selfobject," 65–68.

Chapter Six

1. Luther, *Lectures on Galatians (1535)*, 13–185.

2. As Philip Bosman's rightly notes in his book, *Conscience in Philo and Paul*, "Luther gave a more prominent role to conscience in his theological design than any other exponent of the sixteenth-century Reformation. Furthermore, he deviated from scholastic tradition on the conscience not simply because he was dictated to do so by his theological programme, but also as a result of studying the texts of the New Testament. In this regard he does indeed represent a turn in this history of interpretation. Finally, his views played an enormously influential part in theological discussions and research on the Pauline use of the word [*syneidesis/conscience*]" (20). See Bosman for his cited references that support and challenge this characterization of conscience in the work of Luther.

3. Jaroslav Pelikan, as editor, in his "Introduction" to Volume 26 of *Luther's Works, Lectures on Galatians (1535)*, chapters 1–4 affirms its importance when noting: "If the Epistle of St. Paul to the Galatians is, as it has often been called, the Magna Carta of Christian liberty, then Luther's lectures on Galatians of 1531 (1535) deserves to be called a declaration of Christian independence—independence from the Law and from anything or anyone else except the God and Father of our Lord Jesus Christ" (ix). A major influence upon my decision to select Luther's *Lectures on Galatians* as the text for my analysis of conscience was B. A. Gerrish's book, *Grace and Reason*. Gerrish chose these lectures by Luther as the major text for his study and he carefully delineates the importance of this text in Luther's corpus. Gerrish also discusses the strengths and weakness in relying on this text as a representative work of the mature Luther. See especially chapter iv, 57–68.

4. Martin Luther, "Against the Robbing and Murdering Hordes of Peasants," 50. For the complete online text see the revised translation of Jacobs' text: http://www.scrollpublishing.com/store/Luther-Peasants.html. Accessed August 21, 2016.

Oberman presents a fine review of the historiographical issues entailed in the dominant narratives of Luther's diatribes against Jews and peasants in *The Two Reformations*.

5. Luther, "Against the Robbing."

6. Luther, "Against the Robbing."

7. Luther, "Secular Authority: To What Extend It Should Be Obeyed," 371.

8. Luther, "Secular Authority," 365.

9. Luther, "Secular Authority," 369.

10. Luther, "Secular Authority," 365.

11. Luther, "Secular Authority."

12. Luther, "Secular Authority," 371.

13. Luther, "Secular Authority," 370.

14. Luther, "Secular Authority," 365–66.

15. Luther, "Secular Authority," 371.

16. Luther, "Secular Authority," 371.

17. Luther, "An Open Letter," 69–70. See also Luther's "Admonition to Peace," in which he lays out his unsuccessful attempts to work with the peasants and the princes to avoid warfare. Luther did indeed advise both peasants and rules to act justly. But his attempts were not successful. Only then did he tell the princes to pick up their swords.

18. Luther believes he must give himself as a Christ to his neighbor as Christ offered himself to Luther. Luther thus believes he must "do nothing in this life except what [he sees] is necessary, profitable, and salutary for [his] neighbor." See "Freedom of a Christian," *Martin Luther: Selections from his Writings*, 75–76.

19. Luther, *Lectures on Galatians*, 134.

20. Luther, *Lectures on Galatians*, 59.

21. Bosman, *Conscience in Philo and Paul*, 16–20.

22. See the essay by Murphy, "Martin Luther, the Erfurt Cloister, and Gabriel Biel," for a review of the growing scholarly interest in Luther's Reformation consciousness in the context of his own theological contexts.

23. Bosman, *Conscience in Philo and Paul*, 20.

24. From Medieval Latin *syntērēsis* (in Thomas Aquinas), from Ancient Greek συντήρησις (*suntérēsis*, "careful watching"), from συντηρεῖν (*suntēreîn*, "to keep guard"). https://en.wiktionary.org/wiki/synteresis Accessed August 18, 2016.

25. Pierce, *Conscience*, 16–22, for a fine synopsis of this linguistic history from Jerome through Luther.

26. Pierce, *Conscience*, 118.

27. Pierce, *Conscience*, 118.

28. Pierce, *Conscience*, 118.

29. Baylor, *Action and Person*, 25.

30. Baylor, *Action and Person*, 26.

31. Baylor, *Action and Person*, 26.

32. Baylor, *Action and Person*, 26.

33. Baylor, *Action and Person*, 26.

34. Bultmann, *Theology of the New Testament*.

35. Hirsch, *Lutherstudien*, 11.

36. Hirsch, *Lutherstudien*, 12.

37. Hirsch, *Lutherstudien*, 13. See Baylor's book, *Action and Person*, for a discussion of the ethical ramifications of this concern. As Baylor suggests: "The scholastic view that invincible ignorance excuses from sin arose from the disparity created by the two fundamental axioms of the scholastic position on the authority of conscience: that to act against conscience is to sin, and that to follow conscience is not always good. The ethical dilemma concerned the man with an erroneous conscience who does wrong whether the conscience is followed or violated" (244).

38. Baylor, *Action and Person*, 49.

39. Baylor, *Action and Person*, 50.

40. Oberman, *The Harvest of Medieval Theology*, 65.

41. Baylor, *Action and Person*, 52.

42. Baylor, *Action and Person*, 52.

43. Baylor, *Action and Person*, 52.

44. Oberman, *The Harvest of Medieval Theology*, 65.

45. Oberman, *The Harvest of Medieval Theology*, 65.

46. Joest, *Ontologie der Person bei Luther*, 159.

47. Oberman, *The Harvest of Medieval Theology*, 66.

48. Oberman, *The Harvest of Medieval Theology*, 65–66.

49. See Smith, *Luther's Table Talk: A Critical Study*, 108. Luther also believed thunderstorms were quite literally satanic, and he advocated torture for persons he considered witches (108–9).

50. As Bosman notes in *Conscience in Philo and Paul*, "There is general agreement that Luther's stance on conscience progressed through various stages. Initially, he remained very much in line with late scholasticism, accepting that all humans have knowledge of the basic moral principles and viewing the *synteresis* and conscience as aspects of practical reason, the latter especially oriented to the judgments of human actions. He also, however, expanded the notion of the *synteresis* to include volition and emotional aspects. A person not only has an innate knowledge of the good, but also naturally wants to do it. The *synteresis* of the will is the source of guilt in the sinner and the consequent cry for forgiveness. During the course of his lectures on Romans (1515–16), Luther started to evaluate the scholastic *synteresis* more negatively and he eventually discarded the notion all together" (20). See Bosman for references cited to support and elucidate his claims in this above text.

51. Cited by von Ranke in *History*, 93.

52. von Ranke in *History*, 106.

53. von Ranke in *History*, 106.

54. von Ranke in *History*, 106.

55. von Ranke in *History*, 92.

56. Luther, "Ninety-Five Theses."

57. von Ranke, *History*, 82.

58. Luther, *Lectures on Galatians (1535)*, 57.

59. Luther, *Lectures on Galatians (1535)*, 57.

60. Cited by editor Pelikan, in his "Introduction to Volume 26" to Luther's *Lectures on Galatians (1535)*, According to Pelikan, Luther made this remark at his table.

61. Holl, *What Did Luther Understand by Religion?*, 48.

62. Holl, *What Did Luther Understand by Religion?*, 48n. This quote is taken from *Luthers Werke,*, 40. I. Band, 2. Galatervorlesung (cap. 1–4) 1531 (1535). 21, 1. 12.

63. Lohse, "Conscience," 159.

64. Lohse, "Conscience," 159–60. Lohse is referring here to Theodor Siegfried's book, *Luther und Kant.*

65. Lohse, "Conscience," 159. Lohse is quoting from Rudolf Hermann's book, *Luthers Theologie, Gesammelte und nachgelassene Werke*, I, 219, n.2.

66. Ebeling, *Luther*, 119.

67. Ebeling, *Luther*, 119.

68. Ebeling, *Luther*, 119.

69. Ebeling, *Luther*, 119.

70. Lohse, "Conscience," 164.

71. Lohse, "Conscience," 165.

72. Lohse, "Conscience," 165.

73. Lohse, "Conscience," 166.

74. Einar Billing, *Our Calling* (Philadelphia: Fortress Press, 1947), 8.

75. Lohse, "Conscience and Authority in Luther," 167.

76. Tillich, *Morality and Beyond*, 78.

77. Tillich, *Morality and Beyond*, 77.

78. Tillich, *Morality and Beyond*, 77.

79. Baylor, *Action and Person*, 242, n. 91.

80. Baylor, *Action and Person*, 243.

81. Baylor, *Action and Person*, 243, n. 92.

82. Baylor, *Action and Person*, 253.

83. Baylor, *Action and Person*, 253.

84. Baylor, *Action and Person*, 253. Commenting upon Luther's rejection of the scholastic problem of the conscience, which gives a person incorrect information (namely, the erroneous conscience) and commenting upon Luther's rejection of the *synteresis* as a valid notion, Baylor summarizes these rejections as follows. "In both cases what [Luther] found unsatisfactory was conceiving the relationship of conscience to divine law and gospel in the same way that one conceived the relation of the conscience to a set of ethical precepts or moral principles. But just as the rejection of the *synteresis* did not make the conscience a faculty with an inherent supernatural dimension, intrinsically connected to the divine will, so neither did Luther's rejection of the dilemma of the erroneous conscience give to the conscience more—or less—than the relative and negative authority in ethical affairs which the scholastics had granted it."

85. Baylor, *Action and Person*, 271.

86. Baylor, *Action and Person*, 271.

87. Baylor, *Action and Person*, 271.

88. Tillich, *Morality and Beyond*, 69.

89. Tillich, *Morality and Beyond*, 69.

90. For a comparison of the way assurance was achieved by Calvin and Luther via their distinct understandings of conscience, see Zachman, *The Assurance of Faith*.

91. Panksepp, "A Synopsis of Affective Neurosis."

92. In Bosman's words in *Conscience in Philo and Paul*, the *synteresis* is "discarded ... all together" (20).

93. Jane Dempsey Douglass, in the opening remarks of her presidential address—"Christian Freedom: What Calvin Learned at the School of Women"—delivered at the annual meeting of the American Society of Church History (23 December 1983), notes the impact on the second generation of Reformers of Luther's paradigm-changing focus on freedom and the Christian conscience: "Christian freedom was a major concern for Calvin from the very beginning of his theological career. The very long sixth and final chapter of the first edition of the *Institutes* is devoted to this question. He opens the chapter by calling this freedom 'a matter of prime necessity; ... without a knowledge of it consciences dare undertake almost nothing without faltering, often hesitate and draw back, constantly waver and are afraid ... unless this freedom be grasped, neither Christ nor gospel truth is rightly known.' From this first edition until the last Calvin continues to talk at length about three aspects of Christian freedom: freedom of the conscience and freedom from the law because of justification by grace alone; freedom of the liberated Christian to obey God's will voluntarily and not out of necessity; and

freedom in outward things which are 'indifferent,' that is, in themselves neither necessary nor forbidden. For much of this understanding Calvin is deeply indebted to Luther and Melanchthon" (*Church History*, 53 no 2, June 1984, 155).

94. Emphasis added.

95. Baylor, *Action and Person*, 270–71.

96. Bosman, *Conscience in Philo and Paul*, 20.

97. Schleiermacher, *The Christian Faith*, proposition 172.1.

98. Schleiermacher, *The Christian Faith*, propositions 3.0, 3.1 and 3.4.

99. As neuropsychologist Darcia Narvaez has noted in "Neurobiology," "Perceived threat activates the survival systems: blood flow shifts away from higher order thinking and towards mobilization for fight or flight. As Robert Sapolsky [*Why zebras don't get ulcers*, 3rd ed. New York, NY: Holt, 2004] pointed out, these systems are very useful for zebras (or humans) facing a hungry lion, but modern humans have extended them to the social life. When one is sensitized to the unfamiliar (people, actions, things) as threatening, modern life can keep people in a state of alarm, especially when the self-regulatory systems have been underdeveloped [Allan N. Schore, *Affect Regulation and the Origin of the Self: The Neurobiology of Emotional Development* Hillsdale, NJ: Erlbaum, 1994]. When early life is traumatic or routinely suboptimal, protectionism can become dispositional, dominating personality. Protectionism is problematic as a dispositional way to get along with others because of its self-oriented nature. In self-oriented modes, people are less responsive to helping others. [E.g. M. Mikulincer, P. R. Shaver, O. Gillath, R. A. Nitzberg, *Attachment, Caregiving, and Altruism: Boosting Attachment Security Increases Compassion and Helping*, in *Journal of Personality and Social Psychology* 89 (2005): 817–39.]"

100. Barth, *This Christian Cause*.

101. Barth, *This Christian Cause*.

Chapter Seven

1. Contrary to the basic claim made by Robert P. Jones that "White Christian America … has died," this chapter argues that the unexamined moral values that originally informed the white Protestant conscience remain steadfastly in place.

2. Bennett, "Moral Origins," 276.

3. Kristol, "A Conservative Looks at Liberalism," 290.

4. Tom Johnson, "Garry Wills: Conservatives Consider Themselves 'Superior People' Who 'Have License to Circumvent Democracy,'" January 29, 2016 MRC NewsBusters: Exposing and Combatting Liberal Media Bias [https://www.newsbusters.org/blogs/nb/tom-johnson/2016/01/29/garry-wills-conservatives-consider-themselves-superior-people-who] Accessed February 19, 2018.

5. Himmelfarb, *The Road to Modernity*.

6. Westin, *The Role of Emotion*.

7. Himmelfarb, *The Road to Modernity*.

8. See the discussion of the *synteresis*—man's innate capacity to follow God's Law—in chapter six for details.

9. Levy, "Thomas Reid's Defense," 413, passim.

10. Howe, *The Unitarian Conscience*.

11. Historically, this standpoint brought together medieval scholasticism's interest in the *synteresis* with the ongoing interest in the Christian conscience that was tracked back to Paul and Jerome. See chapter six for the details.

12. This definition of the term *irony* is based on Reinhold Niebuhr's definition found in his book, *The Irony of American History*, vii–viii. According to Niebuhr, *irony* is a term that refers to a "hidden relationship ... discovered in the incongruity" of a personal experience. For example, virtue that turns into a vice. The relationship between virtue and vice in this personal experience is ironic because a hidden relationship between the virtue and the vice is an incongruous element within the virtuous experience itself. A simple example makes this complex point evident. Not over-eating is a virtue of which anorexia is its vice. The relationship between not overeating and anorexia is thus ironic.

13. Reid, "On the Active Powers," 317.

14. Reid, "On the Active Powers," 317.

15. As Sacvan Bercovitch rightly observes in *The Puritan Origins of the American Self*, "Both humanism [a scholarly tradition in which Luther and Calvin were trained] and Protestantism shift the grounds of private identity from the institution to the individual; and it has been said of each movement that its concept of *imitatio* makes every man his own church.... The Reformers demanded that every individual reconstitute by grace a reflection of the church. That every man is *a world* in himself." But those gifts of value, Luther insisted, "the only identity worthy aspiring to, lay utterly beyond man's power" (11). As Bercovitch also notes, among the Puritans, "The High Calvinist Arthur Dent instructed them about the nature of man: 'a glut of grief, a stye of filthiness.'" (13)

16. Bercovitch, *The Puritan Origins*, 319.

17. Bercovitch, *The Puritan Origins*, 320.

18. Bercovitch, *The Puritan Origins*, 320.

19. Bercovitch, *The Puritan Origins*, 322.

20. Bercovitch, *The Puritan Origins*, 322.

21. Rauschenbush, cited by Hunter, *American Evangelicalism*.

22. Hunter, *American Evangelicalism*.

23. Hunter, *American Evangelicalism*.

24. Hunter, *Culture Wars*, 42.

25. John B. Cobb, Jr., personal correspondence (October 7, 2016).

26. Personal correspondence from John Cobb, Jr. to author, (October 8, 2016).

27. Hunter, *American Evangelicalism*.

28. For a general introduction to Pietism, see Herzog's fine summary of six varieties of Pietism in his book *European Pietism Reviewed*.

29. Reid, "On the Active Powers," 306.

30. David Hempton, *Methodism: Empire of the Spirit*, 2005.

31. Cited by Bercovitch in *The Puritan Origins*, 157–58.

32. Bercovitch in *The Puritan Origins*, 159.

33. A stunning analysis of Emerson's social reform and near revolutionary work on slavery is found in Stauffer's *The Black Hearts of Men*.

34. Cited by Metaxas in *Bonhoeffer*.

35. Dowey, *The Knowledge of God*, 60 for references to Calvin citations use in this chapter.

36. Dowey, *The Knowledge of God*, 61.

37. Dowey, *The Knowledge of God*, 56–71.

38. For textual references to Calvin citations used here, see Dowey, *The Knowledge of God*, 60.

39. Dowey, *The Knowledge of God*, 61.

40. Dowey, *The Knowledge of God*, 56–71.

41. Etty Hillesum's description of this enlivening feeling is displayed in her diary entry written in a transition camp in Westerbork, Holland, shortly before she was transported to Auschwitz and killed on 30 November 1943 at the age

of 29: "All I wanted to say was this: the misery here is quite terrible and yet, late at night when the day has slunk away into the depths behind me, I often walk with a spring in my step along the barbed wire and then time and again it soars straight from my heart—I can't help it, that's just the way it is, like some elementary force—the feeling that life is glorious and magnificent and that one day we shall be building a whole new world. Against every new outrage and very fresh horror we shall put up one more piece of love and goodness." *An Interrupted Life.* [http://www.holyhill.ie/etty-hillesum]. Accessed May 10, 2018.

42. Thandeka, *The Embodied Self.*

43. Thandeka, *The Embodied Self,* 301.

44. Cobb, *Spiritual Bankruptcy,* 8. Cobb, however, does not condemn religiousness as a whole. "It often generates excellent community life among those who basically agree." Religiousness, like all human activity, is thus ambiguous (ibid.).

45. Cobb, *Spiritual Bankruptcy,* 8.

46. Cobb, *Spiritual Bankruptcy,* 8.

47. Niebuhr, *The Irony of American History,* 41.

48. Niebuhr, *The Irony of American History,* 41.

49. Niebuhr, *The Irony of American History,* 82.

50. Niebuhr, *The Irony of American History,* 82ff.

51. Niebuhr, *The Irony of American History,* 83–84.

52. Niebuhr, *The Irony of American History,* 172.

53. Niebuhr, *The Nature and Destiny of Man,* 17.

54. Niebuhr, *The Nature and Destiny of Man,* 108–21.

55. Niebuhr, *The Nature and Destiny of Man,* 112.

56. Westen, *The Political Brain,* xv.

57. Westen, *The Political Brain,* xv.

58. Westen, *The Political Brain,* 36.

59. Westen, *The Political Brain,* 36.

60. Niebuhr, *The Irony of American History,* 41.

61. See the "Neurobiology, Emotions and Faith," by Thandeka and neuropsychologist Darcia Narvaez for a case study of how such a system can be established as a new model for race talk and public policy.

62. Thandeka, "Ministering to Anxiety." [Complete reference required for Bibliography.]

63. David Brooks, "Obama, Gospel and Verse," *The New York Times,* April 26, 2007 [accessed February 19, 2018].

64. Niebuhr, *The Irony of American History,* 41.

65. Dowey, *The Knowledge of God,* 56–71.

66. See "Syrian War Magnifies Tension in America's Global Mission," by *The New York Times* reporters and columnists Max Fisher and Amanda Taub for a vivid example of popular discourse of America's moral values as a tendency to divide the world into heroes who support American values and villains who oppose them. The term "conscience" is not used once in this article, but the presence of the easy conscience is very much evident. So, too, the logic of Reid.

67. See "U.S. Torture Leaves a Legacy of Detainees With Damaged Minds," October 9, 2016, by *The New York Times* reporters Matt Apuzzo, Sheri Fink, and James Risen on the torture techniques used on inmates including "victims of mistaken identity or flimsy evidence that the United States later disavowed…. At least half of the 39 people who went through the C.I.A.'s 'enhanced interrogation' program, which included depriving them of sleep, dousing them with ice water, slamming them into walls, and locking them in coffin-like boxes, have since shown psychiatric problems."

68. A concise summary of this tradition is given by Kirk in his book *The Conservative Mind*.

69. Brody, *The Teavangelicals*, 39.

70. The Hamilton Project, for example, found that the full-time, full-year employment rate of men without a bachelor's degree fell from 76 percent in 1990 to 68 percent in 2013.

71. Thompson, "Who are Donald Trump's supporters, really?"

72. See the "Neurobiology, Emotions and Faith" by Thandeka and neuropsychologist Darcia Narvaez for details of the affective and historical contexts for Trump's rise to power.

73. His appointment to this seat by President Trump not only downgraded the roles of the chairman of the Joint Chiefs of Staff, but also that of the director of National Intelligence. As the New York Times noted in its January 30, 2017 edition, "It is a startling elevation of a political advisor to the status alongside the secretaries of state and defense, and over the president's top military and intelligence advisers."

74. Stephen K. Bannon's 2014 Vatican speech and commentary: https://www.buzzfeed.com/lesterfeder/this-is-how-steve-bannon-sees-the-entire-world?utm_term=.px23276Ee#.glyKBjyN3. Accessed January 30, 2017.

75. Niebuhr, *The Irony of American History*, 41.

76. See note 1, page 245.

77. Niebuhr, *The Irony of American History*, 41.

78. Max Fisher's April 8, 2017 *New York Times* article, "Measuring Action Against a Government Already Under Siege," brilliantly lays out how Trump's order to send dozens of cruise missiles launched at a Syrian air base was, at best, a symbolic act to demonstrate American moral values. The intention: to reap the reward of such displays from American voters. The act placed in any other terms, Fisher argues, lacks long-term credibility because it was committed without a carefully worked out foreign policy protocol. As such, it created a credibility gap between the symbolic act and the ongoing realities of the Syrian war. Trump, simply put, was prompted by his easy conscience that conflates the differences among feelings, thoughts, and acts.

79. Contrary to the basic claim made by Robert P. Jones that "White Christian America ... has died," this chapter argues that the unexamined moral values that originally informed the white Protestant conscience remain steadfastly in place.

80. For more on King's increasing radicalism see Thandeka's book, *Learning to Be White*.

81. Epstein, *Good Without God*.

82. Epstein, *Good Without God*.

83. "Here's What We Know About The 2.4% Of Americans Who Are Atheists," Michael Lipka, Pew Research Center's Fact Tank, Nov. 6, 2013, 5:38 PM [http://www.businessinsider.com/5-facts-about-atheists-in-america-2013-11]. Accessed May 10, 2018.

84. Amy Sullivan, "The Rise of the Nones," *Time Magazine*, March 12, 2012.

85. *USA Today*, February 7, 2013.

86. Stout, "Oh, to Be Young, Millennial, And So Wanted by Marketers.".

87. Kelly Taterta, "Gerenation RX Eats Prescription Drugs Like Candy."

88. *New York Times*, February 1, 2013, "Young, Liberal and Open to Big Government."

89. More information about this new congregational development initiative can be found on my website: http://lovebeyondbeliefinc.org/.

About the Author

Thandeka (Ph.D., Claremont Graduate University) is creator of the Love Beyond Belief initiative (lovebeyondbeliefinc.org) for progressive congregations and the founder of Contemporary Affect Theology. Her books and publications have secured her place as a major figure in American liberal theology. Formerly an Emmy award-winning television producer, she is an ordained Unitarian Universalist minister and congregational consultant who was given the Xhosa name Thandeka, which means "beloved," by Archbishop Desmond Tutu in 1984.